Youth as Catalysts and Change Makers

About the Authors

G. Palanithurai, Coordinator in Rajiv Gandhi Chair, Gandhigram Rural Institute, presently heads the Department of Political Science and Development Administration, in Gandhigram Rural University, Tamil Nadu. He is also Associated with Centre Planning Commission, State Planning Commission of Tamil Nadu, Population Foundation of India, Ford Foundation, UNICEF, Rajiv Gandhi Foundation, CAPART, Ministry of Rural Areas and Employment and DANIDA (Danish-Indo Development Agency) in specific areas of activities in connection with empowerment of people.

Prof. Palanithurai has to his credit twenty-nine books and seventy-five articles on three major areas, namely, legislative behaviour, ethnicity and Panchayati Raj system. He was recipient of Fellowship from Sastri Indo-Canadian Institute, New Delhi and World Academy of Art and Science, USA. He is the Chairman of the Tamil Nadu Council for Sustainable Livelihoods. He was a visiting fellow in the MiGill University, Canada in 1989. He is a member of the expert committee constituted by the Government of Tamil Nadu to monitor the training programme for local body leaders.

M.A. Thirunavukkarasu is the Research Coordinator of the Rajiv Gandhi Chair for Panchayati Raj Studies, Gandhigram Rural Institute, Gandhigram. He is an expert in micro-planning and he has facilitated the Panchayat leaders to prepare micro-plan document for their respective Panchayats. Also, he is associated with capacity building exercise for local body leaders and has assisted in evolving training module and manual for local body leaders' training.

YOUTH AS CATALYSTS AND CHANGE MAKERS

G. Palanithurai
M.A. Thirunavukkarasu

CONCEPT PUBLISHING COMPANY PVT. LTD.,
NEW DELHI-110 059

ISBN-13: 978-81-8069-682-4

First Published 2010

Published and Printed by

Concept Since 1974

Concept Publishing Company Pvt. Ltd.
Regd. Office:
A/15-16, Commercial Block, Mohan Garden
New Delhi-110059 (India)
Phones : 25351460, 25351794, *Fax* : 091-11-25357109
Email : publishing@conceptpub.com
Website : www.conceptpub.com

Editorial Office:
H-13, Bali Nagar, New Delhi-110 015, India.

Cataloging in Publication Data--*Courtesy:* D.K. Agencies (P) Ltd. <docinfo@dkagencies.com>

Palanithurai, G. (Ganapathy)
Youth as catalysts and change makers / G. Palanithurai, M.A. Thirunavukkarasu.
p. cm.
Study, with reference to Tamil Nadu, India.
Includes bibliographical references and index.
ISBN 13: 9788180696824

1. Youth in development--India--Tamil Nadu. 2. Youth--Political activity--India--Tamil Nadu. 3. Youth--Government policy--India--Tamil Nadu. 4. Panchayat--India--Tamil Nadu. I. Thirunavukkarasu, M. A., joint author. II. Title.

DDC 305.235095482 22

To

The Divine Mother

Preface

Crisis in India is not that of material but moral in nature. When we were in school we were taught that "If wealth is lost nothing is lost, if health is lost something is lost, and if character is lost everything is lost". We learned this in the moral class. Moral values and high principles were repeatedly taught everywhere by quoting the epics, scriptures and practices of Mahatma Gandhi. One period of forty five minutes was devoted exclusively for teaching moral values in the schools at the dawn of Independence. The basic principles of life were connected with moral values. It was emphasized that human being has to evolve himself or herself and they are treated as humans if they are positively connected with their community. Serving others, living for others, working for others, and roles to be performed. People have to perform different roles as father, mother, worker, son, brother, manager, employer, owner, servant, student, teacher and so on. An individual has to discharge several responsibilities as he or she has to perform several roles. But all the roles have to be performed professionally and achieve the expected results. What are our responsibilities? and how are these responsibilities be discharged? How are they taught in the civic class? Independence day, Republic day and Gandhi Jayanti were programme days for us in the school. Public speeches were arranged, on those days. Students, teachers and public participated in all the functions. We were not informed about any right granted by the Constitution when we were in school. But we were instructed to discharge certain responsibilities in our families, in schools, and among the peers. We came to know about the rights only during our college days. From the school days to the college days and from the college to university, although we were influenced by my teachers on the aspects of connecting oneself with the community positively and proactively for the development of the community. We were taught that the individual interest is taken care of when the collectivity is taken care of. But now we see the society where individual welfare is at the cost of community. People have been oriented to be greedy, possessive, self oriented, career-oriented, profit-oriented, to the maximum level. Today, every one talks about the malady in governance and administration as if they are isolated events. They are parts of the society. Social system is the broader system, in which politics, culture, economics, religion, caste and so on are operating as sub-systems. Hence, the issues are to be seen always in a larger backdrop. When we want a good government, we should have a good society. When we want a perfect administration, we should become good and honest. Everyone talks about the non application of the rules of law. Rule of law will be enforced in a society where people have a culture of obeying the laws. One cannot get a good government and good administration in a bad society. There is a close linkage between the society and governance and society and administration. What is in the society will be reflected in governance and what is in governance will be reflected in society. Both are influencing with each other. One could find the effect of governance in the society and vice versa. Where deterioration starts and where reform starts is yet another serious question as the "chicken or egg" story. Which is stronger in influencing the others? It is also a question. But we see a general trend of declining moral values in all walks of life which needs to be stalled. All the time we have seen in history that unless there is a mass movement against the ills of the society, it cannot be corrected by simple modifications and adjustments of the administrative and governance system. Any step towards reforming governance and administration is a futile exercise as problems to be confronted in the society are mighty and they require a thorough overhauling. It really needs a shake up and for which a mass movement is an imperative.

In this context, where do we begin is the million dollar question. Society brings both good and bad, events bring good and bad likewise all human actions produce positive and negative results in the world. But things have to be seen perspectively and scientifically and then only can we act futuristically. What we see today is top-down activities in every walk of life. For all our activities we expect direction or command from higher ups either political leaders or officials. As a result at every level dependency syndrome prevails. Consequently, initiatives, creative actions and independent actions are totally discouraged. Moreover, such a kind of syndrome in the society creates a new culture in Governance and Administration which encourages the ruling elite to follow the colonial culture and they do not lead the society as leaders. It is always antithetical to democratic culture. People, organizations and institutions have been oriented in this manner. All development activities are owned by the government and its institutions. Nowhere in the world it is proved that Government and bureaucracy alone have developed the society. Government and bureaucracy facilitated the people to achieve development. Old temples and water tanks in the villages are real contributions of the communities. But now, government gets funds from the International funding agencies to desilt the tanks created by the communities. People have got vision, skills, commitment, knowledge and energy. When they are facilitated, they will achieve development. Whenever allowed to take initiative and people are given freedom to act, development has been achieved. Hence, people's involvement and participation are essential for development. Thus development is always people-centric and with the participation of people. In a democratic country, people are the sovereign and they get primacy of importance. Government can facilitate the people to achieve development by harnessing their skills and knowledge. They are to be respected and they are to be valued. In this context, it is argued that people decide their destiny and by which they decide the destiny of the nation. But unfortunately such a kind of preposition has not gained much momentum in India in the past sixty years. People are really the development participants. But in reality it is not so. As a result, people are reduced to voters, subjects or objects, or petitioners or dole receivers or beneficiaries. People are not treated as citizens. Unfortunately people are driven away from governance, administration and development. In the process of expansion of public administration spaces so far occupied by the people have been occupied by the government and Government takes the ownership of development of the people. When people are drawn towards public action as participants, they look for profit or gain. As we are in the market era, people are oriented to look for gains for every action. As a result voluntary initiatives for serving the community has gone. This is the general trend. But on the otherside humanity has finer elements. There are individuals who have got commitments to serve the people. Many exhibited extraordinary leadership qualities when they are in their youth. They exhibit a culture of voluntarism and serve people working with people. Voluntary spirit of the individuals have to be documented for dissemination. Hence, such a kind of individuals voluntary activities are narrated and their activities are covered in this write up.

Their services are unique and their methods of achieving things are special. They are simple but their achievements are laudable. They are youths both men and women, some of them are from the marginalized communities. They are the real change-makers. They are to be brought to the limelight. There is a new opportunity for the youths who want to serve the community through the new Panchayati Raj System. The youths can directly or indirectly participate in regenerating the villages. By contesting in the election or by helping the panchayats, the youths can solidly achieve development. There are a few cases captured in this book and they are the inspiration for the youths. As a youth how they struggled and succeeded have been delineated in this book.

To document all such stories, the Common Wealth Youth Foundation has helped us by providing financial support. The concerned individuals have spared their valuable time and allowed us to consult the records. Our project team in the Rajiv

Gandhi Chair has helped us by providing some analytical input to evaluate the documents. Our academic team has enabled me to concentrate on the outreach programmes and research activities. Hence, I thank profusely the Commonwealth Youth Foundation, research team of Rajiv Gandhi Chair, Academic staff of our Department and finally members of my family for their generous help and support. For all those who helped me to complete this work, I place on records my thanks whole heartedly and sincerely.

Gandhigram **G. Palanithurai**

Contents

1

Introduction

The moment we think of youth, the qualities that come before us are impulsive, emotional, vulnerable, energetic, highly risk taking, rebellious, unrealistic, sensitive, motivated, cheerful, creative, innovative and egoistic. These adjectives refer to both positive and the negative qualities of the youth. The youths are educated, uneducated, skilled, unskilled, men and women, rural and urban, employed and unemployed and organized and unorganized. How many of them are in the process of development, contributing to development and how many of them are becoming problems to the society? These are to be assessed and seen. It is a country consisting of 40 per cent youth as per the definition of the Government of India policy. They fall between the age group 13 and 35. Shaping of the youth is the duty of the government and the society. Youth can be shaped as a resource and potential for growth and equally there is a potential danger for the country and society if they are not properly shaped and oriented. Normally governments used to invest their resources in youth in many ways for their meaningful engagement. By evolving meaningful policies and spending needed amount in youth activities, youths are being prepared to face challenges in life. They will be accordingly educated, skilled, resourceful, employable and organized. By creating such a kind of change and transformation in youth, the society can convert the youth population into a productive population. They are really the assets of the society. To bring such a kind of achievement, a cohesive and coordinated effort is needed. The intensive coordinated activities between the society and the state will reduce the gap between the

Government and the society, and the hold over each other would become strong. Further, it would create informed citizenry.

At present, a very strong perception has gained currency among the public that the values of human life and ethical way of leading life have touched the lowest ebb as every one is in the race for making unlimited profit. Profit making is not unethical, as long as this exercise is carried out well within the ethical framework. But people started making money unethically and unfathomably. Public life and public administration have become dishonest and corrupt. As a result, the society has become dishonest. Unethical and corrupt practices are the order of the day. People have started accepting the unethical way of life. Social concern, values and integrity in public life and serving the people with rectitude are the casualties at present. That is why every one wants a change and alternative and that too through good governance. Good governance cannot be created in a bad society. So, to establish good governance good society is an imperative. Good society is created on the basis of the values which are cherished and followed by people over a period of time.

Globalisation of economy, liberalization and privatization have further worsened the situation by making life more enjoyable to a few who have capacity, skill and capability and it has made the life of the poor miserable, which deprives them and keeps them away from development. It has induced the people to go ahead as free sailors without any restrictions to earn wealth. Profit earned by the companies has been doubled and tripled. Salary of the individuals have increased beyond our imagination. Once it was declared that people have to discharge their duties and responsibilities and they should not expect any returns for discharging their responsibilities. People had accepted it. So "Serve and Suffer" and "Sacrifice and Serve" were the frameworks. Now market puts a new *mantra* "Serve and Prosper", which has become so popular. No one objects the individuals and groups achieving prosperity by serving the people. But, all activities should be well within the framework of ethical values. But while observing society, one can make a statement that the society has dismantled the ethical values which had been evolved over a period of time. This may be the opinion of many and hence, there is a general discussion on good governance and creating a good civil society. These are all observations and perceptions based on the realities. Humanity survives not on unethical pursuit for prosperity. It survives on ethical way of life. The new perceptions and understandings are the outcomes of the media. One cannot underestimate the power of communications in increasing the speed of development. A century of development activities have been completed within ten years because of the the development in communication. The free flow of ideas, products, technologies, capital from one end of the globe to another without any barrier in governance and administration made the humanity unleash the potentials of the people for productive purposes. The media highlights only the negative and unusual. The media also do not want to make the people move into unethical means. It wants to correct the erring collectives and individuals. The media wants the authorities and institutions to take initiatives to undo wrongs. Positive acts are always in the society. They are not captured properly. What is new in it? There is no news. So when something goes wrong then it is news, but if everything goes unethically it is to be corrected for which dissemination of information is needed for mobilizing the people. What we see today in the world is stories full of negatives in the media. There are hundreds of good things happening in the society which go unnoticed. It is necessary to bring to light the better side of each issue. People are looking for models for emulation. Good models are not projected, as the individuals with good character never demand publicity. They are always simple. They do good things not with the expectation that every one will appreciate. They do things as they feel it is their responsibility as responsible citizens and enlightened citizens to do good things.

There is yet another argument which is being discussed everywhere at present. The whole world is looking towards India as India brings with it the power of youth. By building the capacity, skill and capability of the youth, India will make new strides in its economy. But in India, it is attributed that the present day youth do not have a sense of responsibility as the youth of 1950's and 1960's. It has created a values crisis. There is yet another argument: the youths need orientation as they have development urge and motivation but no corresponding mechanism to perform the expected activities. The youth of the country are in deep crises. They are responsible for the dismantling of the unethical ways of life. The existing conditions in the society negate values for which youths are also responsible. There is yet another argument that the youths are not as bad as we project. The youths who are motivated have developed aspirations to achieve things. The youths who are occupying high positions have become achievers. They are fighting for social justice, social transformation and democracy. Even in political parties and pressure groups, the youths are active. The capacitated youths have migrated to different countries. The unskilled youths have migrated to different regions in pursuit of gainful employment opportunities.

We have enormous problems in society to be tackled. Everyone thinks that to tackle the problems, we need more money, and packages of policies and programmes. No doubt these are essential. But more than all these factors, leadership matters much. It is a considered opinion that wherever the leaders are effective and efficient, major problems are tackled very easily and effectively. Whether it is a macro issue or micro issue, it is necessary to have good leadership. In the whole world, it is proved unequivocally that the leadership played crucial roles. Macro issues need macro leaders, micro issues need grassroots leaders. In India over a period of time, grassroots institutions and leaders have been ignored. Over a period of time grassroots institutions have been dismantled, and they remain unappreciated and unrecognized. People who expect major solutions to micro issues should come from the above. At every level people are oriented to be subservient to the state. People have "dependency syndrome" and they look for help from their government for all the issues and problems. But the macro institutions have not solved the problems.

In this country, there are major breakthroughs in the era of globalisation in the area of communication, information technology, industry, scientific and technological innovations, education and infrastructure development. How are these developments achieved? It is a major question. We have leadership in many fields but we lack such leadership at the community level and in political fronts. Leadership is the most crucial aspect for achievement and success. In a democratic set-up, leadership plays a crucial role as it has to manage the people through a democratic process. Leadership has to develop a vision for the society and the nation based on the existing conditions and aspirations of the people. The leaders have to show the way by engaging the people and suitably governing, and administrative mechanism have to be modified depending on the requirements. Hence leadership skill and capacity are the most essential ingredients to be developed in the leaders constantly. Unfortunately, such a kind of exercise is not being done in the third world countries. For all the jobs and responsibilities in governance and administration training is made mandatory, but for the elected representatives and political party leaders there is no such training. Hence, the leaders of the developing countries indulge in fire fighting and they do not act in a futuristic way. In the absence of such a leadership school to orient new leaders and capacitate the leaders constantly to cope with the contextual requirements, the present leaders are ruling the society as colonial masters by adopting the same coloured methods of exploitation.

In democratic countries, the leaders think that election is the only instrument of democracy. Democracy is not election alone. It is a culture by itself. Organisations and institutions have to nurture a culture of democracy. But democratic organizations and institutions have not developed a healthy democratic culture. No doubt, election is part of the democratic culture, but even the election has to be conducted in an ethical way as democracy wants honesty and upliftment. Democracy means leading an ethical way of life individually and collectively. Many of democratic countries which are liberated from the colonial yoke have established internal colonialism which has made the collectives and groups which are marginalized and alienated, who have started movements to work for demanding due representation for them in governance. To tackle this crisis, a series of steps are being taken. There are initiatives from above and below. Policies and decisions are taken from above and they are to be implemented locally. Steps have to be taken from grassroots to implement the policies and decisions effectively and efficiently.

It is interesting to note that there are very many initiatives taken by individuals at the community level, which have achieved tremendously. Despite corrupt policies and administration there are individuals who, without losing hope, relentlessly fight against corruption, change the attitude of the people and make strides in achieving results in their domain of activities. Their vision, commitment, aspiration and methodology are unique and varied. They create records and history. Their achievements are laudable and replicable. As youths they have developed a dream and when opportunity came they captured it and performed. All the individuals who have made unique achievements have unanimously observed that people when they do good work, would find opposition in the initial stages and if they persist with the involvement of the people then everyone will join in and help. This society looks for sincere people for public space. Such people are not coming forward and as a result, bad ones come to the public space and people have no choice but to tolerate them. Against this background, this is an attempt to document the leadership role of the youth at the grassroots. How does new leadership emerge from below, how do they develop new democratic culture, how do they build a new vision for development and how do they shape organizational culture? These are the major aspects covered in this document.

Rani Sathappan is the President of K. Rayavaram Gram Panchayat in Pudukkottai District. She has exhibited a new kind of leadership. She disseminated honesty in administration, extraordinary will power to work with women leaders through self help groups. She developed a practice of establishing partnership with the traditional panchayat in managing the affairs of the panchayats as traditional panchayat is strong in her panchayat. Normally, the traditional panchayat will not allow the gram panchayat leader, especially if the leader is woman, to act independently. But, she made it clear that she would work with them and at the same time, she would maintain her individuality. She kept the panchayat clean, neat and polythene-free and she worked in the panchayat as the panchayat leader. She was given an award for her outstanding works. One can appreciate her strategy of working with women in a society where patriarchy holds sway. Equally, she developed partnership with traditional panchayats tactfully to deliver goods to the society. She emerged as a leader on her own and now she works as a support structure for many women leaders.

Ms. Pappa is the President of Athankaraipatti Gram Panchayat of Madurai District. Being a *dalit,* she managed to establish herself as a leader and was able to help the other gram panchayat *dalit* women leaders in Tamil Nadu. She is known for her collective leadership approach. She demonstrated that the oppressed can empower themselves on their own for which they have to struggle. While struggling for victory the oppressed have to unite together. Her courage and conviction in carrying forward the struggle is a model to be emulated by other *dalit* women leaders. She had been appreciated by institutions for her relentless work for the upliftment of the poor and the marginalized. She fought with the dominant class caste Hindus and a even minister to establish herself as a leader working for the marginalized and the poor. Her extraordinary work and conviction to fight injustice in an organized way has become a model to be replicated elsewhere.

Mr. Chandran is yet another model. He is the president of Kothattai Gram Panchayat of Cuddalore District. Chandran has demonstrated his leadership qualities during the time of *tsunami* in Tamil Nadu. When everyone brought an allegation that the panchayati raj institutions were neglected in relief and rehabilitation activities in the *tsunami* rehabilitation works, whereas in Kothattai Gram Panchayat, the panchayat under the leadership of Mr. Chandran performed all the activities from relief to reconstruction and it was a model for others to show how a panchayat leader was able to take responsibility and exhibit responsiveness in dealing with the needs of the community.

Mr. Elango, is a committed young scientist who resigned his job and contested in panchayat election and became the President of the Gram Panchayat, Koothampakkam in Thiruvallur District. He had been in this position for ten years. He made the Panchayat a role model for creating self-reliant economic activities in the lines of J.C. Kumarappa, a noted Gandhian economist. He created job opportunities for the poor and made them earn and consume their own products. A cluster economy model was being created in his gram panchayat. An academy was created for the local body leaders to teach about rural economy and local governance. Elango exhibited an unusual talent in projecting an alternative model of economic development in the era of economic globalisation. He believes in knowledge economy. He proved the viability of the model. He believes appropriate technological interventions would enhance the status of the rural society. Creating an enabling environment in terms of technological input and credit facility would make the rural society more self-reliant.

Gandhiselveam has created a model when he was the chairperson of Municipal Council of Namakkal in managing waste. Waste management is a difficult problem in both urban and rural areas. Consumerism and technological innovations have complicated the issue. No government is working towards a solution. This gentleman conducted an experiment with great difficulty. He brought about many innovations and engaged the entire municipal council on development issues. He is a role model for local body leaders especially to engage the local body for development politics. When all local bodies face crisis in managing waste, he successfully managed it and it has become a model now. He created a need culture at the bottom among the people to keep the streets clean, keep the city clean. He prepared the people first. For his success, "Putting the last first" worked very well. Believing in the people and working with the people would bring the expected results. He is highly creative, simple, committed and always takes risks and he has succeeded ultimately.

Dr. Valluvan, is a doctor by profession and was the chairman of Virudhachalam Municipality. He helped a candidate to win the Legislative Assembly election when he worked as a manager of the election campaign. He had managed the entire campaign in a systematic and scientific way which prompted him to contest in the Municipal election. He followed the same principle and won the election. He came to the public office with a different object. He wanted to change the system and it should be made people-friendly and people-centric. Initially, all people joined together to oppose him. Then he started the work and in the process the politicians who supported him moved out. He fought against the bureaucratic corruption and put an end to it by his relentless fight. He fought single handedly. He was isolated and yet he fought and won the battle. He approached the court many times as higher administrative mechanism failed to respond to his demands. He unequivocally argued that people had been oriented to act as spectators and the leaders had to act against the corrupt practices. If leaders are able to win, people will join with the leaders and for which the leaders have to be prepared. In the whole process he tried his level best to integrate the people in the struggle. He hardly succeeded because people had been conditioned to perceive that corruption has been integrated in governance and administration. One can get things done with persistent persuasion but one cannot avoid corruption. One can demonstrate that one cannot take bribe but it does not mean that he can survive without giving bribe. People were prepared over a period of time. That is why he opines that leaders have to fight and establish themselves and only then will people be ready to join the crusade against corruption.

Mr. Sundaramorthy is a youth leader who organized the community for development initiative. People's needs have to be met by the government. As we all aware governments are not responsive to the people. People need a small hospital and when it was demanded government quotes only the rules and procedures and never goes beyond it. He mobilised the resources from the people and built up a hospital and proved that community is more powerful than the government in responding to the demands of the people.

Mr. Selvam is the President of the Sitharevu Gram Panchayat in Dindigul District and he has emerged as model in implementing the National Rural Employment Guarantee Scheme. He provided opportunity to the poor to work and he managed the natural resources especially the commons. He acted as a volunteer in the initial stage and he became the president of the panchayat later. His commitment and his involvement in the public activities enabled him to become the president of the village.

People of different castes have crossed the barriers of caste and worked together. Such a thing has never happened in those villages. Women of different castes mingled with others and worked together. By providing transparent administration, he emerged as model among the grassroots leaders.

India is a country of the youths, youth power has to be moulded. Youths are on their own shaping their destinies. The youth who have contributed substantially for the transformation of the poor and women in general have to be captured and analysed case by case. These youth leaders are the real change-makers.

2

War against Corruption

The 73rd and 74th amendment to the Constitution of India is a sincere and committed attempt to use the potentials of the decentralization of powers to achieve what has not been achieved so far in strengthening democracy, administering social justice, developing the economy through a process of people's participation by which the problems of participation and governance could be tackled very effectively. There are a number of essential features in the decentralization of powers and among them a few are so vital from the perspectives of the citizens. Primarily, service delivery is the most important feature of this new dispensation. It is proved throughout the world, that empowered local bodies have delivered quality service to the people without causing much cost and hardship. After the introduction of the new system of local governance based on the above amendments, the public expect effective, efficient quality service delivery by the local bodies as well as transparency in the administration of the local bodies. In this task the leadership matters more. An efficient leadership oriented in development involving people can create a model in governing local bodies. Dr. M. Valluvan, a dentist by profession joined the services of the Vridhachalam municipality with a sense of commitment with his own agenda as chairman. He first took steps to contain corruption in the municipal administration. The process was not so easy and it was full of relentless struggle. In this monograph an attempt is made to analyse and explain the strategies he adopted as well as the process of his initiatives so that one could gain a comprehensive knowledge in making initiatives to contain corruption in local bodies.

Profile of Valluvan

Valluvan (48) is basically a dentist. He belongs to Vanniar Community. After his studies, he had his specialization in ophthalmology and started his clinic in Virudhachalam in the year 1985. Valluvan's native place is a remote village namely Neivasal, located about 25 km across Virudhachalam. Neivasal is a village in Mangalore block which is one of the most backward areas of Cuddalore District. His father was a teacher; being an educated person as well as a teacher by profession, his father gave much importance to his son's education. After primary school education, Valluvan was sent to the Christian Mission School in Cuddalore for his upper primary education. He was oriented to prepare himself to score high marks in an examination conducted to identify talented students in the eighth standard. Valluvan got through the examination and availed himself of a special scholarship of the Government of India for his further studies in a model school at Pudukottai. Thus in his entire school life, he was a hosteler which helped him to have a better understanding of the various facets of life from his friends. Moreover, the discipline inculcated by the teachers of these two schools during his hostel contributed a lot in moulding his personality. Valluvan when recalling his hostel days referred to an experiment of running a "Honesty Shop" in the model school of Pudukottai by the management of the school. The concept of honesty shop is that there should not be any salesman in the shop, the students have to verify the price of the article they intend to purchase and they themselves have to put the amount in the cash box and take away the article. No one was to check the dealings. It is a call to the consciousness of the students. Valluvan opined that the significance of upholding honesty became a habit through this process. Further Valluvan recollected that his parents especially his mother used to advise him not to covet others' possessions. The trait of honesty was strengthened through home and school which enabled Valluvan to become a distinguished personality. In Thanjavur Medical College, where he contested in the election for the Student's Association and served as the General Secretary of the Association, Valluvan showed honesty in all his dealings in respect of expenditure incurred from the common fund collected every month from each student. The expenditure for the activities like screening of movies, etc. were met from the common fund. The faculty who facilitated the student's association appreciated Valluvan for his honesty and accountability. Yet another event which spoke of the determination in upholding honesty by Valluvan was the Medical Exhibition 1980 organized at the Thanjavur Medical College. At that time of the exhibition, Valluvan was in the final year. Though there were representatives of the association who could assist in organizing the exhibition, the authority of the Medical College selected Valluvan to lead volunteers of one hundred students. An entrance fee to the visitors was collected from the various counters as well as special fees for special stalls. It was a hard task of supervising and monitoring all the collection centres, pooling of all collected money and finalizing the total daily collection. Though there was a faculty, the Professor of Statistics, who served as the Faculty in-charge of these activities, Valluvan was made accountable for all the collections and other miscellaneous expenditures incurred during the exhibition days. Valluvan properly executed all the responsibilities entrusted to him and very promptly and honestly handled the cash dealings to the fullest satisfaction of the authorities. Valluvan thought that since his boyhood days he had enjoyed being a trustworthy and honest person.

His Involvement in Public Life

Valluvan, though basically a political person, as many of his close friends are in Pattali Makkal Katchi (PMK), he also used to share his feelings in respect of the welfare of the public when he had chances to interact with the leaders of the local unit of PMK. His association with the PMK local leaders enabled him to be one of a dedicated persons of the PMK party. He offered his suggestions and ideas in the activities of the PMK party wherever he was asked to do so by his friends who were active in the PMK party. Realising his potential, the PMK party high command made him serve as the PMK party election convenor of the legislative assembly when the general election for parliament and assembly were held. He discharged his duties and responsibilities as the election convenor of the PMK party very honestly and successfully. Thus he become a notable personality among the public as well as among the PMK party cadres.

Moreover, Valluvan was a popular figure as he is in association with Christopher Blind Mission of Trichy which served in their eye camps/operations and post-operation activities. Thus Valluvan, though a practitioner in the field of Medicine, slowly became a popular person in the field of politics also.

His Entry into the Municipality of Virudhachalam

During election for the local bodies held in the year 2001, the PMK party proposed Valluvan for the position of Chairman. But Valluvan did not have any interest in active politics as he had to devote his time to his medical profession. He even contacted the high command of the PMK party but he could not say no to the high command as they publicly declared his name as the PMK candidate. So, Valluvan had to take part in the campaigning activities. Valluvan reported that along with a few well wishers he contacted each and every householder in the jurisdiction of Virudhachalam municipality. He understood that the voters in general preferred his candidature for chairmanship and in respect of the ward councillor, the public had the idea of supporting their own political candidates. Out of 33 wards the PMK councillors managed to win only in three wards and the remaining seats were more or less equally divided among the DMK, AIADMK and the independents. Valluvan promised the voters that he would discharge his role and responsibilities honestly without giving any room for corrupt practices. Further, basic minimum facilities like drinking water supply, drainage system, cleanliness of roads and streets, better roads and street lights would be provided systematically. Valluvan won in the election with a majority of about 1300 votes. Though the PMK party fielded a candidate for the chairmanship in 14 municipalities all over Tamil Nadu, only in the municipality of Virudhachalam, Dr Valluvan, the PMK candidate won in the election.

The party high command appreciated his success and advised him to use the opportunity to gain popularity among the other political parties. As Valluvan defeated his strong opponent who was an ex-MLA as well as the Secretary of the Virudhachalam town unit of the AIADMK party, every citizen of Virudhachalam expected a straight forward and beneficial administration as he had promised so.

Status of Virudhachalam Municipality

The total population of Virudhachalam municipality was about 60,000 in the year 2001. Issues like lack of adequate drinking water supply, street lights, road facilities, and drainage were brought up by the councillors during the council meetings. The commissioner used to reply that as there was no adequate income to the municipality, provision of public amenities was delayed. Valluvan told that it took about six months to comprehend the real issues prevailing in the administration. It was not the lack of resources, it was rather maladministration, lack of planning and corrupt practices that failed the people, Valluvan ascertained.

During the council meetings, a few councillors brought his notice that there were illegal water supply connections to the houses and several households used electrical motors to pump water despite the ban on the use of motors. Valluvan passed a resolution to personally inspect each house in all wards. Along with the officials, Valluvan and the other councillors physically verified each house service connection of water supply and the same was further checked up with the official records to ensure legality of the connections. It was found that there were 114 illegal connections and many legally availed householders revealed that they had to pay more than the amount officially fixed to get a water supply connection to the houses.

Valluvan's Efforts to tune up the Administration

The issue of 114 illegal water supply connections was discussed in the council meeting. Valluvan worked out the loss of revenue to the administration in this respect. Moreover, due to the use of power motors in many pockets of various wards the water supply was inadequate. Hence, the municipal administration had to provide water supply through lorries. This added to the expenditure in the head of water supply. It was calculated about rupees five lakh was lost every year due to maladministration in the provision of water supply. Valluvan immediately took action to set right the activities. The license of the plumber who involved in illegal activities was cancelled immediately. Then Valluvan sought the advice of the state authorities of municipal administration in Chennai to let him know the procedure in dealing with the issues of illegal house connections and illegal use of motors to pump up water directly from the municipal supply system. An order was issued by the Government of Tamil Nadu in this regard. It was instructed to impose a fine of Rs. 5,000 to the illegal connection holder in addition to the payment for legal connection. Rs. 7,000 was fixed as fine to those who have unofficially used motors to draw water directly from the water pipe connection. Further, it was instructed to fix regulatory valves to each house service connection to ensure the equity of water supply. Valluvan informed the Commissioner to take action based on the government order already issued in this connection. But, being a part of the illegal transactions, the official did not come forward to take action against the illegal connections.

Planning for Sustainable Provision of Water Supply in each Ward

Based on the analysis of the trend of population growth, projection for the incoming fifteen years in the jurisdiction of

Virudhachalam municipality, it was calculated that in the year 2016, the population would be 95,000. Hence, with a plan to ensure adequate and sustainable water supply, construction of four new overhead tanks was decided. By proper mobilization of resources the construction of the four new OHTs was successfully completed. Moreover, by fixing an additional motor to pump water from the source to the overhead tank, an additional one lakh litre of water was pumped out. Along with the two lakh capacity the OHTs distribution was enhanced to 3 lakh litres. This innovative effort of extra pumping was undertaken in three existing overhead tanks out of a total of four tanks.

Struggle against the Corruption in Administration

Though Valluvan's effort to ensure adequacy and equity in the distribution of water succeeded by fixing additional motors as well as by construction of new overhead tanks, the resolution of the municipal council passed which instructed the commissioner to take legal action against the illegal connection was not yet initiated. Valluvan's repeated reminders to the higher authorities did not bring any impact. Realising the mindset of the corrupt officials, and the inactiveness of their superiors in taking action against them, Valluvan lodged a complaint to the Anti-corruption and Vigilance authority.

Further, the construction of an overhead tank was completed in the year 2002, but new connections to the householders were not given in spite of resolutions already passed to give new connections. The officials failed to take the initiative to give new connections as the public were aware of the honest and straight forward administration headed by Valluvan and he would not yield to the practice of bribery more than the fee officially fixed rate to get water connections. Hence, providing the new connections was delayed, the municipal administration had to spend money for the distribution of water supply through lorries in which the officials indulged in corrupt practices. Valluvan had to struggle in this regard also.

Valluvan continued his struggle by taking the facts and figures to the public. He explained the problems, the corrupt practices of the officials, the unnecessary delays in taking action against the corrupt officials, the slackness of the municipal officials in taking action against the householders of illegal pipe connection and the consequences of revenue loss to the municipality as well to the general public. He organized street meetings, organized *dharna* and observed fasting against the corrupt practices and the corrupt officials of the Virudhachalam municipality. Valluvan got moral support from the Anti-Corruption Movement of Tamil Nadu. A local unit of Anti-Corruption movement was also formed in which about 60 persons enrolled themselves immediately. Valluvan was of the opinion that in general, the public officials, traders, and businessmen felt unhappy over the initiatives against corrupt practices in the municipality administration as the unfair activities in other sectoral departments and business sector would also be brought to the public notice. Hence the segments from intelligent and other educated persons did not come out openly to support the cause for which Valluvan had been struggling.

Streamlining the Expenditures

Valluvan found that major expenditure was in the sector of water and sanitation. Hence, he closely monitored the expenditure on each item under these heads. The commissioner submitted the details relevant to the expenditure incurred during the period, July 2000 to August 2001, and sought the approval of the council in respect of items like mosquito control, repair and maintenance of motors meant for water supply, telephone charges, diesel expenditure for vehicles, handgloves for sanitary workers, and expenditure on the erection of Mark II hand pumps etc. Valluvan got the files and registers maintained in this respect and found that Rs. 25.27 lakh was spent to control mosquitos. He further looked into the monthly details and came to know that about 20,000 litres of chemicals pertaining to mosquito control were procured altogether. To ensure correctness, Valluvan verified the receipts, way bills for transportation etc., and it was found that there were misappropriation of funds. There was no proof in respect of the transportation of the chemicals, no stock entry of cans or empty cans and the receipts were bogus, handgloves were not distributed to the sanitary workers and the expenditure shown for the repair works was incorrect. And in respect of maintenance of two motors, one 20 HP and another 7.5 HP was purchased spending Rs. 39,450. When physical verification was undertaken, it was found that the motors were not available at all with 20 HP and 7.5 HP. The bills in this regard were also bogus; and the maximum expenditure in respect of erection of one Mark II hand pump was estimated about rupees fifty thousand, whereas it was shown as rupees one lakh. Further, Valluvan shared that in the audit report of 1999-2000 financial year, objection was raised for Rs. 2,39,304 under the head of the expenditure on sanitation. The commissioner did not give any explanation to the above findings brought to the notice of the council by Valluvan. He brought this to the notice of the higher authorities, but no concrete action was initiated to punish the corrupt officials. Resolutions to set things right and to take necessary corrective steps to improve the water supply and street lighting facility were not taken up by the commissioner.

Sensitizing the Public and Steps to ensure Transparency

Valluvan verified the receipts of the expenditures and found bogus bills, in the procurement of electricity equipments, misappropriation in expenditure towards erection of hand pumps, and wastage of municipality funds due to failure in disconnecting the telephone connection extended to the then vice-chairman even after the completion of her tenure. He organized a demonstration demanding the recovery of the public money from the corrupt official on 28.05.2003. Notices and handbills were printed and circulated among the public to sensitize and making them understand the corruption in the administration and the need of their participation to contain corruption.

Valluvan took necessary steps to ensure transparency in the administration so the public would exercise vigil during any transaction with the municipal administration at the personal level as well as at the public level. He formed six committees in which apart from the council members, noted public persons were also enrolled as members. He invited representatives of the Anti-Corruption Movement and other reputed non governmental organisations to witness the proceeding of the council meetings, and their suggestions were obtained to improve the administration. As roles and responsibilities of the committees formed in respect of monitoring the sectors like finance, water supply, sanitation, electricity, construction of buildings and other infrastructures and roads, the members were advised to physically verify the quality of the materials, quantity of the materials, execution of work as specified in the tender sanctioned and the members were asked to bring to the notice of the chairman if any malpractice was found. Valluvan reported that the committee members of the road sector, actually verified the quality of the stones when the roads were laid. Due to these opportunities, the participation of the public in the administration of the municipality was improved, he claimed.

To reduce the wasteful expenditures, Valluvan disconnected the phone personally given to him at the office and phone connection given at his home. Further, Valluvan ordered to disconnect the phone connection extended to the vice-chairman at her home which was allowed to continue even after the tenure of her office for which payment was made. Thus a considerable amount of monthly expenditure was saved.

System in Assessing the Property Tax

Usually one of the major items of transactions where corrupt practices in existence was in the fixation of property tax. The officials of the municipalities instead of making assessment based on the guidelines of the government, used to undervalue the properties in favour of the householders after receiving bribes from them. This resulted in loss of revenue to the municipality. Further, public were not properly informed what the rules and procedures the government fixed were in respect of the assessment of property tax. Valluvan brought this to knowledge of all the public through distribution of notices as well as by holding meetings with the public in all wards. The whole jurisdiction of the municipality was grouped into three categories and the property tax was fixed based on the models developed in the corporation of Patna, in the State of Bihar. The formula for assessment was framed taken into consideration three basic aspects in respect of properties. The place in which building is located, the characteristic features of the building and their utility: all the three items have been calculated in the Patna model and the formula has been selected as the best one at the international conference held in Dubai. Accordingly, the three categories of area were referred as region A, B, C and the rate of tax per square foot was fixed at 0.70 P, 0.50 P and 0.40 P respectively. This system was in existence since 01.10.1998, but the general public were not aware of this formula.

Valluvan took all possible steps to disseminate this information to the public. The anti-corruption movement and the association of various habitations joined in this endeavour with Valluvan. They made appeals to the public not to be the victims of cheats and corrupt officials and their practices and at the same time not to cheat the municipality. By this initiative a revenue loss of about five lakh per year was avoided. Moreover, when visits were made physically to verify properties, it was found that more than four thousand buildings were left unassessed and tax was not levied. The cunningness of the corrupt officials were brought to the notice of the public as well as the higher authorities of the Municipal Administration. Inspite of these efforts the commissioner failed to collect the taxes from the evaders. Valluvan made a complaint to the Anti-Corruption Commission in this respect also.

Ending of Corrupt Practices in issuing Certificates, Licenses and Other Services to the Public

As several complaints were received from the public about the undue delay in issuing licenses, certificates and delivery of services, Valluvan sensitized the public through the local cable network. Details like time limit and fee fixed for each and every service rendered to them by the municipal administration were announced to the public. Public were advised to obtain receipts for all payments made by them. In the mean time, misappropriation of a bill collector was reported. And as it was proved Valluvan made a complaint to the police. But the police officials failed to file an FIR. Hence Valluvan approached the court and then the bill collector was suspended. He claimed that it was not his victory but it is the victory of the people who were vigilant. If public came forward to keep vigilance, the corrupt practices of the selfish officials could be easily contained, Valluvan reiterated. After the action taken against the corrupt bill collector, the undue sufferings of the public in obtaining receipts for taxes paid, for the building license, for name transfer, birth and death certificates etc. were set right successfully, Valluvan explained.

Valluvan pointed out yet another successful attempt in preventing the corrupt practices of the officials. Even after a prompt assessment of tax for the properties was undertaken there were complaints from a few public persons and so they made an appeal to the chairman to look into the fixation of taxes. The chairman discussed that issue with the commissioner and instructed him to constitute a committee to look into the complaints. But the commissioner refused to oblige by stating that there was no such provision for that. In the mean time, the commissioner sought the help of the chairman in constituting an appeal committee as he had a complaint from the proprietor of a marriage hall that tax fixation was very high for his marriage hall. The chairman reminded the commissioner that earlier he had failed to oblige the chairman due to his personal interest he tried to intervene, and influence the municipal council. Valluvan was very alert and refused to bring a resolution in this regard. The attempt of the commissioner to give undue favour to the owner of a 'marriage hall' was successfully thwarted.

Sustaining the Spirit of Struggle against Corruption

By passing resolutions periodically, collection of evidence in respect of the corrupt practices of officials and the continuity in sensitizing the public, Valluvan sustained the spirit of the struggle. The moral support and guidance extended by the anti-corruption movement helped a lot to contain corruption. Valluvan ensured consistency in all his statements/complaints without any prejudice or favour. He wished to establish a system in the administration of the local bodies as they were meant for self rule, self-regulation and swift action against corruption. His determination yielded the desired impact. The anti-corruption and vigilance department engaged an inspector to conduct detailed enquiries. As Valluvan exercised extra vigil, he was able to identify bogus bills submitted in respect of the purchase of stationery items to the tune of Rs. 2,68,570. A resolution had been passed in the council meeting to sanction the purchase of 33 items of stationery at an estimate of Rs. 2,50,000. But the commissioner submitted bills for 37 items and the total expenditure stood at Rs. 2,68,570. When the records and vouchers were verified, it was found that certain items were purchased without obtaining quotations. In the bills double entry of materials was found; though bills were brought from the shops located at Thambaram and material was told as forwarded through parcel lorry service, there was no evidence to prove that there was a forward of materials to the municipality. All these misdeeds of the officials were brought to the notice of the councillors, public, representatives of the people, belonging to the Consumer Forum, Anti-Corruption Movement and welfare associations of the habitations. It was resolved to file a case with the police. The police delayed to file a case and refused to register the FIR based on the complaint given by the Chairman. And then Valluvan filed a case in the high court.

Ensuring Provision of Basic Amenities to the Newly Established Habitations

Residents of new habitations appealed to the municipal administration to provide minimum basic amenities in their area. Resolutions were also passed by the councillors in this regard. But the commissioner did not take necessary action as per the resolution. The staff of the municipality also did not show any real interest to execute their responsibilities as public were alert and not ready to pay any extra money in respect of any transaction to be made with the administration. As the ways of corrupt practices were plugged, the officials resorted into non cooperation with the council. In the mean time, the residents of new habitations organised *Dharna*—public agitation against the municipal administration. The officials reported that the house sites were not the approved ones. Valluvan undertook a fasting on 13.07.2005 demanding the right to live. The *tehsildar* convened a consultative meeting in this regard and at last the commissioner agreed to take the initiative for sanction of approval to the house sites.

The councillor and the chairman quickly and openly worked to fulfil the felt needs of the public. At the same time due to the absence of honesty and straight forwardness among the officials, delivery of services to the public was denied. Deliberations of the public meetings were videographed and broadcast through the local cable network to sensitize the public, the financial transactions of the municipality were distributed every month to the representatives of the habitations, press persons and to the general public. Valluvan's efforts to speed up action on the resolutions were deliberately delayed due to the non-cooperation of the officials.

Valluvan made a good system of communication to redress the grievances of the public. Cell phones were distributed to the electricians, plumbers, sanitary inspectors and the staff, office manager, town planning building inspector, revenue inspector, assistant engineer, municipal engineer, commissioner, the vice-chairman and the chairman of the Virudhachalam municipality (totally 14 in number under a group system of communication). This system of communication was successfully executed and people's accessibility with the officials become very easy and effective Valluvan confirmed.

As the fixation of property tax was promptly done, the revenue of the municipals augmented. Due to the availability of funds, many amenities like exactly 500 street lights, additional buildings to schools, road facilities and drainage system were executed at the cost of Rs. two crore.

The Concept of Local Body System

Valluvan informed that the provision of drinking water, street lights, public health utilities, quality roads and quick, prompt and kind ways in delivering the services to the public were the major expectations of the public from the system of the local bodies.

As Valluvan's efforts to sensitize public about the corrupt practices of municipal officials gained momentum, the officials wantonly delayed the prosecution of crooks as they did not get extra money from anybody including the contractors. Due to non cooperation of the officials, the council meetings were not convened. Several councillors instead of joining hands with the chairman, endorsed the activities of the commissioner and tried to dethrone the chairman. Valluvan referred that the council did not have any power to implement the decisions and at the same time, it could not punish the corrupt officials. It was high time necessary amendments were made in the Act to strengthen decentralisation and government has to be influenced to share its power and responsibilities, with regard to finance, functions and functionaries to the local bodies, Valluvan emphasised.

Involvement of Public in the Struggle against Corruption

Valluvan's struggle against corruption was an innovative one. He first sensitized the public in respect of the principles of governance namely accountability, transparency, equity and equality. His strategies of formation of standing committees and involvement of public opinion, telecasting of deliberation of the council meetings, inviting NGOs and the representatives of NGOs like Consumer Forum, Anti-Corruption Movement to attend the council meetings. Publication of hand bills, notices, and street meetings to empower the community created an atmosphere conducive to the process of participatory governance. Further, Valluvan filed a case against the Secretary of Government of Tamil Nadu Municipal Administration and Water Supply, Chennai, the Commissioner of Municipal Administration, Chenglepet and the Commissioner of Virudhachalam Municipality. The case was filed at the High Court during the year 2004. Valluvan collected rupee one from each voter to meet the expenditure. Valluvan never regretted the delays as he had already witnessed success in containing corruption. He continuously reminded the court to speed up the enquiry proceedings. At last he succeeded. The High Court delivered a judgment in April 2007 by which the respondents were directed to consider Valluvan's representation and in accordance with law asked to pass appropriate orders thereon within a period of three months from the date of the receipt of the copy of the order of the High Court. Though Valluvan's tenure was completed on 24th October 2006, his struggle against corruption continued. He demanded to speed up the enquiry of the authority of Anti-corruption and vigilance against the corrupt practices of the officials brought out with evidences. And criminal cases filed against five corrupt staff were also perused by Valluvan in respect of the misappropriation in the purchase of stationery items. The enquiry is still in progress.

Exercising e-governance

To ensure transparency, an information centre was established, at the initiative of Valluvan. Storage of information in respect of all 21 types of activities undertaken in the various sections of the municipality was attempted. But due to non-cooperation of the officials, this system of full fledged e-governance was yet to be implemented. Valluvan took efforts to sensitize the public about the 207 works carried out at the cost of rupees two crore extended by Tamil Nadu Urban Finance and Infrastructure Development Corporation through e-governance.

Exercising the Right to Information Act

Valluvan sent an appeal to the higher authority of the municipal administration to give information in respect of solid waste management activities, process of e-governance system and audit reports in respect of all municipalities in the State of Tamil Nadu. He was able to get a reply. Hence, Valluvan had the opinion that if awareness of the public was improved, the corrupt practices of the officials would be brought under control. He added that by proper utilization of the Right To Information Act and by influencing the government to strengthen the e-governance system a considerable impact could be made in maintaining transparency.

Overcoming the Problems of Selfish Traders

When there was a proposal to undertake special works in respect of the beautification of Virudhachalam town, the district collector convened a consultative meeting in which representatives of the various associations were invited to participate. During the meeting there was a reference to the road accidents frequently occurring near the junction of the market area. It was told that there were so far 64 accidents of which 12 were fatal ones as per the police records. The cause of these accidents was traffic jam due to unauthorized shops and other commercial establishments in spite of the fact that a pucca market had been provided separately. The merchants erected their shops along the roadsides which was the main reason for the accidents. The District Collector ordered the removal of all shops and it was decided to construct a compound wall so that the unauthorized ways could be closed. Valluvan immediately convened the council meeting and passed a resolution in this regard. But the commissioner in connivance with the selfish traders did not take any step to remove the encroachments and to build the compound wall as per the resolution of the council. The vernacular daily *Dinamalar* highlighted the undue delay in carrying out the resolution of the council passed as per the instructions of the District Collector. The District Collector summoned the commissioner and instructed him to take immediate steps as per the decision. The encroachments were removed. In the mean time, the traders organized themselves and staged a *dharna* against the construction of the compound wall. About 65 of them were arrested and the construction of the compound wall was continued throughout the night and successfully completed. The selfish designs of the traders were dismantled, though the municipal officials were reluctant to discharge their responsibility in this regard, Valluvan explained.

But the traders had resorted to another method to deal with that issue. The market area was located very close to the garden area of the temple. Hence, the traders influenced the temple administration to demand a pathway to have easy access to the garden. The temple administration went to the District Court to give an interim stay against the municipality but the court refused to oblige. The temple administration made an appeal to the High Court. In the mean time the traders succeeded in influencing the councillors. And the majority of the councillors demanded that a council meeting be convened to pass a resolution to provide a pathway in the compound wall. But Valluvan refused to oblige. The municipal staff and the commissioner supported the councillors. The councillors convened the council meeting in the absence of Valluvan and passed a resolution to provide a pathway as demanded by the traders. The resolution was submitted to the notice of the High Court but the High Court refused to yield to their demand but ordered the District Collector to hold a detailed enquiry and to submit the findings to the Court. The Collector submitted the details and the High Court gave an order to cancel the resolution of the council and to build the compound wall without any provision for a pathway. Valluvan felt for the anti-people stance taken by the majority of the councillors. He insisted that only through sensitizing the public, activities of the local bodies could be streamlined.

The Mindset of Officials

Valluvan is of the view that the bureaucracy in general did not give real concern to the public causes. Many officials calculated the scope of illegal income they could get through the activities carried out in the municipality. Valluvan found that the license holders of shops and establishments located inside the bus stand failed to pay the fixed amount properly to the municipality. Hence a resolution was passed to cancel the license of those who failed to pay the due amount to the municipality. But the commissioner did not take any step to take action as per the resolution. Moreover, the commissioner passed orders to extend the license for a further period to a few wrongdoers despite the resolution to cancel them. Valluvan cited as an example, the case of a license holder who withheld the due fee of Rs. 70,251. Instead of cancelling his license, the commissioner extended his license and then the due was accrued in about rupees ten lakh. Valluvan brought the issue of the revenue loss incurred due to the dishonest practice of the commissioner and tried to appoint an honest officer in his place. Though the dishonest commissioner was transferred, the new person failed to join. He applied long leave as he was not ready to fulfil his responsibilities in a straightforward way. Valluvan said that until there was an autonomous body in each district exclusively to take action against the dishonest corrupt officials, the bureaucracy would never be afraid of indulging in corrupt practices, as the function of the anti-corruption and vigilance department was very slow and cumbersome, Valluvan added. Further, he suggested that in the new body as referred above, membership should be given to the representatives of non-governmental institutions which try to contain corruption in public life.

Valluvan explained that in spite of the functioning of local fund audit department, the municipal administration was not serious in taking action against the objections raised in their report. Valluvan by exercising the Right to Information Act, obtained the report of the local fund audit from 1965 to 2000 and found that there were 1945 objections raised in respect of expenditures of a total Rs. 6.9 crore in the Virudhachalam municipality during the period.

Moral Supporters

Valluvan informed that he gained strength and support from organisations like Anti-corruption Movement, and the Consumers Forum. They published the experiments of Valluvan in struggling against corruption in the municipal administration. Popular dailies like *The Hindu* and *Dinamani* featured his strategies introduced in ensuring transparency and handling the corrupt officials. Valluvan indicated that the media could play a significant role in ensuring good governance.

Scope for Local Bodies in the Socio-economic Development of the Citizens

Valluvan is an optimist in respect of the scope of good governance through local bodies. He opined that there is a lot of opportunities to understand the system of governance and administration by the elected representatives as well as the public after the introduction of the 73rd and the 74th amendments to the Constitution of India. Now, a number of elected representatives including women have a direct interface with the system of governance. As the council is closely to work with the bureaucracy, the councillors have opportunities to understand the governing system, politics, plans, programmes and the procedures by which they will improve their leadership skills, Valluvan added.

Scope for People's Participation

Valluvan considers that through strengthening the local bodies, the concept of participatory governance could be more effective. Activities like constitution of standing committees, encouragement to the public representatives apart from the elected ones to attend the council meetings, dissemination of the decisions of the council to the people in sensitizing media as well as distribution of notices, and undertaking direct action on the issues faced by the municipality would encourage the participation of public, Valluvan explained.

By ensuring transparency through periodical interface with the public, explaining the procedures in the fixation of taxes and other fees, the municipal administration has increased its income. Moreover, public welfare activities like running of hospitals, dispensaries, maternity centres, schools, libraries and public parks could be successfully managed though the income generated along with the grants of the government, Valluvan stated. Valluvan further pointed out that by proper assessment in the fixation of property tax, and other revenue sources, any municipal administration can contribute to the development of the adjacent village panchayats.

Valluvan further pointed out that steps to contain corruption at the local level would be possible when compared to act at the higher level. He cited examples from his own administration. He said that he was able to set right many things in the functioning of the municipal administration. His efforts to book the corrupt officials was fruitful though there were delays in this aspect, he added. As income from the educational tax was properly pruned, at a stroke, provision of additional buildings to many schools was possible, Valluvan quoted. Moreover, many wasteful expenditures were properly curtailed due to the close monitoring which would be possible only at the grassroots governance, Valluvan added.

The Importance of Building Good Citizenry

The establishment of good governance is possible only through the active participation of the citizens and it is ensured through enlightened citizenry who would alert the good leader, develop self interest in the affairs of the governance system and make use of opportunities available in the governance system for participation. Further, controlling and stopping of the misdeeds of the bureaucracy could also be easily undertaken by the effective participation of efficient citizens especially when pro-activeness of the councillors/chairman is viewed as anti-government. But the pro-activeness of the public will have its own impact not only on the higher administrators in the government system but also on the rulers themselves, Valluvan reiterated. He emphasized that awareness building on citizenship, action against corrupt officials and non-cooperation with corrupt and self-interested councillors and vigilance activities of non governmental organisations like Anti-Corruption and Consumers Forum movement, and Catalyst Trust could lead us towards the dawn of good governance.

Valluvan's experiments in these aspects is an eye-opener to all concerned as he had achieved success in containing corruption, in ensuring transparency, in bringing public participation through standing committees, in augmenting resources and in improving the basic amenities to the public. When Valluvan assumed office of the Chairmanship there were inadequate funds to undertake the development works in the municipality of Virudhachalam. At the end of his tenure, there was a balance of 2.45 crore rupees with the municipal administration. He accomplished a lot of development inspite of the antipathy of the corrupt officials and the stand of opposition taken by majority of his councillors. It was because of his determination and solidarity shown by NGOs, representatives of the Habitants' Associations and the judiciary, he acknowledged.

3

A War on Dust

Sri. S. Gandhi Selvam (32) is a young and energetic leader. He hails from Namakkal town. He belongs to the Konguvellala Gounder Community. His father who is a sympathizer of the DMK party evinced interest in public life. But as he concentrated on his business, especially lorry transportation he was not able to involve himself seriously in party work or public life. At the same time he did not criticize the social activities of his son Gandhi Selvam. Gandhi Selvam even during his student days had opportunities to participate in the political activities especially of the DMK Party during the Assembly elections. He was attracted to the personality of the DMK party leader Kalaignar Karunanidhi. Though he did not get much orientation in the ideology of that party he slowly moved towards the core activities of the DMK party and become an active cadre of the student's wing of the party. He was elected to the position of secretary of the student's association and later at the college as the chairperson of student's union. His association with the party leaders brought him to the limelight. Gandhi Selvam realized the importance of the recognition and respect extended to him by the community, and so he developed positive qualities of leadership like respecting others, practicing group-based activities, maintenance of self-discipline and character and keeping honesty in all public activities.

Entry into the Local Body

Gandhi Selvam steadily improved his public image and intensified his social activities through his involvement in party affairs. As his presence was not seriously needed in his father's business, Gandhi Selvam utilized much of his time for party work whereas some of his colleagues gave more importance to caste-based activities. Gandhi Selvam opined that though caste had it own impact on the socio-political views of any individual, one should have ideological orientation in politics so as the individual could better serve the society.

In the year 1986, when the election to the local bodies was announced, Gandhi Selvam contested in the ward election in the municipality of Namakkal. He had just come out from college, after completing his graduation in science. His activities as a student wing leader prompted him to serve the cause of Sri Lankan Tamils. It helped him to become a publicly-known personality. He won in the election. As a municipal councillor he was not able to undertake any concrete activity due to his limited exposure to development activities. But he improved his knowledge and understanding of the functioning of the municipality and the felt needs of the public.

He consolidated his position in the party and became the district convenor of the students' wing and then became the district secretary of the party unit. In the mean time, in 1993, he got married. His wife is a post graduate. She and her family already knew the political activities of Gandhi Selvam and they never stood in his way. Even after marriage, Gandhi Selvam was able to devote much of his time to political activities. He has two children, one son studying in the eighth standard and one daughter who is in fifth standard. To provide quality education, Gandhi Selvam put his children in hostels.

New System of Local Governance and his Second Entry into Municipality

Being a well-informed young man, Gandhi Selvam gained more knowledge in governance, administration and development.

At this juncture, the 73rd and 74th Amendments to the Constitution of India were introduced. He went through the newspapers and comprehended the scope of 73rd and 74th Amendments. In Tamil Nadu, during 1996, when election to the local bodies was announced under the new system, Gandhi Selvam contested again for the councillor's position in the Namakkal Municipality.

Being a popular person, Gandhi Selvam easily won the election, and became a councillor. Though he could become the chairperson, due to the coalition with the Congress party, as the chairman position was earmarked for the elected councillor of the Congress party, realizing the situation, Gandhi Selvam shifted his attention and efforts towards the cooperative institutions, namely the Namakkal Urban Cooperative Bank. As elections to the cooperative institutions were also conducted immediately after the elections to the local bodies, Gandhi Selvam contested in the cooperative election, won and became a director. And as majority of the directors were from the DMK party, Gandhi Selvam was able to climb to the position of the Chairman of the Urban Cooperative Bank of Namakkal. He decided to take this opportunity to serve the community better.

Gandhi Selvam as a Person with Dual Responsibilities

Gandhi Selvam understood the significance of the position and power as the chairman of the Urban Cooperative Bank, he devoted much of his time to the activities of the bank. Moreover, he thought that as a councillor he could not do much. He valued the bank's activities as it directly helped the public. He attended the municipal council meetings and once a special fund for local tourism development was available, Gandhi Selvam worked for the provision of sodium vapour lamps along the road leading to the famous Anjaneyar Temple which attracts thousands of people from different towns and villages. It is the culture of the local people to bring their newly purchased vehicles to the temple for conducting *poojas* with a belief that the ritual would ensure the safety of the vehicles.

Due to this culture, this particular road is always crowded. Hence, he claimed that sodium vapour lamps should be fixed in the lamp posts located along the road side. He succeeded in getting an allocation of 12 sodium vapour lamps and the public appreciated his efforts as a councillor. He used to bring to the attention of the officials the grievances of the people in his ward. Issues related to the drinking water supply, removal of waste and mosquito control was also emphasized by him.

Gandhi Selvam, when performing his roles and responsibilities as the chairman of the Namakkal Urban Cooperative Bank, made use of every opportunity to enhance his leadership qualities. As the chairman's position is a respectable one, he used to improve his efficiency. He visited the bank office everyday during the working hours and spent two to three hours to carry out his duties. He understood the various problems of the customers as he used to show patience when hearing the grievances of the customers. The Namakkal Urban Bank is a reputed one, serving the customers for the past one hundred years. The office building is a hundred years old and it was in a dilapidated condition. The local engineers advised him to demolish the old building instead of undertaking any renovation. But it was a huge estimate to construct a new building, the decision on the same had been pending for more than a decade, and Gandhi Selvam decided to build it during his tenure. He took all efforts to construct a new building and made consultation with the district officials as well as the higher authorities of the cooperative department. He met the then cooperative minister Thangapandian. Gandhi Selvam's efforts bore fruits. He got the permission to construct a new building at the cost of Rs. 80 lakh. Though the blue print for building the structure was undertaken under the guidance of government functionaries to give a face lift to the frontage of the building, he engaged an architect in Chennai, by spending money from his own pocket. He personally monitored the execution of the building construction and felt proud that during his tenure, the construction of the new building was completed.

In respect of service delivery of the bank, Gandhi Selvam related that the main service of extending loans for the construction of houses, establishment of small scale industries and promotion of existing businesses as well as industrial activities have been properly executed. To ensure the speedy delivery of credit, Gandhi Selvam developed a new practice. He moved with the staff and officials of the bank, enabled them in the process of loan applications and involved himself in finalizing the issue pending in respect of the inspection of house sites, business sites or other concerned activities of the customers and ensured that the decisions were taken without any delay. He claimed that no untoward incidence occurred in the transaction of bank affairs during his tenure. His service as the chairman of the Urban Bank was very much useful to him to climb up the ladder of leadership.

Gandhi Selvam's Trial in the Assembly Election

During 2001 assembly election, Gandhi Selvam got the ticket to contest in the Kapilarmalai Assembly constituency as the DMK candidate. The Kapilarmalai is not a familiar constituency to him though he had been the district secretary of the DMK party. The constituency of Kapilarmalai was very carefully nurtured by the bigwigs of AIADMK Party, especially by an ex-minister of the AIADMK party. Hence, the PMK candidate who had coalition in election with AIADMK won in the election.

Gandhi Selvam as Chairman

Gandhi Selvam utilized the opportunity in the position to serve the community through the municipality. He contested for the position of chairman during 2001 election. His opponent candidate's family background was very strong. The father of the opponent candidate contested for the Chairman's position twice but could not win. Hence this family fielded a younger person. The competition was very tough. Gandhi Selvam had confidence that he would win as he gained the support of the voters of different castes and religions, whereas his opponent was a key member in the caste association. Gandhi Selvam won in the election by a difference of 550 votes. He managed to get more votes from the downtrodden community. As chairman, he went to the office regularly and was available himself to meet the public

Overcoming of Political Groupism

There were a total of 30 councillors, and nine councillors belonged to the DMK party and as there was direct election to the Chairperson at that time, he was able to become the chairman. Moreover, the vice-chairperson was from the AIADMK. Due to minority status, for about a period of four to six months, there he had difficulties in running the administration. Decisions on common issues were not able to be finalized due to this. Moreover, the ruling party of that time was the AIADMK. Hence, the higher officials of the municipal administration as well as the other departments were not friendly with Gandhi Selvam. But Gandhi Selvam understood the situation. Instead of blaming anybody, he thought over how to bring development in that context. He made use of the deliberations in the council meeting to share his development ideas of improving the civil amenities in all wards and the importance of working together. He was able to win the hearts of two independent members who had ties with the DMK. Further, by-election was conducted in four wards and Gandhi Selvam made use of this chance and ensured the victory of the candidates fielded by his party. Moreover, two more independent members also joined the DMK and the strength of the DMK and its Alliance had a considerable level of strength to carry out the deliberations of municipal meetings more meaningfully. In the mean time, the councillors of AIADMK realized the good efforts initiated by Gandhi Selvam and extended their support.

When introducing any proposal for the common cause, Gandhi Selvam always made his position clear that his interest was to bring development to the municipality. His performance was closely observed by the councillors. He was born and brought up in Namakkal city, has the full details of every nook and corner of city. He used to make frequent visits to all the 30 wards and personally monitored the programmes implemented by the Municipality. He visited the areas where grievances had been reported. He brought them to the notice of the concerned ward members and asked them to go along with him during the visits. He encouraged the participation of all. Against this background, he was able to take right decisions on issues and that too to the satisfaction of all concerned. His unbiased approach to the issues brought up in the council meetings projected him as an efficient leader.

Rapport with the Officials

Gandhi Selvam opined that the bureaucratic delays and its red tapism could be handled successfully if the leader is straight-forward and matured in public life. Gandhi Selvam got the support of the officials and staff. He did not have any misunderstandings with them. He brought to the notice of the concerned officials/staff the details of any issue related to their administration and told them about their shortcomings, instead of threatening them. His official dealings were transparent. He understood the nature of the complaints brought to his notice by the public in connection with tax fixation, name transfer, registration of births and deaths and issuing of any other certificates etc. and personally went to the concerned section of the administration and ensured the clearance of the pending issues as early as possible. This is the most important issue in the municipal administration. The municipal officials used to get money as bribe for all these things. Gandhi Selvam smoothly handled these issues and forced the officials to deliver such services without getting money from the public. He earned a good name through this. He maintained a very good relationship with the officials and hence, they cooperated with the chairperson and delivered services.

Gandhi Selvam came to understand the issue of variation in the fixation of house taxes. He learnt that house tax for the poor was properly fixed whereas the middle and higher income households were able to influence the concerned staff and got reduction in the fixation. Gandhi Selvam got the list of the demands and he personally visited the house sites, took the measurement of the houses and verified with the original demands list. In many of the cases the measurement was not correct and the officials had wantonly reduced the rates. He openly challenged the concerned staff and succeeded in making necessary corrections in accordance with the original measurement and fixed taxes. He prevented tax evasion in some wards. This was yet another vexatious problem in municipal administration throughout Tamil Nadu. Not only officials but people were also involved in the corrupt practice. By bribing the officials people got the rates fixed at the lowest. As a result the Local Body lost its revenue. But he was not able to continue these operations due to various reasons.

Setting right the Issues in the Provision of Water Supply

There were about 850 house service connections in this town and distribution of water supply was not to the satisfaction of the public. Water was provided to the public once in four days. Further, there were complaints about the water supply during the municipal meetings. Gandhi Selvam proposed to inspect all the areas to know about the real situation and then to adopt solutions for the problems. All councillors, officials and technicians were gathered together and visited the municipal area and the real situation in each area was noted. There were 72 points to regulate the distribution of water supply. Areas where the water supply was in excess and wherever distribution was inadequate due to the nature of the topography of the area, ups and downs, were identified. The technicians failed to meet the problems when they laid pipelines earlier. The necessity of relaying of pipelines to correct the distribution issue was discussed. Some councillors raised their apprehension that the existing system in their ward might be disturbed. Gandhi Selvam ensured all councillors that equal distribution of water to all areas would be maintained. Even after the relaying of pipelines, it was found there were some problems in some pockets. Then it was decided to do pumping for all the 24 hours and water supply was provided on alternative days and all pockets received adequate supply. Within a period of two months, the adequate distribution and timely availability of water supply was ensured to the public. All the issues in the distribution were properly dealt with only because of the cooperation extended by the staff and officials of the municipality and the role of councillors had a special impact, Gandhi Selvam observed. The councillors visited the households who objected to relaying of pipelines and explained in detail the new system of distribution and pacified the public. Due to this pro-activeness of the councillors irrespective of their party affiliations, the issue of uneven distribution of water supply was successfully dealt with, Gandhi Selvam explained.

Gandhi Selvam ascribed to socio-cultural values the prevalence of positive climate in Namakkal city inspite of political differences. The socio-cultural system practiced in Namakkal was a unique one. Namakkal is famous in the transportation industry, especially for lorry transportation. It is estimated that there are more than 10,000 lorries and about 3000 LPG tankers owned by the Namakkal business men, which ply throughout the State and country. This progress was achieved over the past forty years by the inhabitants of Namakkal. Lorry owners were once farmers and due to drought and famine slowly and wisely preferred to go into the business of transportation. Now they are lorry owners and own the private financial institutions financing 'to purchase lorries' and so more lorries operate in Namakkal. Gandhi Selvam told that every adult man in all families used to think how to become rich. Hence, they do not indulge in any petty issues and always engage their mind and energy towards acquiring wealth. This atmosphere enabled even economically weaker sections of the community who used to toil themselves and slowly obtained higher standards in life. Of course, there are many political parties, caste and religions in Namakkal town but the citizens of Namakkal gave less importance to them and gave much importance to earn a standard life through their own hard work.

Further, the industrial sector has developed into new phases in the Namakkal area, including textiles, poultry industry. All such business activities demanded full involvement and attention of the stakeholders, the employers as well as the employees. This pro-activeness among the individuals is the secret of the prevalence of harmony in all four taluks of Namakkal district namely Namakkal, Thiruchengodu, Velur and Rasipuram. There is yet another activity that of establishing private educational institutions by enterprising individuals in Namakkal. Further, in the above mentioned business activities there are opportunities for more interface between the citizens of Namakkal district and the citizens of other areas; mutual learning and understanding also were strengthened. This contributed to the improvement of socio-cultural life in Namakkal area.There are occurrences of inter-caste marriages between the BC and SC communities. It is learnt that marriages between different castes in backward communities are not considered as unwanted whereas in the case of SC, the inter-caste marriages are not encouraged. And due to economic progress, many youths who belong to SC community prefer white collar jobs. These youths after school education continue their college education or technical education and try to get jobs instead of becoming manual labourers. Earlier, they were cleaners and unskilled workers and now-a-days they have become clerks, computer operators, supervisors or mill workers. Education and cultural development are aimed at by the members of all castes. Hence, one cannot find individuals other than very aged persons sitting idly in the jurisdiction of Namakkal District, Gandhi Selvam informed.

INNOVATION IN SOLID WASTE MANAGEMENT

Namakkal city is famous for Sri Hanuman Temple which is located along the National Highway going through the heart of the city. Devotees used to throng in large numbers every morning and evening to get the *darshan* of the main deity, Hanuman. Further, the owners of motor vehicles also bring their new vehicles and perform *pooja* to ensure the blessings of the Swami Hanuman for their safety. Due to this, the premises of the temple and the road sides near that temple are filled with wastes and it became a threat to the environment. As the waste was dumped in heaps, Gandhi Selvam made arrangements for a cleaning campaign which was followed by strict regulations for the parking of vehicles on the temple road, as well as prohibiting performing *poojas* to the vehicles near the temple area. Further, the solid waste discarded by the dwellers of ward number two in which the jurisdiction of the temple, lay was dumped along the road. As it was a bigger menace than in any other ward, Gandhi Selvam discussed that issue with the commissioner and the officials of the sanitation division. Gandhi Selvam involved the councillors in this matter. Though it was a special discussion, a majority of the councillors suggested the possibility of making the whole city of Namakkal clean and tidy. The commissioner took a special interest and it was decided to pay attention to ward number two where the removal of solid waste had to be ensured every day and at the door step of each house. It was proposed to have a hand-pull cart to transport the collected waste. Hence, to ensure the proper design of the cart, various types of hand-pull carts were put into use in places like the railway station and hospitals. And then, all the hand-pull carts were purchased by the municipal authority.

Sensitizing the Community

Collection of solid waste at the door step was a new practice which was never attempted in the city of Namakkal. To ensure the cooperation of the households an appeal notice to all individual households of ward two was distributed asking them to put the waste only in the dust bins. Sanitation workers were engaged privately for the assignment. They were instructed to collect the solid waste each day in the morning from all the dust bins. But the households did not properly carry out this process and the efforts taken by the Municipality did not bear fruit even though there were twelve dust bins available in the streets of ward number two.

Failure in the safe removal of solid waste was discussed in the council meeting. The councillors suggested removing the dust bins so that the waste could be collected directly from the households. But the households had to keep the waste in polythene bags or in other containers. The sanitary workers engaged in this work used to keep the cart in the street and rang the bell to announce their arrival. The households had to give the waste the sanitary workers who stocked the same in the carts. To introduce this system of daily collection of waste door to door, initially for a period of ten days, Gandhi Selvam had arranged for demonstrations and he along with the commissioner and the concerned councillor accompanied the sanitary workers when they were on their job. It was a rare scene to the public of Namakkal, that of the group consisting of commissioner, the Chairperson and councillors of Namakkal municipality accompanying the sanitary workers. They visited each street, stood before each house, helped the households to put the solid waste in the cart and briefed them about the novel attempt of the municipality to keep the second ward as a model in the safe disposal of solid waste.

The issue of collecting waste during holidays/festival period was a great challenge due to over dumping of wastes and inadequacy of the labour force. And it was decided to engage more sanitary workers. To remove the heap of waste stored during the festivals, extra labour force was engaged and the streets became clean and tidy.

Replication of the Model to Other Wards

The door by door collection of solid waste became a success in the ward number two, as the inhabitants understood the importance of sanitation and the availability of a system. After discussing the success, all the other councillors of the remaining wards came forward to replicate the experiment in their own wards also. And within a period of 20 days, the households were properly sensitized and slowly extended their cooperation. Many households had come with a separate bag for organic wastes. But there were a few who still dumped their solid waste into the drainage. They were advised to use the dustbins with the personal involvement of the ward councillors as well as the youth volunteers. Those who failed to obey were given a warning and later imposed fines. Public witnessing the procession of the councillors, officials and the Chairman of Namakkal criticized their efforts, and those who had been defeated in the election made mockery of their efforts. Even the members of his in-law family felt for the plight of the chairman, who had to work along with the scavengers. But the councillors realized the importance of making the city clean, extended their cooperation and with a new enthusiasm they conducted the activities of solid waste management successfully.

Role of Mass Media

The media covered the activities widely and through the local cable channel, and the significance of the safe disposal of solid waste was stressed. The officials extended their cooperation made periodical visits to the streets, met the households and ensured the sustained cooperation of all concerned.

Improving the System

As of now, the collection of solid waste is extended to all wards, and the municipal council decided to make it a more efficient system. As there was a necessity of more labour force, more number of carts and systematic regulation and monitoring their activities, a tender was called from competent institutions to engage the labourers and the safe disposal of all solid wastes in all wards of the Namakkal Municipality.

The number of households in each ward and in each street was properly counted and the number of labourers to be engaged in the collection was announced. It was found that for at least hundred houses a pair of labourers was needed;

and a hand-pull cart had to be available to transport the waste. On an average four labourers were needed to each ward and the boundary of each ward was properly notified. To collect waste, a lorry was procured by the municipality. The contractor was asked to meet the fuel expenses and the wages to the workers. A daily wage of Rs. 50 per worker was paid.

The process of collection of solid waste was demonstrated and it was a surprise to note that many women from poor families of SC community came forward to work. The assigned work to these contract labourers was only collection of solid waste. The maintenance of drainage was done by the sanitary workers of the municipality. The householders were severely warned not to put any solid waste in the drainage.

The Problems of Collecting Solid Waste of Uneven Size

When this novel system of collecting solid wastes was put into practice, the public raised the following questions :

- Will the sanitary workers come everyday without any break ?
- How can the unclassified waste be disposed ?
- In the event of any festival/social celebration as a large quantity of solid waste is accumulated, how can this waste be removed in a day ?

The issues raised by the public were deliberated at the council meetings. The contractor was instructed to engage adequate workers when some workers absent themselves for work and in respect of the collection of miscellaneous items of solid waste, the households were asked to inform well in advance so that the lorry would be brought to collect those items whether they had unwieldy waste. Yet another issue of collection of large quantity of solid waste from the house where there was any celebration, such households were asked to inform well in advance and adequate number of drums/pins/ jute bags would be provided by the municipality. The inhabitants of all wards witnessing the successful implementation of the system oriented themselves and extended their full cooperation. Though here and there, there were some problems, the councillors were able to attend personally to such issues and set things right. After a period of six months, the system became a success. Nowhere in any ward there was any dust bin. The solid waste was collected every morning in each street of each ward and dumped in the manure yard. The segregation of waste was done by the labourers themselves and the organic waste was converted into manure and the few inorganic waste items were sold and the whole accounting was maintained by the labourers themselves.

Environmental Cleanliness in Hamlets

Four areas were identified where the number of hutments was large. Altogether, about 4,000 huts were in the above referred four areas. These areas were located in ward number two, under the jurisdiction of Namakkal Fort near the main town. The majority of the inhabitants belonging to SC community eat beef. Hence, there is slaughtering of cows in these areas and beef is sold. Due to this practice, this locality was unclean. Orienting the inhabitants of these hutment areas was very challenging. The councillors of the concerned wards took personal interest in giving an orientation to the households. The staff of the municipality and the commissioner frequently visited and educated the public. Gandhi Selvam himself spent time with the ward members and staff personally and discussed matters with the community leaders and youths of the locality. The slaughtering of cows in a public place was prohibited and the license holders were asked to do the slaughtering away from public places and the wastage was kept inside polythene bags instead of throwing it outside. To prevent open defecation, public toilets were constructed separately for men and women under the Central Rural Sanitation Programme. Moreover, provision for bathing as well as washing of clothes in the toilets was also given. Slowly, the poor families of these hutments adhered to the activities as instructed by the municipal council.

Now sanitation and public hygiene is well maintained in these hutments too.

Maintenance of Sanitation in the Bazaar and Market Places

The owners of the commercial establishments and shopping area were called for a meeting to enlist their cooperation in making the town clean. The system of collection of solid wastes was explained and the proposal for the collection of solid wastes from the commercial establishments with the help of an auto was explained. The shopkeepers were asked to keep the solid waste in the premises and not to dump at the side or in front of their firms. Everyday, a morning public announcement was made about the arrival of the auto and the labourers were told to go to each firm and collect the waste materials. There were two autos going around the streets and market places every morning to collect the solid waste directly from each establishment. At times, a few firms failed to adhere to the procedures and dumped the waste near their shops. The sanitary workers did not remove this waste and allowed it to be kept for two or three days. Then the issue was solved successfully and the concerned traders agreed to adhere to the rules framed by the municipal authorities. Gandhi Selvam met the erring traders and briefed them about the steps and efforts taken by the municipality and sought their cooperation for their own sake as well as for the sake of the other people. Gandhi Selvam was severely criticized by some well-to-do traders for being strict in this aspect. Gandhi Selvam told that he never felt sorry for the criticism as some of the people did not have proper civic sense. He was optimistic that by pursuance one could change the mindset of the public. The waste in the market place was removed daily and a clean atmosphere was ensured especially in the market places.

From Waste to Wealth

The old manure yard was at a distance of two kilometres. Heaps of waste was dumped here for the past ten years. Now the solid waste was properly collected, the segregation of waste was properly attended to. A contractor was engaged in this regard. The segregated organic waste is converted into manure. Forty tubes were provided for vermi-culture. And the contractor was permitted to get 50 per cent share from the sale of the manure. Now, about Rs. 4 lakh is earned annually through the sale of organic manure, Gandhi Selvam added.

A New Change

The inhabitants of Namakkal town became used to keep plastic buckets in their houses to put the solid waste; the menace of stray dogs and pigs was severely dealt with; majority of the households practiced the segregation of waste at the house level; contract labourers as well as municipal workers properly discharged their duties and responsibilities; in all the commercial establishments, owners themselves kept the solid waste; the drainage was smoothly functioning without any complaint of blocks; the entire town of Namakkal has been clean and neat. And in marriage halls the wastages are properly kept and removed systematically.

Sensitizing the Public

To sensitize the public in respect of their perception in the maintenance of sanitation and public hygiene, a slogan was coined, viz. 'A clean city is equal to a temple" (Kuppaaiyilla Nagaram, Kovilukku Samam). In all advertisements, whether permanent or temporary, one-third of the space in the total area of advertisement had to be earmarked to make writings on the significance of maintaining environmental sanitation and public hygiene. The painters and the artists extended their help in this regard. They used to get the writings/slogans from the municipal authorities of Namakkal and highlighted them along with the text of the advertisement. In the jurisdiction of Namakkal city this practice was followed strictly as small family norm was insisted by the government through the advertisements on the vehicles.

Infrastructure Facilities in the Burial Ground

The burial ground is extended in an area of 3.5 acres. As it is located near the slum area, the public made use of this place for open defecation. Due to the absence of power connection, the entire area is infested with antisocial elements, Gandhi Selvam explained. Moreover, there are many graveyards which occupied larger spaces. The issue related to the burial ground was exposed through the media and public were encouraged to give a solution to those issues. The municipal council resolved to remove the encroachments. Using JCB machine in spite of challenges, the encroachments were removed. A compound wall was constructed from the municipal general funds of Rs. 10 lakh as well as from the grant Rs. 2 lakh given by the then District Collector. The encroachers lodged complaints that they did not have adequate space for their habitation.The municipality came forward to provide public toilets to those houses. At the cost of Rs. 13 lakh two sanitary complexes, one for men and one for women were provided. Five hundred saplings of different kinds were planted inside the burial ground and they are properly protected. Now the burial ground is in proper use.

Removal of Debris during Building Constructions

Construction is one of the main activities especially in urban areas. In Namakkal, the removal of debris is a major problem. The issue of removal of debris was seriously discussed and the municipality resolved that the owners of the construction sites would be held responsible to remove the debris safely and if any one found guilty in his responsibility, his license to construct new buildings would be withheld. As this rule was strictly enforced, the debris are properly transported from the construction sites by the contractors themselves, Gandhi Selvam explained.

Removal of Biomedical Wastes

Urbanization brings many new issues like safe disposal of bio-medical wastes. The municipal council realized this problem of safe removal and management of bio-medical wastes. The doctors of Namakkal municipality were advised during the meetings of the Indian Medical Association, that they should make their own arrangement to collect and dispose of the bio-medical wastes. The IMA has engaged an auto to collect and transfer bio-wastes from its member establishments, Gandhi Selvam added.

Civic Sense

The initiatives and practices of public participation in solid waste management experienced in the municipality of Namakkal should be properly documented and disseminated to all. It is quiet encouraging news. Hence, from various corners people representatives and officials of civic bodies go to Namakkal for field trips for learning from the experiment successfully carried out. Keeping the city clean is a consistent, honest and sustained contribution of the responsible civic representatives, accountable bureaucracy and the public of Namakkal aware of civic sense.

A Milestone in Development Politics

Though civic bodies are represented by the cadres of various political parties, at one stage, these representatives were working together to address the common issues, forgetting their political differences. In the municipality of Namakkal, due to the effective leadership of Gandhi Selvam, the councillors came together and attained success in making the town a clean and neat area when compared to any town in the whole of India. In spite of these good developments, Gandhi Selvam had a sense of sorrow to share. The then State government did not come forward to give a helping hand to the Namakkal municipality in its efforts to maintain sanitation and public hygiene. The commissioner who extended his fullest cooperation to Gandhi Selvam was transferred abruptly. There was no special fund as an incentive to the efforts taken by the municipality. Gandhi Selvam did not feel sorry at such neglect. He maintained good rapport with sincere and committed officials, the collector and the councillors. With the participation of the public, the efforts so far taken would not go unnoticed and unrewarded. The experiment is now a system which continues even after the assumption of office by new councillors. Since 2006, Namakkal municipality is the only municipality in the country which received the ISO certificate as it has provided civic amenities very effectively and to the satisfaction of the people concerned.

4

We Participate, therefore, We Govern

Mr. Sundaramurthy is a young and energetic post graduate youth of Vavipalayam Village Panchayat in Palladam Block of Coimbatore District in Tamil Nadu. He hails from a farmer's family. His grand fathers were the active leaders of the Farmers Movement of Tamil Nadu. His father was a hard working farmer who dedicated his whole time to agriculture and he became a big landlord with 30 acres of landholding. After the demise of his father, Sundaramurthy, along with his brother, has been managing the agriculture activities which involved mainly coconut and vegetable cultivation.

His Public Orientation

During his school days Sundaramurthy spent his leisure time by reading novels and stories. The writings of famous writers of Tamil Nadu such as Pattukottai Prabakar, Kannadasan and Jayakanthan attracted Sundaramurthy. The writings of Dr. M.S. Udayamurthy inspired him a lot. Dr. Udayamurthy visited the Higher Secondary School at Vathambacherry when Sundaramurthy was a student and he interacted with the NSS students during this visit. Sundaramurthy said that it was a memorable event in his life. His passion for reading took Sundaramurthy to other areas of human life as well as the affairs of the State. He read in detail the history of the Indian freedom struggle, the role of Gandhiji and the other national leaders.

His college life was a turning point in respect of his reading subjects. He took interest in reading books on Tamil culture and civilization. He had a friend who was his classmate, hailing from Sri Lanka. Sundaramurthy had an opportunity to visit Sri Lanka along with his friend to attend a marriage. He witnessed the scenario of war and life of the Lankan Tamil community. Moreover, their seriousness and commitment to uphold the rich tradition and culture of Tamils impressed him. After his return from Sri Lanka, Sundaramurthy could not remain calm. He discussed the spirit of the Sri Lankan Tamils and compared it with the status of rural youths belonging to the poor families of Tamil Nadu. The local youths were stirred by Sundaramurthy's view and, as a result, they created a new organisation named 'Sinthanai Sirpigal' (Thinkers Forum) in the year 2000.

The youth of Vavipalayam village commenced their village welfare activities. They were involved in organizing medical camps and night school. They mobilized the community and oriented the people to claim their entitlements. Their aim was to make the people citizens rather than petitioners and beneficiaries. If people become citizens they would become assertive and claim their entitlements.

Village Panchayat Elections 2001

When the election for PRIs was announced for the second term 2001-2006, and reserved the position of the president for their village for women, the young members of Sithananai Sirpigal were disappointed. Yet, they proposed to field at least 10 youths to make entry into the PRIs. All the members persuaded Sundaramurthy's wife to contest the election. With much expectation the young members fielded Sundaramurthy's wife in the election. The youth group met each family in all the hamlets and assured them that they would give priority to providing proper drinking water supply, ration card to all eligible families, compulsory education to all, maintenance of water resources. The opposition candidate belonged to the AIADMK and two ministers themselves seriously engaged in the election campaign to canvass for the AIADMK candidate.

The husband of that candidate was holding a party position in the district unit of the AIADMK. By a difference of 93 votes, Mrs. Sundaramurthy won the election. Sundaramurthy enabled his wife to administer the panchayat. He said that he would serve only as personal assistant and never exercise any authority over her.

Brush with the Bureaucracy

Sundaramurthy once raised his voice against the corruption prevailing in the government departments at a meeting convened by the District Collector. It was flashed in the media. Getting angry over his remarks, in retaliation, the government authorities arranged for a special audit of the accounts of Vavipalayam Panchayat. They could find only a few omissions, not any big mistake or misappropriation of funds. From this one could understand the mindset of the officials. The officials wanted the elected leaders to take up the routine work of administration. If any one came out openly against the corrupt practices, they were driven out. In such a way a corrupt culture had developed.

Village Development Activities

During this tenure, 'Sinthanai Sirpigal' enabled the Panchayat to effectively address the issues of water supply. The Panchayat was able to mobilize funds from the MLA and the MP and a new borewell to a depth of 850 metres was sunk. After fulfilling the immediate felt need of the villagers, the Panchayat focused its attention on augmenting ground water sources so as to sustain ground water availability. In this respect, deepening of tanks and construction of new ponds and tanks were undertaken. Even owners of private tanks were encouraged to desilt and deepen their tanks and ponds. This resulted in improvement in the ground water source within two years. It was considered a remarkable achievement.

Demonstration against the Opening of Liquor Shop of TASMAC (Tamil Nadu State Marketing Corporation Limited)

When the Government of Tamil Nadu included the name of Vavipalayam and Kazhuverypalayam to open liquor shops, the womenfolk of Vavipalayam Village Panchayat were mobilized and they organized a demonstration to oppose the decision of the government officials. The District Collector called the representatives of the womenfolk and discussed with them. Then the Secretary of TASMAC came and held a discussion with the women. But the womenfolk stood very firm on their demand that there should not be any liquor shop in their Panchayat area. At last the government withdrew its earlier decision. Sundaramurthy said that the habitual drinkers could go elsewhere to drink, but once the non-availability of liquor shop at the village itself is ensured, the temptation would be avoided and so there would be less number of new drinkers.

Interface with Isha Centre of Yoga

Sundaramurthy interacted with some yoga masters for understanding the spiritual side of life. He visited the Isha Centre and learnt yoga. The Isha Centre has an innovative programme helping the rural masses through a 'Rural Rejuvenation Programme'. He wished to make use of this opportunity and explored the scope for the working of the Isha Centre in and around Vavipalayam. Then came the concept of a mobile clinic to ensure the health of the villagers. The management of Isha Centre agreed to sponsor the expenditure of one doctor provided a vehicle was arranged. Sundaramurthy and his friends held discussions with the villagers and the villagers suggested that instead of a mobile health clinic a permanent building could be more useful. The idea of a permanent building for the health clinic was supported by all the hamlets' households. To take further steps an association named Grama Makkal Nala Amaippu (Villagers Welfare Association) was formed in which two representatives form each hamlet (totally 6 hamlets) were enlisted as members.

The villagers took serious thought about the establishment of the health clinic since the primary health centre was located 17 km away from the village. The concept of a health clinic was sensitized by Sinthanai Sirpigal, involving all the village farmers, youth, women SHG members. As the Isha Centre management came forward to sponsor one doctor, the idea of the health clinic got the attention of the village community and there was a good response from the villagers. Moreover, there were two neighbouring village panchayats which could also make use of the services of the health clinic. The villagers of the neighbouring villages came forward to strengthen the hands of Vavipalayam Grama Makkal Nala Amaippu. A committee of 15 members, including two women, was constituted to work on the project estimate for establishing a health centre at Vavipalayam.

A door to door visit was made to mobilise contributions of cash or materials from each household. The list of outsiders known to Vavipalayam village who would contribute to this cause and yet another list of non-resident villagers of Vavipalayam were prepared. They were provided with the project details—need, the efforts so far taken, and the estimate. The total estimate was Rs. 30 lakh of which Rs. 15 lakh was targeted through local mobilization. First, rupees one lakh was mobilised quickly. Further, the Isha Centre of Yoga helped the committee. The land site for the health clinc was identified and four farmers came forward to part with their land at a comparatively lower cost than the original land value.

The President of Tamil Sangam in the USA, who is a doctor known to another doctor of a nearby village of Vavipalaayam, came forward to help. He came to the village from the USA along with two members of the Tamil Sangam. After a period of six months, they announced the happy news that they would donate Rs. 7.5 lakh. The construction work was commenced with the hope that the total estimated amount could be collected. The villagers witnessed the progress of the construction and came forward one by one and donated their share. About Rs. 8,90,000 was mobilised from the people of 15 villages in and around the village panchayat of Vavipalayam.

The 30 committee members representing 15 villages donated Rs. 10,000 each, totaling Rs. 3 lakh. Now about Rs. 13 lakh was mobilized.

The mobilization campaign was intensified as the overall cost became high due to cost escalation of construction materials. At last the committee was able to mobilize Rs. 40 lakh but the expenditure rose to Rs. 45 lakh. The committee members took the responsibility to pay the balance amount of Rs. 5 lakh. An ambulance was donated by a doctor. Yet another doctor donated hospital equipments.

The Commencement of the Health Centre

14th March 2007 was a day of celebration for all the villagers of Vavipalayam. Gurudev Jakki Vasudev, Dr. M.S. Udayamurthy, Sri Tamilaruvi Manian and Sr. K.R. Karthikeyan (former Director of the Vigilance Commission) graced the function. The Isha Centre of Yoga made arrangements to provide the services of two doctors. The doctors decided to study at the centre itself as the necessary facilities are provided to them.

The villagers volunteered themselves in the activities of giving the final touch to the buildings and the campus two or three days ahead of the inauguration. They made arrangements for planting of tree saplings, *pandal* erection and other decorations. When executing the odd works the villagers did not look for any instruction or advice from the members of the committee. Rather they considered the function as their own and involved themselves fully and showed their own interest and talent to decorate the campus. It was a wonderful thing to watch the performance of the villagers in this respect. Sundaramurthy said that he witnessed the spirit of public service on that occasion.

Any patient who visits the centre, has to meet the cost of the medicine prescribed by the doctors. Rs. 10 is collected as hospital fee from each patient. The salary of the doctors is met by the Isha Centre and the Makkal Sakthi Iyakkam. The cost of electricity charges is met by the Isha Centre. There are other staff, three nurses, one attendant who assist in the running of the centre. On an average one hundred patients visit the centre each day. The cost of medicines is very high, it is learnt. The villagers who are mostly poor are not able to meet the cost of medicine.

Sundaramurthy held a brainstorming session with the fellow members of Sinthanai Sirpigal to find an answer to the question of 'sustainability'. He proposed to meet the local village health nurse so that her services could be fully utilized through the health centre; he also decided to meet the government officials to explore the possibility of making use of the services of the government health department.

The Continuity of the Public Spirit of Sinthanai Sirpigal

Witnessing the impact of voluntarism especially the initiative of their own spirit in respect of establishment of the health centre, the next attempts initiated by the youths were the upgradation of the elementary school into a middle school, the provision of a community hall and application of the technology of solid waste management.

The Impact

The success attained by the youth of Vavipalayam inspired the youth of nearby villages and they have been contacting the youth of Sinthanai Sirpigal for effective development in their own villages.

Panchayat Election 2006

During the election to PRIs in the year 2006, one of the youths, namely Parthasarathy, who was associated with Sinthanai Sirpigal contested. He was opposed by another youth who was comparatively lagging behind in public spirit and public service. The villagers preferred the public spirited youth. Parthasarathy won in the election by a margin of 10,000 votes.

The Way Forward

Sundaramurthy has his future plan on two important issues, namely, welfare and rehabilitation of street children and the progress of farmers. He is of the view that the voice of farmers is not properly echoed in the forums of policy makers. The community of business and trade has its own influence over the policy making whereas farmers' views are not properly taken into account by the government, he said.

5

Gandhian Model of Development

Background

Kuthambakkam Gram Panchayat in Poonamallee Block of Thiruvallur District in Tamil Nadu is headed by a *dalit* youth, Mr. Elango, since 1996 under the New Panchayati Raj System. By profession he was an engineer earning Rs. 25,000 per month from a central government Institute meant for research at Karaikudi. He is married to a chemist working in the ONGC. They have two daughters. He has three brothers. Being the eldest, he had the responsibility to support his family and bring up his brothers. He was groomed in a social transformation movement for *dalit* emancipation and empowerment. As he was oriented in the Ambedkar Movement, he was looking for an opportunity to serve the *dalits*. But his family commitments made him serve the family first. To support his family, he started an industry (KSI Laboratories) with an investment of rupees fifteen lakh, for his brothers. When his family was well set to march forward economically through his earnings, his wife's and the industry, he was drawn towards the election to grassroots institutions as it provides as opportunity to transform the lifestyle of the people, particularly *dalits*. He has a firm conviction that, of all the institutions, grassroots institutions are the most powerful instrument to transform the life of *dalits* by mobilizing them for socio-economic transformation. A gram panchayat president can achieve many things for *dalits*—more than what a *dalit* MLA can achieve. All the livelihood issues can be easily addressed through panchayats if the panchayat presidents are sensitive to the problems of the *dalits*. His plea is that the *dalits* should occupy their positions in the gram panchayat on their own and perform their roles and responsibilities independently. Allowing the industry to see to its own fate and resigning from his job, he contested in the election. However honest and dedicated he was, the election process would not spare him, as it had its own inbuilt weaknesses. As he was identified with the *dalit* movement and oriented in *dalit* mobilization, he was branded as a *dalit* fanatic and the opponent candidate, though hailing from the *dalit* community, took the political support of the Tamil Manila Congress Party. His opponent relied on the votes of the non-*dalits* with the support of that political party. But Elango won the election. He won the election as the people expected more from him, since he is an educated youth. He got the support of the *dalits* in the first election.

Village Setting

After he was elected President of the Gram Panchayat, he observed the village scenario. There are about 1,110 families, with a population of 5250, of which 52 per cent are *dalits* and the rest non-*dalits*, comprising of Vanniars, Naidus and Mudaliars. Of the lands available in this Panchayat, 90 per cent are with the upper caste groups. Both *dalits* and Vanniars are totally agricultural labourers, barring a few who have small parcels of land. The cultivable lands are with Naidus and Mudaliars. Agricultural labourers who do not find jobs most of the year started brewing illicit liquor and it became the practice of the poor. No one has come from other areas to ruin the life of the *dalits* and it is the *dalits* who ruin themselves by taking part in the illicit *arrack* trade. *Dalits* have no other option except to lead a life of sub-human conditions. They had been lured into all kinds of antisocial activities under the leadership of mafia gangs from the urban areas. When action is initiated against the antisocial activities, the *dalits* of this village are the victims. They have no leader at their village level to show them the path to lead a decent human life. They have political leadership at the State level and no way to improve their life through their political leadership. The *dalits* are being mobilized, for political struggles but their living conditions in the rural areas have not changed. They still face what they had faced all along. They live in poverty, penury and miserable conditions. The need of the hour is leadership for *dalits* to achieve development. The panchayat provides this opportunity and hope.

About Panchayats

The Gram Panchayat has four wards, nine ward members and seven hamlets. It has roads of 10,500 metres. Of them, 8,000 metres have been made concrete. The total number of overhead tanks providing water is seven. There are 320 street lights. The panchayat has 1,175 households having a population 5,250. There are five anganwadis, two schools, one primary and one higher elementary. Totally 530 students are studying in different schools in the village. Eighteen SHGs are functioning in the village. There are five youth groups which are very active in the panchayat area.

On Development

In his perception and opinion, *dalit* emancipation can be possible not through mobilizing them for political participation but through their socio-economic transformation. Unless their livelihood pattern is changed, their perception and behaviour is changed, *dalit* emancipation will reamin only a pipe dream. His target is the marginalized—and the vulnerable families. He feels that the *dalits* are far away from the basic facilities which have been created for livelihood security. *Dalit* children are deprived of development aspirations. *Dalit* women are the worst affected in the whole of society. By giving doles one cannot develop the *dalits*. Only by protecting their self-respect, creating awareness, upgrading their skill, linking their skills with production of marketable commodities, linking their economic activity with banks one can create an opportunity for *dalits* to come up in life. Cinema, lottery and liquor are the three evils which have eaten away the vitals of the *dalits,* of which liquor is the major factor which has completely ruined their life. Thus he started his work with stopping the brewing of illicit *arrack.* The *dalits,* though belonging to his caste, started arguing what the alternative was and started opposing him. *Dalit* leaders instigated them to oppose him saying that he is working against the *dalits.* But he successfully stopped the brewing of illicit liquor and he was in search of employment opportunities for those individuals and families who lost their jobs.

On Panchayat System

He considered the panchayat a powerful instrument for transforming the life of the rustic folk, provided powers and responsibilities are given to the panchayat system. He regretted that, in Tamil Nadu, the panchayat is considered only an instrument to carry out the schemes of the Central and State governments. The New Panchayati Raj System provides scope and opportunity for the deprived, marginalized and neglected to come up in life, provided good leadership is readily available at the grassroots to overcome the barriers in the institution and to work for the community. Otherwise the new system will also work for the privileged. The success of the New Panchayati Raj System largely depends on the leadership of the panchayats and their relationship with the people. To overcome the problem which arose out of stopping the brewing of illicit liquor, he had to seek some solution in the schemes of the governments. He found out a major scheme, namely, Samathuvapuram, along with other schemes to be carried out in this panchayat area. In his estimate, he said that he has mobilized nearly rupees one crore forty lakh for various schemes implemented in the panchayat. The panchayat has got Rs. 90 lakh for the Samathuvapuram scheme (housing and other infrastructural facilities for the poor of all caste groups to live together) and Rs. 45 lakh for concrete cement roads. He has determined that no work should be given to contractors and that all the works are to be carried out only by the people who have lost their jobs of brewing illicit liquor. He strongly believes that panchayats have to take up works which are less skill-oriented and more manual oriented, as rustic folk have only energy and not much of refined skills. Any scheme will provide employment opportunity to the rural poor if it is less skill-oriented. There he found out the technology of mud block making. People are involved in making bricks through this technology and construction of houses for the Samathuvapuram. The entire construction was done by the people on their own. Likewise, laying of roads was also done by the people. Their livelihood security was ensured by the Panchayat by providing jobs in the implementation of government schemes. As per his calculation, 350 families are in the vulnerable category. They need continuous manual work for their livelihood security. Yet it was not smooth sailing. Beneficiaries who got houses in the Samathuvapuram scheme raised opposition to this mud block construction as it was thought that the mud block has no strength. He tried his best to convince the people and it took nearly six months. His import of mud block technology was born out of a need but people did not accept it. He took pains to convince the people. Now they have realized that they have done the right thing. He is going in for the same technology to construct 200 houses to make it a katcha-house-free village. He felt that the *dalits* have a very strong mindset on all aspects of life. To break the mindset of the *dalits* one has to struggle a lot. Moreover they have a strong belief that they cannot improve their living conditions.

When these works came to an end, he was in trouble as those involved in construction and road laying works would turn towards the preparation of illicit liquor. His second journey started in search of technology to provide sustainable job opportunities to the people in his village at an affordable cost. The cost of the technology should be small, and any individual should be able to operate and simultaneously should provide to the poor people for continuous employment opportunity . He visited a number of places like Gandhigram, RTRC, Mundur, Kerala, Sevagram, Wardha, CETRI, Mysore. He found out several technologies suitable to his village, but cost reduction was needed. He thought that he could do it and improvise the technology. While looking at the type of activities that are to be undertaken and the way in which panchayats are taking shape in Tamil Nadu he felt that all these activities cannot be done by the panchayat. Totally panchayats are under the control of the bureaucracy and the bureaucracy are never oriented to deliver services but oriented to look at rules and procedures. At the panchayat level social audit is more important than the audit of the chartered account. In the panchayat it is not the chartered accountant auditing the panchayat but someone from the Block Development Office. This panchayat has no space for experiments, innovations and creativity. But, to carry out all those creative works, the panchayat has no flexibility and space and hence he started a Trust called Trust for Village Self-Governance. Because of his activities, vision and commitment, he was invited to the USA and the UK and NRIs contributed a small amount and with the small amount he improvised tools and machines. He identified mud block making as a technology and hence he got it from Auroville of Pondicherry by paying Rs. 40,000. He further identified soap making, both toilet and detergent, dairying, bakery, *thoordhal* preparation, oil extraction, jute bag preparation, handmade paper, preparing energy efficient lights as activities to be carried out, for which technology has to be improvised. Both mud block making and jute bag preparation have been carried out.

The panchayat president has created the following units to generate employment opportunity in his Panchayat area under the banner of the Trust.

Jute Bag and Cotton Bag Production and Training

In this unit the villagers are producing ecofriendly, value added jute bags and cotton canvas bags. One self help group of 12 members is running this unit. They are producing 82 models of jute and cotton bags. Some of the models are being exported to European countries like Switzerland. This unit is functioning as a production-cum-training centre.

Fig. 5.1: Mud Block Making

Fig. 5.2: Jute Bag Production

Fig. 5.3: Jute Products ready for Sale

The particulars of the tailoring unit to produce jute bags, cotton bags, shirts, petticoats and uniforms :

Total investment needed—Rs. 1,00,000
Working capital—Rs. 1,50,000
Profit to be generated—Rs. 30,000 p.m.
Debt services—Rs. 10,000 p.m.
Profit for the people—Rs. 20,000 p.m.
No of persons employed—10 persons

Thoordal Production Unit

In this unit the raw *thoordal* is purchased from Vellore and Dharmapuri Districts. It is properly cleaned and soaked in water and dried. This is taken for milling where the *thoordal* is deskined. It is collected, sieved and sold. The skin is collected and sold as cattle feed. The *thoordal* processor is purchased from the Central Food Technological Research Institute, Mysore. This is a simple model run by one HP single-phase motor. One SHG of 12 members works in this unit. This also is a production-cum-training unit.

Particulars

Machinery etc.

(a) Mini *Thoordal* mill (1 HP prime driver and ½ HP for classifier—Rs. 80,000
(b) Soaking tanks and decanters—Rs. 24,000
(c) Drying yard—800 sq ft
(d) Working capital—Rs. 1,20,000

Other

The capacity is 300 kgs/day and 7 tons/month
Local market will consume 4 tons and the rest will be sold to the nearest villages.

Expected profit—Rs. 28,000 per month
Debt services—Rs. 7,000 per month
Profit for people—Rs. 21,000 per month
Employment opportunity—12 persons
By-product—Thoordal dust—2,100 kg (good cattle feed)

Fig. 5.4: Energy Efficient Street Light Spare Parts Production

Fig. 5.5: Thoordal Processing

Groundnut Products Unit

In this unit there are hand-operated groundnut breaking machines available to deshell the groundnut. Each machine can crush 6 to 7 bags (40 kgs) of dry groundnut. From the broken mass the shell is removed by physical separation.

Fig. 5.6: Groundnut Oil Extraction

Fig. 5.7: Groundnut Oil Extraction Machinery

The deshelled material is sieved to separate the bigger sized kernels. The smaller size kernels are sent for oil production. The bigger sized ones are roasted and taken for burfy and chakkie production. Sometimes the bigger sized ones are sold as seeds. This also is a production-cum-training unit.

Oil Extraction Unit

Capacity : 3000 kgs groundnut oil
4000 kgs gingelly oil
2000 kgs coconut oil

Machinery

(a) Rotary extractions—3 Nos.—Rs. 1.8 lakh
Power—30 HP
(b) Oil filling system—Rs. 20,000
(c) Hand decordicators—3 Nos., Rs. 20,000

Expected profit—Rs. 30,000 per month
Debt Services—Rs. 8,000 per month
Profit for people—Rs. 22,000 per month
Employment opportunity—12 persons
Byproduct—Oil cake and ground nut shell (cattle feed)

Groundnut Processing and Eatables

Machinery

Roasters, packing machine—Rs. 50,000
Profit expected—Rs. 10,000 per month
No. employed—5 persons

Soap Making Unit

In this unit a simple soap making system is developed. No machine and no electricity is used. Using this new device, varieties of toilet soaps are produced. This is one of the activities for the SHGs. This unit consumes coconut oil which is produced

Fig. 5.8: Soap Making Process

Fig. 5.9: Soap Production

by the local oil extraction unit. This also uses the locally available herbs. This unit generates employment for 10 members. This also is a production-cum-training unit.

Production of Soap

No. of soaps—10,000 per month
Cost of machine and materials—Rs. 40,000
Raw materials—oil is obtained from oil unit—alkali and chemical from market
Expected profit—Rs. 25,000 per month
Debt Services—Rs. 5,000 per month
Profit for the people—Rs. 20,000 per month
No. of people employed—10 per month

Dairy Processing Unit

This unit consists of mini jacketed vessel for heating and cooling the milk, a refrigerator, an open pan evaporator and stainless steel vessels for curd making and storing. In this unit 300 litres of milk can be processed per day. This gives opportunity for one SHG to work. To feed milk to this unit we are promoting groups of cattle growers. This will in turn give employment to about 60 people. This also is a production-cum-training unit.

Milk Processing and Milk Products

Capacity—to process—300 litres milk a day

Machinery

Baby boiler—1
Pasteurizer—1
Chiller—1
Packing system—1
Pan evaporation—1; and
Trays and utensils
Total investment—Rs. 2.0 lakh

Fig. 5.10: Milk Processing

Profit to be gained—Rs. 30,000 per month
Debt services—Rs. 8,000 per month
Profit for people—Rs. 22,0000 per month
No of employed—10 persons

Cattle Feed Unit

Capacity—15 tons/month

Machinery

(a) Ball mill 1 No.—40,000
(b) Grinder—20,000
(c) Packing system—10,000

Power—10 HP
Expected Profit—Rs. 30,000 per month
Service to Debts—Rs. 8,000 per month
Profit for people—Rs. 22,000 per month
No of people employed—10

Village Bakery Unit

This is a small bakery unit to produce basic baked items—biscuits, cakes, puffs, bun and bread. This also is a production-cum-training unit.

Production of Food Items

1. Sambar Powder
2. Pickles
3. Other food items

Machinery—Rs. 3,00,000
Profit to be generated—Rs. 35,000 per month
Debt services—Rs. 10,000 per month
Profit for the people—Rs. 25,000 per month
No of persons to be employed—10 persons

Energy Efficient Street Lights Unit

This unit produces street lights using energy efficient CFL bulbs. It produces the metal boxes, glass cover, holders, plastic components, bolts and nuts. These lights save 75 to 80% of electric power. This gives employment to a group of 20 people. This also is a production-cum-training unit.

Fig. 5.11: Fixation of Energy Efficient Street Light

Energy Efficient Street Lights and Electro Mechanical Gadgets

Investment on machineries—Rs. 4.0 lakh
Working capital—Rs. 2.0 lakh
Profit generated—Rs. 50,000 per month
Debt services—Rs. 10,000 per month
Profit for people—Rs. 40,000 per month
Number of employed persons—18

Fig. 5.12: Mat Weaving

Construction Materials Production

(a) Mud blocks
(b) Ferro cement panels
(c) Toilet materials
(d) Roofing materials

Investment on machines—Rs. 1.5 lakh
Working capital—Rs. 1.5 lakh
Profit generated—Rs. 40,000 per month
Debt services—Rs. 10,000 per month
Profit for people—Rs. 30,000 per month
Number of employed persons—15

His Vision of Integrated Sustainable Rural Development

He strongly feels that people-centric activities can be generated only when people are mobilized and conscientised on development. To perform the above task a strong leadership with a sense of commitment is needed. Once people are mobilized they are to be conscientised on the process of development. If they are conscientised on development, they will start critiquing the current development scenario and decide what type of development they want. Based on the awareness, the need of the people will be assessed and available skills will also be assessed. By assessing the available opportunity to meet the requirements of the society, steps will be taken at the panchayat level to prepare a plan to achieve development. Panchayats and NGOs and CBOs will work together to address the issues of the people. Continuously people will be mobilized for all activities from assessing the need to plan and implement the same. Thus development becomes the people's subject by which government agencies will be relegated to the background.

He is of the opinion that, to generate employment opportunity, the Kumarappa model is the only solution. Many of the products coming from outside for consumption in the villages can be produced locally by introducing a new device by which money flow from the village to outside can be arrested. Products produced by the villagers have to be consumed by the villagers. Hence he feels that critiquing of the process of development is key for village development and that, by doing so, the mindset of the people can be changed.

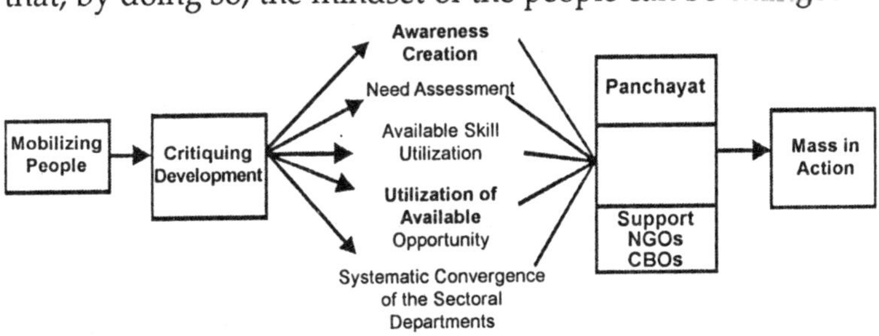

His Vision of Integrated Sustainable Development

Panchayat Academy

He is not content with the activities carried out in his panchayat. He is interested in and committed to creating a cadre of panchayat leaders dedicated to achieving economic development and social justice. He considers that his panchayat is a laboratory and all experiments successfully carried out in his panchayat should be replicated in other panchayats also by which his model will be emulated and a new movement can be created for development. For this kind of activities he wants to create an academy called the Panchayat Academy. It is not a mere teaching academy. It is a doers academy. Panchayat presidents have to come to Kuthambakkam and discuss with people who are working different units of production and get to know the details. As the president, he will explain the whole process to the panchayat leaders. He is the head of the academy and other SHG women are the co-teachers in this academy. Already he has started this work. Seeing his activities the academy is supported by the British Council. Panchayat leaders have started coming to this panchayat in large numbers.

A village, by making itself a role model for total development using the Panchayati Raj System is becoming a learning centre for other villages. Based on this concept, it was decided to invite 20 to 30 panchayat leaders from various districts to Kuthambakkam to witness the developmental process taking place here. What they are given in the programme are :

Only from his experience in this Panchayat →

Decentralization
Democracy
Development
Social Justice
Empowerment
Economic Development
Village Level Planning
Participatory Planning and Village Development
Conflict Resolution
Changing the mindset and living conditions

Training Programmes Conducted

1. Training in village industries and sustainable development—Panchayat Leaders from Thiruvallur District.
2. Training in jute products and weaving—for women and girls from Kuthambakkam and surrounding villages—May 2003.
3. Training in toilet soap production—SHG members and panchayat leaders from Kancheepuram District—June 2003.
4. Panchayat Leaders training and workshop on sustainable development through Panchayati Raj System—August 2003.

Fig. 5.13: Training of Trainers

Fig. 5.14: Panchayat Presidents Workshop

5. Panchayat leaders training and workshop on sustainable development through Panchayati Raj System—September 2003.
6. Panchayat leaders and NRIs meet on village industries and Panchayati Raj System.
7. Outstanding Panchayat Leaders meet for Pudukkottai District Panchayat Leaders—October 2003.
8. Panchayat Leaders and NGOs joint training in sustainable village development, November 2003.
9. Outstanding Panchayat Leader meet for Thiruvallur and Kancheepuram District Panchayat Leaders, December 2003.
10. Panchayat Leaders and NGOs from Coimbatore District meeting, January 2004.
11. Women Panchayat Leaders training in village industries and women's rights, February 2004.
12. Visit to role model villages, Odanthurai and Semmipalayam in Coimbatore District. He took panchayat leaders from his district to other areas to show other success stories.

Apart from the above programmes, meetings for youths and SHG members were organized when people visited the village industries complex. Other than this, there is an intensive research and development programme on village industries and village level marketing. Due to this a revolutionary breakthrough has happened in energy efficient street lighting and water pumping. This is going to lead to a situation wherein every panchayat will save 65 to 70 per cent of energy in street lighting and water pumping. This will certainly liberate the village panchayat from the debt trap because of electricity changes. Many of the village industries programmes are successfully prototyped and the process of commercialization is going on. The support rendered by the Hunger Project and the Tamil Nadu Foundation has really helped to reach a situation wherein the Trust for Village Self-Governance has gained full confidence in the village industries packages.

Photo Gallery on various Capacity Building Programme

Influencing NRIs

By visiting various countries in the west on invitation, he sensitized the NRIs in all those countries. So far some of the NRIs have contributed their mite towards rural development activities through NGOs. Now they have started working with the communities directly with the help of the panchayats. He helps a lot of NRIs in their activities.

Finance of Kuthambakkam Panchayat

(a) Panchayat Fund Account for one year

Sl. No.	Particulars	Amount (in Rs.)
1.	House tax	2,63,000.00
2.	Library tax	26,300.00
3.	Professional tax	1,05,000.00
4.	Surcharge on stamp duty	5,55,000.00
5.	House tax matching grant	1,65,000.00
6.	Building plan approval	27,000.00
7.	Advertisement tax	10,000.00
8.	Miscellaneous	20,000.00

(b) Scheme Fund Account

Sl. No.	*Particulars*	*Amount (in Rs.)*
1.	Sampoorna Grameen Rozgar Yojana	2,36,000.00

(c)Earmarked Grant Account

Sl. No.	*Particulars*	*Amount (in Rs.)*
1.	Eleventh Finance Commission Grant	63,000.00

Table 5.1: Last Eight Years' Panchayat Fund

Year	*SSS*	*SFC*	*HTMG*	*LC*	*Funeral Grant*	*Thiru-valluvar Library*
97-98	3,60,066	1,20,868	40,440	—	—	—
98-99	3,46,245	1,78,830	4,01,055	—	—	—
99-00	2,98,907	3,37,454	1,33,375	6,600	2,500	5,000
00-01	5,90,811	2,58,723	2,04,990	5,783	500	—
01-02	2,31,861	2,92,889	71,615	5,847	2,500	—
02-03	11,67,761	3,88,377	1,34,670	6,077	—	—
03-04	24,69,457	3,49,218	—	6,177	—	—
04-05	1,64,560	35,694	—	—	—	—
Total	**56,29,668**	**19,62,053**	**9,86,145**	**30,484**	**5,500**	**5,000**

Table 5.2: Panchayat Earmarked Grant Account

Year	*11th*	*E/Grant*	*Funeral Grant*	*11th (Toilet)*
97-98	29,020	—	—	—
98-99	—	—	2,200	—
99-00	28,208	—	—	—
00-01	43,318	23,40,000	—	—
01-02	—	—	—	—
02-03	1,21,266	—	2,000	—
03-04	—	—	—	—
04-05	60,632	—	—	9,000
Total	**2,82,444**	**23,40,000**	**4,200**	**9,000**

Table 5.3: Panchayat Scheme Account

Year	*IAY*	*CRSP*	*JVVT*	*JGSY*	*PMGY*	*SGRY*
97-98	3,00,000	28,000	67,122	—	—	—
98-99	7,900	—	84,000	—	—	—
99-00	4,57,075	81,364	—	1,63,761	—	—
00-01	1,39,330	—	—	7,34,433	1,66,860	—
01-02	-	—	—	65,419	—	—
02-03	2,11,911	—	—	3,52,566	—	—
03-04	—	—	—	2,41,081	—	—
04-05	—	—	—	—	—	2,07,070
Total	**11,16,216**	**1,09,364**	**1,51,122**	**15,57,260**	**1,66,860**	**2,07,070**

Special Grants

1. Construction of Samathuvapuram Government of Tamil Nadu	Rs. 35,00,000
Government of India (Dovetailing various Government of India Schemes	Rs. 55,00,000
2. Namakku Namme Thittam (for laying CC roads)	Rs. 44,00,000
3. Innovative Habitat Development (hutless village):	Rs. 50,00,000
Government of India, RD Department Trust for village self governance (from donations and grants)	Rs. 50,00,000
4. Solar power facilities for the Panchayat office	Rs. 1,10,000
5. Solar Street lights (from MNES and TEDA)	Rs. 1,00,000
6. Furnitures for the school children	Rs. 4,00,000
7. Computers for the school children	Rs. 1,00,000
Total	Rs. 2,41,10,000

Noto: SSS = Self Sufficiency Scheme.
SFC = State Finance Commission Grant.
HTMG = House Tax Matching Grant.
LC = Local Cess.
IAY = Indira Awaas Yojana.
CRSP = Central Rural. Sanitation Programme.
JVVT = Jawahar Velai Vaippu Thittam.
JASY = Jawahar Gram Samridhi Yojana.
PMGY = Pradhan Mantri Gramodaya Yojana.
SGRY = Sampoorna Grameen Rozgar Yojana.

In his first tenure, he spent near about rupees one crore forty lakh through various kinds of activities. But he provided maximum opportunity to the people to use their energy and manpower. His mud block preparation was born out of this vision of providing employment opportunity. It was an ordeal for him to convince the people that mud block construction will have strength equal to chamber bricks. People accept the mud block preparation when they are employed. But they refuse to accept them to be used to construct their houses. With great difficulty he convinced the people. All his technological improvisations are made only with the aim of providing livelihood security to the poor, that too vulnerable sections of the society.

His first period was full of struggles and learning to build his vision and mission. While performing his role and responsibilities he had to face a volley of problems from many sides. Officials at lower level did not understand the works that he carried out. They issued one notice after another to book him under clause 205 of the Tamil Nadu Panchayat Act of 1994. He had to struggle a lot to convince people on each and every issue as the awareness level of the people on development is low. There is no ready-made improvised technology for adoption. Working for economic development and social justice is the basic task of the Panchayats. Neither the Panchayat Ward Members nor the officials understood this. He had to work alone as he had developed a vision. Even Panchayat ward members were not sensitized to the roles to be performed in the Panchayats. Everyone was interested in carrying out the activities if schemes and programmes were sanctioned by the government. Throughout the period, his transactions were made transparent and everything was written on the Panchayat display board, including the bank balance. His transparency has brought more people to his fold. Equally, his firm action in removing encroachment of Panchayat lands meant for the Samathuvapuram kept nearly 60 families away from him because he removed them from the Panchayat lands. The sixty families who had encroached the Panchayat lands were *dalits* and hence they thought that he would not touch them in order to keep their support to him in tact.

In the beginning he was perceived as a *dalit* activist and subsequently he was perceived as a facilitator of community development. One section of the people who had closely watched him admired him for his evolution from the *dalit* fold to the community level. Another section felt that being a *dalit* he was expected to provide job opportunity to *dalits* but instead of adopting a *dalit* perspective in Panchayat administration he brought community perspective to it. As a result a minor section of the *dalit* families determined to defeat him in the next elections. But a major chunk who had opposed him in the first election, mostly non-*dalits*, came close to him and were determined to support him in the next election. In the second election for local bodies he contested by reporting his activities and vision. Families which were involved in illicit liquor brewing and selling and families who had been evicted from encroachments joined together to oppose him. Equally the families, mostly non-*dalits*, who opposed him in the first election with the perception that he was an active *dalit* movement representative came together to support him since he emerged as a facilitator of community development. Four candidates contested in the election and he won the election without any expenditure. Even a handbill was prepared by some one and printed by one NGO. He said that providing job opportunity to 450 families through government schemes, keeping the panchayat administration transparent, acting as a facilitator were responsible for his victory.

In the second period he wanted to consolidate his proposals and concretise his actions towards economic activities. He strongly believes that by proving opportunity to the people to work and earn their livelihood, the self-respect of the people could be protected.

When asked about the annual income and expenditure he said that it is around rupees 28 lakh and Rs. 18 lakh respectively. He is not interested in spending money but he is interested in studying the process of development and people's perception of their participation in the development process. He wants to change the process of development from the hands of the officials to people's hands. He said that through the Gram Sabha a healthy democratic culture could be developed at the grassroots. He gets the agenda in the Panchayat council for discussion in the Gram Sabha. He conducts the Gram Sabha on the basis of the agenda set by the Panchayat council. All issues are people-centric and hence the Gram Sabha attracts the people. He has got sanction from the central government to construct houses for the poor under the innovative housing scheme for Rs. 50 lakh.

He has developed a scheme for economic activities of the poor and it can be sustained if a cluster of villages join together. A cluster of Village Gram Panchayats have to join together to form a consortium. This can be achieved through improvised technologies. It needs lot of work with other Gram Panchayat Presidents. For the development of the poor and the well-being of all, a perspective plan is needed. He has developed a plan for the development of his Gram Panchayat. He has developed it from the beginning of the first term itself. In fact it is a plan prepared by him and it was approved by the Gram Sabha. It is not a plan document prepared with the participation of the people. It is almost a vision document prepared by the President. There are a few industries emitting waste by which they pollute the entire area and for which he has to struggle against the industries.

He has evolved this development perspective based on the writings and speeches of Rajiv Gandhi, Kundrakudi Adigalar, Anna Hazzare and Kumarappa. His belief and ideas got concretized only after his visit to Gandhian institutions. He believed that *dalit* development rests not on political mobilization but solely on the mobilization of *dalits* for development. Their skills have to be upgraded. Their energy has to be used productively. He concentrated his attention on the service delivered by the primary health centres and primary schools. A Parent Teachers Association has been facilitated by the Panchayat President. He provided needed furniture to the schools. He got all the furnitures as donation from a donor agency. He made special arrangements for interaction with school students.

Analysis

Mr. Elango's main objective is not to work with the people in achieving economic development and social justice. His intention is to create a model in his Panchayat and the same can be upscaled. The process of development which we see today has to be reversed from the government domain to the people's domain. People should feel that they can develop on their own. He further envisages the fact that a cadre of Panchayat leaders could be created with a new mindset with a sense of commitment and honesty to perform the above task. Even in the path of development, he realistically feels that an alternative development model has to be projected which should rely on people's skill, people's knowledge and be need-based and not growth based. It should be always employment oriented, equity oriented and gender oriented.

It should have sustainability. The Panchayat cannot function in isolation. It has to work with other institutions. Now he has brought visibility to his model. To bring this model to this level of visibility he had to struggle a lot both personally and publicly. The Panchayat system which is in vogue is neither in the hands of the people nor in the hands of the elected representatives. It is in the hands of the unskilled, rusted, corrupt officials who continue to look at the Panchayat as an implementing agency. He looks at only the provisions in the Constitution, not in the system created in Tamil Nadu. People's needs and the vision of the leader cannot be addressed in the existing system. The Panchayat leaders, by building up their capacity and performing their genuine role by assuming power would generate a heat in the system which would pave the way for decentralization. As in other Panchayats, he performs the role in laying roads, providing streetlights, taking care of water supply and sanitation, and maintaining clean environment in the village. To him these are all the routine functions and no Panchayat can escape from them. He feels that Panchayats have to show the path to development for which Panchayats have to break new ground as there is enough space. But one has to understand and build the capacity to struggle against the barriers in the process of development.

He is of the opinion that social audit is the only option for creative leaders working in the Panchayats.

Conclusion

Kuthambakkam has started a movement which is a new Gandhian model of development which will gain momentum as he already started taking this model to other Panchayats. In fact other Panchayat leaders have started visiting Kuthambakkam. For Panchayats, it is Sevagram. The Panchayat leader is a neo-Gandhian worker. In the days of *dalits* attacking Gandhi, a *dalit*, in a convincing way, shows a practical model for the upliftment of the poor and *dalits* through the model of Kumarappa. His technology driven activities will bring the needed solutions to the existing crisis in Panchayats. It is a basic question that, as he is an engineer, he can do all these technological innovations in his Panchayat, but, in other Panchayats, the leaders are not able to do the same. Here he breaks the myth and he says that anybody can use these devices. The technologies are very simple and in no way they are complicated. Already a number of Panchayats have picked up this model. For him the infrastructural facilities are very simple and, even without the Panchayats, these things could be achieved. Panchayats have to address the issues of the poor and the marginalized. The mandate of the Panchayat is to achieve economic development and administer social justice. He has addressed the two issues. He is emerging as a leader of leaders at the grassroots.

6

Struggle for Gender and Social Justice

Her Background

Mrs. Pappa aged 33 is a science graduate. She hails from the *dalit* community. Her father is a progressive farmer who preferred Pappa to be an educated woman. To ensure proper and conducive atmosphere for her study, Pappa was sent to a Government Arts College, Palani where she stayed in the hostel. During her college days she took part in sports and acquired proficiency in athletics and games. Her college education helped her to understand the sufferings of the *dalit* community. Being a cadet of the NCC unit in her college, Pappa had the opportunity to live in villages other than her own. Pappa informed that the plight of *dalit* in the villages around Palani was agonising. They lived in sub-human living condition. Moreover they lived in abject poverty, completely depending on the caste Hindus. Pappa expressed her concern for that status of the *dalits*. She was longing for an opportunity to help *dalits*.

After successfully completing of her graduation—B.Sc. (Zoology) she learned computers. In 1995 her marriage was arranged with her close relative. Her in-law's family is a reputed one. Her father-in-law was the ex-president of Athankaraipatti Gram Panchayat three times. Being aged, he withdrew from public life and paved the way for the entry of his son, Pappa's husband. Pappa's husband served as an employee in the local cooperative. Moreover he is a key member in the Traditional Committee which looks after the social activities of the caste group. Of the four key members in the

Committee, her husband is the 'Kaladi', the traditional position of Secretary/Treasurer in the activities of the Committee. The other three positions are Kudumban, Varian and Nattanmai. This is the practice of the 'Pallar' community of SC in Athankaraipatti. Thus Pappa has a strong support base besides her education and family.

Pappa as a Social Worker

Pappa did not want to sit idle in the house. She is a highly motivated, committed and educated woman among the members of the *dalit* community. She used to render assistance to her neighbours by offering guidance and counselling in their family affairs. In the mean time she came to know the activities of Dr. Ambedkar Development Society functioning in Perungudi near Madurai, which called for the service of young and dedicated men and women to contribute to the advancement of education of the *dalit* students. She applied and got the post and served as animator. She conducted coaching classes for school students in her house. Further she used to mobilize adults and elderly women, shared their concern and created awareness among them about the conditions of the poor and especially women. She helped them

Fig. 6.1: Pappa with Members of Dr. Ambedkar Society

to acquire literacy which is considered a main factor for empowerment. Realizing the potential of Pappa, many women used to visit her and get her guidance for many matters relating to their family. She was paid for these activities also by Dr. Ambedkar Development Society. Her in-laws expressed happiness over the development. They even appreciated her for her approach and method of doing services. Her husband also encouraged her activities. Being a politically oriented person of the Congress Party, her husband used to involve her in public welfare activities. Thus, Pappa slowly prepared herself to shoulder higher public responsibility in ensuing days. Her family stood as a support structure for her public activities.

In the service as animator, Pappa had the good company of students and youths. She spent from her pocket to meet the educational needs of poor *dalit* students. She organized excursions and picnics for students to the nearby mountains, religious places, and dam sites. Parents of these children witnessed the attitudinal and behavioural changes among the school students and used to frequently visit Pappa and express their gratitude. Pappa became a significant woman in the village of Athankaraipatti. She came into the public space on her own.

Panchayati Raj Election in 1996

Athankaraipatti Village Panchayat had two hamlets namely, Subbulapuram and Kamatchipuram. Athankaraipatti and Kamatchipuram are exclusively of *dalit* habitation. Families of backward class communities live in Subbulapuram hamlet. The major communities are Thevar, Naicker, Vellalar and Brahmin. When the election under new Panchayati Raj System was held in 1996, a middle-aged *dalit* woman became the President as the seat was reserved for *dalit* women. She was a proxy. Her father was the Union Councillor at that time. The woman President was not approachable to the public. The delivery of services was not effective during her administration. Moreover there was misuse of Panchayat funds and she was dismissed at the fag end of her tenure after an enquiry conducted by the district administration. Villagers stood in solidarity against the misdeeds of that woman President.

Pappa as a citizen used to attend Gram Sabha organized in her village. She recollected that she was just attending along with other women, as the proceeding of the Gram Sabha was not so serious. In the mean time, she became an agent in the LIC and actively engaged herself in that assignment. Within a short duration she achieved high position among the agents of LIC as she achieved the highest target. Her approach and sincerity in follow-up, with regard to LIC work as well as her counselling and guidance in the family affairs of those premium holders who sought her opinion were very useful to her in gaining recognition. Moreover she learned a lot as an insurance agent, she claimed, which helped in the administration of village panchayat after she became the President.

Panchayati Raj Election in 2001

When the election to Panchayati Raj Institutions was held in 2001, villagers suggested Pappa to file her nomination. Though Pappa had the mind to serve the community, with regard to contesting in elections she had some reservations. The villagers influenced the in-laws of Pappa. The family members of Pappa finally agreed to the suggestion of the villagers. There were four candidates in the fray who were not at all oriented to social activities. Moreover they were less educated than Pappa. The villagers suffered a lot during the first tenure in the hands of ill-equipped leadership. So they were determined to elect a woman with more potential this time. Pappa and her team of women and young men projected the necessity of a better qualified, independent and easily accessible leader in the village panchayat. The propaganda worked successfully. Pappa won the election in the four-cornered contest. Pappa told that she was also able to get more votes from the backward community.

Pappa as the Village Panchayat President

Pappa has shared that though she was not well versed with the Panchayati Raj System, she had her own perceptions over the issues of underdevelopment. She proposed to carry out activities in three important areas, namely; (i) education; (ii) women's development; and (iii) economic development as she realized that her villagers did not encourage girl children to continue their studies after schooling and most of them have been living in abject poverty. Due to rainfed irrigation, there is no successful agricultural practice and so poor landless labourers and marginal farmers used to go a distance of over 20 km to get employment in farms or to fell trees in the forest area so as they could earn for their livelihood from the sales proceedings of wood as fuel. Moreover, due to the lack of awareness, women failed to make use of services like pre-natal and post-natal care available in the health centre. They did not have the practice of prompt reporting and registration of pregnancy. They did not adhere to the small family norm. There were many couples who had five and even eleven children. Further, there was the practice of female infanticide problems especially among the Pallar and Kallar community, Pappa pointed out. She decided to work against these issues and hoped that the village panchayat would be a suitable place for this activity.

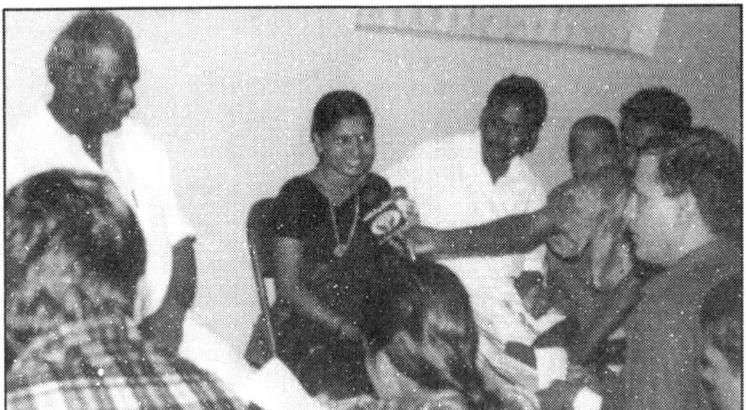

Fig. 6.2: Pappa's Interview

But in practice village panchayat presidents were asked to carry out the plan programmes drafted at top level. Moreover, the villagers were also of the opinion that basic amenities like drinking water supply, roads, other infrastructure facilities had to be carried out by the village panchayat. There are a large number of issues and problems in the rural areas which were not discussed in public fora and she had decided to discuss all those issues with the people. She is of the opinion that unless the poor, *dalit* and women are sensitized and conscientised, social transformation cannot be achieved.

Improvements in the Basic Amenities

1. ***Drinking Water Supply*** **:** Availability was not adequate in the panchayat when Pappa assumed position. There were only six public taps. Pappa in consultation with the development officials was able to get TWAD (Tamil Nadu Water and Drainage Board) assistance and two borewells were sunk. From the village fund three mini power pumps and a Sintex tank for storage were provided. Now, there are 23 public taps in the village panchayat, Pappa claims. The drudgery of women has reduced a lot, she adds.

Fig. 6.3: Removal of Encroachment

2. ***Road and Transportation Facility*** : From the village fund, at a total cost of Rs. 5.35 lakh, five road works have been carried out in the village panchayat jurisdiction. Priority was given to the replacement of gravel road into metal road and to provide Cement and Concrete (CC) road in streets and lanes, Pappa pointed out. As a large number of young girls and youths came forward to take part in labour works in the panchayat and village youths were given employment. Athankaraipatti is located in a remote area. There was no public transport facility. Public pleaded with the district administration and transport corporation officials, and succeeded in geting bus facilities, two trips a day from Peraiyur and Usilampatti.

3. ***Educational Development*** : Pappa's family is closely associated with Indian National Congress Party. Her husband is serving as the Vice-President of the SC cell of the Madurai District Congress Party. She along with her husband assisted the candidate in the election campaign of Lok Sabha election 2001, and is personally known to the sitting MP. She availed funds from MPLADP and a school building was constructed at the cost of Rs. 2.60 lakh. From the MLA fund, toilet and water supply facilities were provided to a Balwadi in her panchayat. Further the women sanitary complex, and village community centre 'Chavadi' were also provided under MLA constituency development fund at a total cost of Rs. 3.15 lakh in her panchayat.

4. ***Common Property Resources Maintenance*** : The supply channel for Manickapuram Kanmoi meant for Kamatchipuram farmers had been desilted at a cost of Rs. 1.60 lakh. The work was successfully completed with the involvement of farmers. With about fifty irrigation wells, the water table has improved as the rainwater reached properly and was stored in the *kanmoi* which resulted in the percolation of ground water into nearby irrigation wells.

After witnessing the improvement in the water table, villagers suggested making a new *oorani* as a *porambokku* land was available in the hamlets. A suitable place was identified involving the farmers of Kamatchipuram. During the discussion, the farmers suggested to have a retaining wall at the side of the proposed new *oorani* so that it will be a *pucca* arrangement. It was decided to form the *oorani* first and in the mean time approach the PWD to get funds for the construction of the retaining wall. When the formation of new *oorani* was in progress, the PWD officials inspected the site and agreed that they themselves would construct the retaining wall. Accordingly, with people's participation from planning to the stage of implementation, an *oorani* was successfully formed at a cost of Rs. 0.70 lakh, Pappa explained. Livelihood of the poor was so important and hence natural resource management was given priority and also the water bodies. She is conscious of the world to be done for poor by the panchayats.

Her Struggle for Entitlement

Athipatti is a nearby village panchayat. There is an irrigation *kanmoi,* benefiting the *ayacatdhars* of these two Village Panchayats located in that area. When they experienced severe drought during 2003-04 the government decided to undertake maintenance work in that *kanmoi.* Accordingly, at a total estimate of Rs. 2.60 lakh the work was given to Athankaraipatti Village Panchayat by an administrative sanction earmarked to that panchayat. But, in the mean time, the work of desilting and strengthening of bunds have been executed by a contractor without the knowledge of the Athankaraipatti Village Panchayat. Hence Pappa raised her objection against the contractors work. Moreover, the work was very unsatisfactory as the desilting was done only to a limited extent. It was easy to observe that a cost of Rs. 2.60 lakh work was not really carried out when compared to the quantum of work and removal of earth which existed there. The issue was brought to the notice of the union as well as the district officials. But it was unnecessarily dragged on to find out the truth, she complained. In the mean time, due to poor and sub-standard work, there was a breach in the bank and the rainwater flooded into the fields causing heavy damage, Pappa added. When the issue of damage was highlighted the union administration re-engaged the contractor who did surface work instead of strengthening the bank. Till today the administration played hide and seek in the issue of giving the work to a contractor by the union administration despite administrative sanction given to the village panchayat, Pappa remarked. The bureaucracy used to play second fiddle to the ruling party men, Pappa commented.

Issue in Selecting the Beneficiaries of Indira Awas Yojana

Pappa used to show real concern in selecting the eligible poor families under IAY. The allocation and the details of norms, procedure and rules and regulation were properly explained to the villagers in the Gram Sabha meeting with regard to all schemes and programmes assigned to the village panchayat, she informed. So far about 40 poor families (34 SC and 6 BC) have been provided with IAY house. There was no procedural lapse in this regard and the work was completed successfully, Pappa shared. During the year 2005-2006 10 houses were allotted. But, a list of beneficiaries was sent by the union administration instead of the written rule that the selection had to be in the Gram Sabha meeting. Hence Pappa did not yield to the pressure made on her to pass resolution in this regard.

In the mean time, the Gram Sabha was convened at the marriage hall owned by the backward community and Pappa sought police protection. Pappa had the practice of availing police protection whenever she convenes Gram Sabha meetings as there would be anti-social elements or drunkards who try to disturb the proceedings. On that day of Gram Sabha where the issue of list of beneficiaries sent from the union administration was taken up for discussion, Pappa availed police protection.

Pappa maintained the procedure with regard to the seating arrangements during the Gram Sabha meeting, and thereby avoided any special importance to anybody. But, the officials resorted breach of customary practice. When the Union Chairman came to attend the meeting (he is a local resident) the officials arranged the seating arrangements giving preference to him and those accompanying him. Pappa refused to have a break in the system and the proceedings of that Gram

Sabha was disturbed. She was instructed to convene another Gram Sabha. In the mean time Pappa discussed the issue of denying the legal right entrusted with Village Panchayats and Gram Sabha in respect of selection of IAY beneficiaries, with institutions like Rajiv Gandhi Chair for Panchayati Raj Studies, and at last she decided herself to seek the direction of the court in this regard. She moved the petition in the Madurai bench of High Court of Tamil Nadu and the court ordered the stoppage of activities in this regard, Pappa informed. Realizing the consequences of legal action, the union administration and the Union Chairperson agreed to adhere to the list of beneficiaries selected by the Gram Sabha. Among the ten beneficiaries proposed by the union administration six of them were found ineligible and they have been replaced with 6 eligible families identified by the Gram Sabha, Pappa told.

Issues in the 2004 Parliament Election

In 2004 when the election to the Parliament was held, Pappa joined her husband and assisted in the campaign for the success of Congress candidate of Periakulam Parliamentary Constituency. The Congress candidate pooled 6000 votes more than the AIADMK candidate in the union of Sedapatti, she told. After a few days, a group of opponents gathered and forcefully entered into the house of Pappa, assaulted their in-laws. Her husband was beaten when he was in a tea shop and was hospitalized. A false case on Pappa was also registered by her opponents. But Pappa went to the local police station and explained the furious attack made by the opponents and demanded to register her complaint. As the local police officials delayed Pappa approached the district officials in the police department and Pappa resorted to *dharna* with a majority of her villagers. The case was filed and two among the accused were sent to jail for further investigation. The case was registered only after an agitation and a *dharna* by Pappa and her relatives and villagers. The case is still pending, Pappa shared.

Panchayat By-Election to fill the Vacancy in her Panchayat

As a SC woman ward member expired, a by-election was held in the Athankaraipatti Village Panchayat. To challenge the leadership of Pappa, her opponents fielded a SC woman in the by-election as their proxy. But Pappa identified a woman volunteer who really showed interest in public life. It was the toughest election. Heavy expenditure was incurred by the opponent party of Pappa, she explained. But the local villagers knew the potentials of Pappa and the significance of her team. So majority of villagers in that Ward cast their votes in favour of the candidate supported by Pappa. At last with a 40 votes margin, the opponent was defeated, she added. Pappa reiterated that it was politics which stood against decentralization and women's empowerment. Money and muscle power play an important role in panchayat elections. But she courageously faced and tackled all these threats successfully. She acknowledged that it was the confidence building and guidance received from Gandhigram that equipped her to overcome all the hurdles. She claims that support structure is very important for women and *dalit* leaders.

Her Contribution to the Welfare of Women

Pappa explained that she was constantly working to create a social climate in which her village women would be in a better position. She told that she could observe a change in the mindset of her village women. They never used to come in front of unknown male visitors and always showed inhibition in conversation. They wouldn't undertake a journey independently even to nearby cities and towns. They never individually visited government offices and other public institutions like banks etc., Pappa pointed out. Self help group activities and personal encouragement given by her brought a new life to the majority of womenfolk in her village, Pappa claimed.

The number of girl students who continued their studies after primary school increased, the practice of early marriage has decreased, the participation of women in SHG activities is enhanced, girls are permitted to undergo professional courses like nursing and computer study, and the women in general courageously express their opinion in families as well as in public forum; Pappa listed out the attitudinal and behavioural changes occurred among women of her village within a short span of five years, thanks to the reservation for women, especially SC women, in Panchayati Raj Institutions, she reiterated. She herself is a role model and she constantly interacts and facilitates women to move further in the public space.

Pappa further cited the process of transformation among the women. Pappa recently organized a women's meet under the aegis of the Catalyst Trust, a non-governmental organization promoting civil society, through establishing a "people's centre" in villages. Pappa is running one such centre in Athankaraipatti Village Panchayat. In the women's meet, the response was intensive, Pappa quoted. Women cutting across age mingled among themselves and keenly participated in folk songs and games programmes. They shared their feelings and aspirations frankly and they staged cultural programmes without any inhibition. The rural women are coming away from the routine life of manual labour, cooking, eating, and personal time with husbands. Now-a-days they spare time for SHG activities. Moreover, in that connection they go to various places away from the local area for training and exposure. They undertake entrepreneurial activities, discuss profit and loss, market, stock and registers etc. They visit banks, government offices and fearlessly meet authorities and share their opinions with them, Pappa remarked. The women's sanitary complex is in full use. Even elderly women are taught to make use of the toilet properly and without hesitation Pappa spends her time in early morning and late evening to motivate and to create awareness about public sanitation and personal hygiene. Informal discussions are held on topics like reproductive health care, HIV-AIDS, waterborne diseases, importance of literacy and education to girl children, Pappa explained. It was found that there were four dropouts among the girls. The parents have been contacted and after coaching the children were admitted in the same school to continue their study.

Witnessing the involvement of Pappa in creating awareness through formal and informal gathering of women, the union officials made use of her voluntarism in the IEC activities on AIDS awareness and ills of alcoholism. In all the 31 Village Panchayats of Sedapatti Union, Pappa participated and influenced the women participants in the above topics. These experiences capacitated Pappa and she mobilized women of her village at once when the government introduced sale of liquor in the rural pockets, through TASMAC (Tamil Nadu State Marketing Corporation Limited), and showed stiff opposition against the TASMAC officials to open and run a retail liquor shop in their Village Panchayat. She met the District Supply Officer in this regard and succeeded in their attempt. There is no TASMAC retail liquor shop in her village, Pappa shared.

Pappa herself was instrumental in the formation of a self-help group in her habitation. The name of her group is Sarvodaya Women Group No. 56. There are twenty members in that group. The members have a system of mutual help and assistance for the social activities of fellow members apart from their joint venture in entrepreneurial activities. It is told that during the events like marriage, pubetry, death, hospitalization, etc., each member contributes rupees 200 and the consolidated total Rs. 4,000 is used to procure useful household utensils, furniture and jewellery. It is a lottery to the recipient member, Pappa remarked.

Moreover, Pappa used to spend her time on the promotion of SHG activities in all hamlets of her village panchayat. She assisted a few women to undergo training in marketing of articles of companies like Hindustan Lever. Rearing of milch animal is economically viable to rural women, Pappa observed. There is a cooperative milk society at T. Ramanathapuram, a nearby village panchayat and so marketing of milk is easily done, Pappa added.

Promoting Social Harmony

Athankaraipatti is a multi-caste village panchayat. The relationship among the various communities of Athankaraipatti

Village Panchayat is a cordial one. It is reported that there is no communal clash in this area. Pappa shared that there is a village temple Samathi Pattaiya situated in a site belonged to SC community, but the temple affairs are managed by Naicker and Vellalar community. There are common temples, Mariamman Temple and Vinayakar temple where all the communities participate in the celebration. Moreover, each member of SC community contributes to the *pooja* activities during the annual celebration where meals prepared from the contribution of paddy by each SC member and all communities irrespective of castes partake in the feast. It is a grand celebration of two days. Villagers from 18 villages located around the area participate in the celebrations. The temple *poojari* belongs to Naicker community. Inspite of a huge congregation of people from different castes, the celebrations was observed peacefully, Pappa explained. Pappa told that as the President of the village panchayat she was serious in promoting communal harmony in her panchayat area as many villages witness communal conflict among the castes.

She uses her good office and position when dealing with issues which involve more than one community to ease tensions by personally visiting the houses of both communities, freely sharing with men and women and assessing their feelings and emotions related to issues and instead of projecting the negative feelings if any shared, Pappa used to project positive feelings of the opponents. Hence she acted wisely to reduce tension and contributed to the promotion of communal harmony. Pappa opined that it was all possible because, being a woman President it is easy to get into touch with the female and youth members among the disputed families, she pointed out.

Her Contribution to Social Reform Activities

Pappa has another dimension as an agent of Life Insurance Corporation of India. In connection with enrolling policy holders she maintains a wide contact with a large number of families in many village panchayats of Sedapatti Union. Pappa shared that it was a great opportunity to mingle with family members and she was able to share in their emotions, especially the women. She facilitated successful widow remarriages. In one incident a widow member in her group with one child got married. It took about two years to pacify the parents of the bridegroom. Now, that women is pregnant and Pappa and her group members participated in the celebration. Another marriage was for a widow of backward community with two children. Both couples are living happily, Pappa remarked. Being a woman she was able to realize the emotional problems of women, Pappa pointed out.

Promoting Small Savings Account among Rural Populace

Pappa, through personal contacts explains the significance of small savings among poor families. With the help of the local postal department staff, she made 400 families open small saving accounts in the post office. Appreciating her efforts in mobilization of small savings account, Rs. 3 lakh was awarded to her village panchayat as an incentive.

Her Achievement in Namathu Gramam

When the innovative scheme of 'Namathu Gramam' was introduced in all the village panchayats of Tamil Nadu, Pappa with the cooperation of villagers undertook activities to

Fig. 6.4: Award is presented to Ms. Pappa

accomplish the seven components targeted in Namathu Gramam. She had given attention in the following activities :

1. Maximum utilization of women's sanitary complex.
2. Cleanliness in streets and lanes.
3. Segregation of wastes-organic and inorganic.
4. Tree planting in all houses, public lands, school campuses and tanks.
5. Cent per cent school enrolment.
6. Education of girl children.
7. Eradication of child labour.
8. Creating awareness about the age of marriage.
9. Prevention of female infanticide.
10. Transparency in panchayat administration.

Pappa informed that all details of finance and works proposed to be carried out, and even the details of her tour programme have been written on the notice board. Her village panchayat was graded as 'B' and Rs. one lakh was awarded under Namathu Gramam incentive. Pappa, during the interview promised to improve further in the above areas anticipating to achieve 'A' grade.

Welfare of the Marginalized Section

Pappa is acting quickly in assisting eligible persons among the marginalized section to avail their entitlements. She got personally involved in getting marriage assistance earmarked for daughters of widows, widow's remarriage, old age pensions to 12 elderly persons, disabled assistance to 7 persons and under the free rice scheme to ultra poor pledged rice for 35 families, Pappa listed out.

Pappa informed that in her village panchayat a hostel-cum-training/production centre for persons with special needs is under construction. She assisted the union administration in conducting camps for persons with special needs and distribution of identity cards for them in other village panchayats of Sedapatti Union.

Pappa as a Winner of the Heart

It is a well known that female infanticide is in practice in the area of Sedapatti Union of Madurai District. Government of Tamil Nadu has taken a series of steps in preventing the inhuman cruelty of female infanticide. The law punishes the guilty and apart from programmes like creation of awareness, a cradle scheme of adoption of unwanted female infants is implemented by the government. Pappa being an educated woman as well as in the capacity of woman President took much efforts in this regard. She used to associate with the village health nurse in meeting mothers who delivered female children and offered guidance and counselling to rear the female children. Pappa narrated her experience in this respect. In a family there is a delivery of one female child. The above said mother already has two female children. Having a third female child, the grandma of the child advised her daughter to desist herself from feeding the child and let it die itself naturally avoiding the accusation of female infanticide. Pappa having known that, informed the village health nurse and accompanied her to that house with an intention of getting the female child admission under cradle scheme for adoption. But the family members refused to give the baby and even resorted to reacting angrily towards Pappa and the nurse. The grandma of the baby threw away the loincloth on the nurse. But, the nurse showed patience and both advised all the members of the family to immediately save the baby otherwise they would face legal action. Finally, Pappa and the family persuaded the mother to feed the baby. At last she won the heart of mother. The mother fed the baby and as the baby eagerly waited for the mother's love and care enjoyed her feeding. A lamp is protected to extinguish, Pappa quoted.

Pappa used to share that she herself was a successful woman and so she assured the rural womenfolk that there was a great scope to all women in ensuing years provided they are empowered. She learnt to drive motor bike and she was known as 'bike lady'. It is an inspiration to several young girls, Pappa observed.

Linkage with Line Departments

Pappa maintains good rapport with the officials of line departments. She helps her villagers to avail services from Agriculture Department, THADCO, Electricity Board, Education, PWD, Women Development, Social Welfare and Revenue Departments. She successfully availed the Land Purchase Scheme of THADCO and 4 landless agricultural labourers in her village and 6 landless labourers from nearby Village Panchayat benefited in this regard.

Fig. 6.5: Awareness creation programme

In consultation with the government doctor, she helped a poor wage earner to undergo a brain operation at Chitira Thirunal Hospital, Trivananthapuram. She accompanied the patient to the hospital and pleaded with the committee of doctors regarding the case of the patient. Now after the operation, he has returned to normalcy. The family of the concerned person were very thankful in this regard, Pappa shared.

Under the scheme 'Single Light to Hut' 40 hutments obtained electricity connection by her efforts. The Parent Teachers Association activities were strengthened. The school children adhere to the ten commandments of personal hygiene promoted under Total Rural Sanitation Programme, Pappa highlighted. The distribution of free noon-meal was monitored

Fig. 6.6: A Function Organised in the Village

and the quality of food was ensured. Additional building for the school have been provided by the Union Chairman.

Pappa informed that the various trainings and exposure she had at the aegis of institutions like Gandhigram, Vivekananda Kendra, RETC, SIRD, ISS and training given by Women Development Corporation for SHG animators helped to shape her personality. Further her service as an agent of LIC was very much helpful in sharpening her approaches in dealing in public affairs, she added. She used to organize legal awareness programme under the aegis of Department of Law and Justice and helped women to get justice by the intervention of Women's Commission and Human Right Commission, she pointed out.

Activities in the Federation of Women Panchayat Presidents

Pappa is serving as the President of Madurai District unit of the Association of Elected Women Representatives of Panchayati Raj Institutions. She is the treasurer in the union level committee of Village Panchayat Presidents of Sedapatti Union where both men and women presidents were members. She is the Secretary of the Dalit Women Presidents District Unit, Madurai District.

Pappa informed that though education is very essential to the empowerment of women, it was her active involvement in public affairs that brought her to the limelight. Her struggles and achievements have been featured in many newspapers and electronic media. She opined that even less educated women could perform well provided they got needed orientation and guidances whenever they demanded. It is by performance only women Presidents could get recognition in the community and the society. In this regard she acknowledged the services of supportive institutions functioning in the State of Tamil Nadu.

Fig. 6.7: She received honorary doctorate from Sri Lanka

Fig. 6.8: She received honorary doctorate from Sri Lanka

Honour on Pappa

Pappa's struggles have been brought to the wider public through media. In several newspapers and magazines the details of her struggle and her courage to uphold the truth and commitment in public life were published frequently. Colombo University of Sri Lanka recognizing the struggle of Pappa came forward to honour her by offering honorary doctorate (D. Litt.) on her. She was invited to go to Colombo to accept the doctorate. Pappa visited Colombo University along with her husband and she recollected that it was an evergreen memory. She shared that she came to realize the power of media in the contribution of grassroots democracy. She expressed her heartfelt thanks to the media.

Her Future Vision

She is seriously contemplating on the ways and means for the socio-economic advancement of the villagers of her area. She pointed out that they needed support to start self-employment ventures and vocationally trained youths could get employment elsewhere, she added. She proposed to have youth centres, meant for physically and mentally challenged persons.

Villagers assured their support if Pappa contested in the next election to Panchayati Raj Institutions. If opportunity is available, Pappa is ready to move further, to be the Member of Legislative Assembly in her constituency. She gained popularity by her bold and courageous steps which she carried out after planning and in the support of all concerned, she added. She has a positive feeling that the future is bright and full of scope for her active involvement in the public space in the context of under development and poverty in her area.

Conclusion

Primarily she is an educated and motivated individual who has a passion for public service. Even before contesting in the election, she has come out for public service with the support of the family. Moreover the family has got political connections.

Her husband is also supportive. One important factor which helped her to assert herself as leader is that she has gone to police station, she has gone to court and she went to different offices. Finally she won in all her ventures and that provided confidence. She got strength from her family and external agencies like Rajiv Gandhi Chair to overcome the barriers created by a political class and bureaucracy. But she was always on the right path. Her moral strength and community support made to face all her ordeals. Many popular articles have been written about her struggle and success and some of the articles got awards also. Her story is both a struggle and success. The moment she gets success in one struggle, she begins another. In the whole process, she has built up her capacity. She is conscious of *dalit* problems and her commitment towards the issues of *dalit* is visible and yet her approach is that *dalit* problems could be solved with the support of the caste Hindus. She said that it is possible and it is happening in her panchayat.

She has moved further frontiers in socio-political transformation of the villages. She has not confined her activities only to her panchayat areas. She has expanded her activities in and around the Sedapatti Block Panchayat areas. She is not looking into the powers assigned to Panchayats. She has a tendency to respond to the demands and calls of the people. As her administration is transparent, non-corrupt, she has been fighting against injustice. She is being supported by the community. Her movement with higher officials and support agencies helped a lot to strengthen her position in Panchayats. She is a role model for other *dalit* women leaders. She is the head of many associations including *dalit*. Her multifaceted role enhanced her capacity and capability.

7

Harmony and Development

Socio-Economic Background

Ms. S. Rani Sathappan, aged 32, is the President of K. Rayavaram Village Panchayat. She is married and has two sons. Her husband is serving as an overseer in Kallal Union of Sivagangai District. She has studied up to 10+2. After her school final, she joined the B.Lit. course, but discontinued it as she got admission to the teacher training course. That course also she discontinued as she was married at the age of 19 years. Even though it is more than 12 years, her interest in studying is not gone. Now she is studying for her M.A. (History) through a correspondence course. She was a sportsperson during her school days. Volleyball was her favourite game. She served as a district player. Moreover she showed interest in celebrating Pongal and temple festivals along with the villagers. From these experiences she understood public affairs. She belongs to the Vallambar caste. It is one of the components in the Mukkalothor community (one of the most backward community).

After her marriage she was away from K. Rayavaram as her husband served in various block offices for 10 years. But she and her family used to visit her own house in K. Rayavaram village frequently. Her husband, who is an engineer, showed interest in village life. Whenever he visited K. Rayavaram, he met the village elders and shared his views with them regarding the village development activities initiated by the Village Committee (traditional). Her father-in-law showed interest in village activities. He belongs to the All India Anna Dravida Munnetra Kazhagam (AIADMK). His constructive participation during the Village Committee meetings brought him a name. Due to this reputation Rani's name was suggested when the Village President's position was reserved for women (general). Rani Sathappan was a sympathizer of the Indian National Congress for long.

Recruitment

The Village Committee met to take a decision on the selection of a candidate unopposed. But there was opposition to this idea. So the Village Committee did not take any decision. Rani's father-in-law was told to field her and the majority of the members agreed to support her. The opponent belonged the Dravida Munnetra Kazhagam (DMK) Party. Though her father-in-law was a cadre of the AIADMK Party, she never projected herself politically. Moreover, the villagers openly encouraged her candidature as she was better educated than the opponent. Rani's husband readily agreed to this proposal as his wife would be a better choice to make use of his expertise for village development. Rani had no reservations and agreed to contest in the election.

Rani and the six contestants for the Wards joined together as a group. They made two rounds, house by house and visited all the families. The opponent also belonged to her community and was also her relative. There was a tough competition, but they observed peace and so there was no untoward incident.

The villagers had a lot of expectations from the New Panchayati Raj. Earlier, during the period of officials, no one represented the village and so no development activities were carried out in the village. The Government officials did not have an opportunity to understand the socio-economic problems of the village as the village is located on the border of Sivagangai District. Moreover, there is another village named Rayavaram where the business community of Chettiars live. Generally, if any reference is made to K. Rayavaram, officials used to remember the other Rayavaram. So, this village could not get any attention from the Government officials.

Against this backdrop, Rani's entry into the village panchayat might change the scenario, the villagers felt, and so there was a lot of expectation from the election. At least the name of K. Rayavaram could easily come to the memory of officials, the villagers hopefully believed.

Though her father-in-law belonged to the AIADMK Party, she was a staunch supporter of the Tamil Maanila Congress (TMC). The simplicity of G.K. Moopanar attracted her. But she could not become a full time politician. When the opportunity was given to her, she was happy to contest in the election as her husband explained to her and asked her to give the best of her ability to bring about a new name and fame to the village by serving as a good President under the New Panchayati Raj System. With this expectation the villagers elected her by a difference of 174 votes.

Leadership Sustained

The first tenure under the new Panchayati Raj System came to an end by September 2001. Rani decided not to contest again due to family responsibilities. But the villagers preferred her for the second term also, as the seat had once again been reserved for women. The Village Committee met and decided to unanimously elect the same President and Vice-President for the second tenure. Rani respected the feelings of the villagers and accepted.

In the mean time, one of her close relatives decided to field his wife, who is an elderly woman. He came to Rani and advised her to contest for the Union Councillor's position. She frankly replied that since the villagers had decided to field her she had to respect them and so she would not withdraw her nomination. There was a straight contest. As per the advice of the village elders, she made arrangements for bringing voters who are living away from the village. The election campaign was effectively handled by Rani with the support of SHG members. She won again with a margin of 184 votes—this time 10 votes more than the pervious time.

The reasons behind her success are:

1. The Village Committee expected someone who would be an active President.
2. Her father-in-law is an active and constructive participant during the Village Committee meetings.
3. Her husband is educated and working in the Panchayat Union.
4. She is better educated than the opponent and her social commitment is known to other women.

Village Setup

K. Rayavaram is a small panchayat which does not have any hamlet. About 200 families of Vallambar, 50 families of Udayar, 30 families of Valayar and 20 families of other castes like Vellalar, Velar, Asari and Pandaram are residing in the village. It is said that there is no family from the SC community. Vallambars are the dominant caste and Udayars are the second majority. They have a separate residential area just away from the main settlement. There is no caste association in the village. The youth tried to organise themselves as an asscciation, but, due to poverty and unemployment, their spirit diminished and so they failed in their attempt.

Political Parties

The DMK, the AIADMK, the TMC and the Marumalarchi Dravida Munnetra Kazhagam (MDMK) are the parties in the village. There are no serious activities from the side of the political parties. The TMC cadres give their time for public activities as she is one of the three district secretaries nominated by the TMC Party.

Village Temples

Ayyanar Kovil and Perumal Kovil are the important temples. A Vellar and an Iyyangar are the *poojaris* in the Ayyanar and the Perumal temples respectively. The Perumal temple was renovated recently. Though it is common to all, a few families of the Udayar community spent a lot of money for the renovation. Pachaiamman and Mariamman are the Amman temples. Mariamman is common to all, whereas Pachaiamman is only for the Udayar community.

There is a Kaman Kovil in which an Asari is the *poojari.* The celebration of the Kaman festival is a popular and memorable event in the village. It draws people from nearby villages also. The Ayyanar temple celebration is facilitated by the Panchayat with the suggestion to maintain peace and to settle differences of opinion among the villagers.

Village Committee

A traditional Village Committee exists in the village. The Ambalam is the head of the Committee and there are members from the major communities. The Committee meeting is usually convened near the *oorani,* under a tree. Only men are allowed to participate in the meetings. Village affairs like organising of temple festivals, maintenance of public assets like *oorani,* trees in *poramboke* lands, conciliation between disputing parties are the major dealings of the Village Committee. When the goat

Fig. 7.1: Traditional Panchayat leader facilitates the Gram Panchayat President

rearers entered the Iyar *oorani* and the PWD *kanmai,* where a number of saplings are growing and damaged the saplings, the issue was brought to the notice of the Village Committee. The issue was discussed in the Gram Sabha meeting also. The Village Committee asked those families who rear the goats not to enter the *oorani* and damage the saplings. Rani's interaction with the Ambalam is very limited, as she is not permitted to attend the Village Committee meeting. Her husband attends the Village Committee meetings and explains the details.

Fig. 7.2: Gram Sabha Meeting

Sections and groups in a village community are used to conflicts due to difference of opinion, particularly in respect of temple celebrations. K. Rayavaram is not an exception. Two different groups claimed that the 'Muthal Mariathai' i.e., the first honour, had to be given to its leader. This resulted in the stoppage of temple celebration for a decade.

The Panchayat Council decided to try its best to bring the two opposing parties to a peaceful solution. Rani took special interest in this regard and she played a vital role in bringing about a settlement between those groups and, at last, the temple *kumbabisekam* was performed successfully along with the festival celebrations. The villagers felt very happy about the restoration of peace and harmony.

Since then, the traditional village community started to share formally and informally with the village panchayat and vice versa. The mutual understanding and cooperation between these two institutions created a healthy working atmosphere for the village panchayat administration. Activities like tax-collection, selection of works, worksite and beneficiaries, protection of community assets, participation in Gram Sabha meetings, SHG functions and social control in the monitoring of drinking water supply distribution etc., are being effectively and successfully carried out to the satisfaction of the villagers and officials. Rani acknowledged that she could impress the higher officials only by good performance, for which the traditional committee extended support.

Common Property Resources

There are three *ooranis* and four *kanmais.* Two *kanmais* belong to the PWD and two *kanmais* are under the Union. Under the Social Forestry Scheme trees are planted and a watchman is employed by the Panchayat. In the *oorani poramboke, velikaruvel* trees are grown. As they are more than three years old, the Panchayat decided to auction the trees and approached the RDO for getting permission. Some officials expected a bribe, but Rani was determined not to give any. In the mean time, in

Fig. 7.3: A desilted tank

the presence of the BDO, through an open tender, the auction was conducted for Rs. 16,950. The tender was awarded. But the RDO did not respond with the sanction order to cut the trees. At last, after the transfer of the field officials by chance, Rani met the higher officials and got the order. In the mean time, more than two years had gone by. Red tapism in the Government departments is a handicap in bringing about development. But, at the same time, people are not ready to hear excuses from the President. The people wish to achieve immediately what they want.

Fig. 7.4: A desilted inlet channel

When there was an encroachment on the inlet channel by an individual belonging to a nearby village, the panchayat decided to deal with the issue carefully. Otherwise there would be a clash between the two villages. They petitioned the District Collector and the Chief Minister. Rani attended the monthly grievance day and brought the matter to the attention of the District Collector. When the District Collector arranged for an inspection by the revenue officials, the revenue officials twisted the matter. They threatened that they would become enquiry officers and book the panchayat President, if she did not obey the officials. But the President complained against the revenue officials. Due to this difference of opinion and egoism, it was all delayed. At last the inspection was done and the officials agreed to arrange for the removal of the encroachment. As there was no action, again the issue was reported. Whenever the higher officials asked for a file/paper, the department officials used to reply negatively. As the Panchayat maintained photocopies of all their correspondence in this regard, they immediately produced them and again the issue became alive. In spite of that, the encroachment is not yet removed. It is more than three years of struggle with the bureaucrats. These trials and tribulations led to her belief in the maximum "Efforts will bring about change". This slogan is printed on her official letter pad.

During the initial period, her focus was on the provision of minimum basic amenities to the villagers. In course of time she came to understand the problems of farmers. On several occasions, during the Gram Sabha meetings, the village elders and the members of traditional committee urged her to take up activities related to protection and promotion of common properties, especially irrigation tanks and *ooranis* in the village. Hence, she was determined to work on that aspect more seriously.

Table 7.1: Tanks and *Ooranis* in K. Rayavaram

Sl. No.	*Name*	*Category*	*Total Extent Average*	*Ayakat Average*
1.	Pappankulam	PWD	21.00.0	48.66.5
2.	Pudu Kanmoi	PWD	24.91.0	66.80.0
3.	Narathar Kanmoi	Union	9.29.0	36.66.0
4.	Sivan Kanmoi	Union	10.62.0	14.92.0
5.	Nachiar Oorani	Village Panchayat	0.54.5	—
6.	Iyyar Oorani	Village Panchayat	0.32.0	—
7.	Nambakulam Oorani	Village Panchayat	2.55.0	—
8.	Nambi Oorani	Village Panchayat	1.81.50	—
9.	Peevetti Oorani	Village Panchayat	0.49.0	—

Source: Computed.

As agriculture in the major source of the village economy, after realizing the expectation of the villagers through Gram Sabha meetings, the Village Panchayat President Rani gave priority to improving the above mentioned tanks and *ooranis*.

Whenever there was a scope for availing of any scheme fund not only from the Department of Rural Development but also from other sectoral departments like agriculture, agricultural engineering, agro forestry, etc., the Village Panchayat made all necessary attempts to harness the fund assistance. Accordingly, desilting and deepening of tanks and *ooranis,* strengthening of *bunds,* removal of thorny bushes and wild weeds, protection of standing trees and planting of more trees, maintenance of supply channels, and construction of a *ghat* for public utility were carried out successfully, involving the village community in the planning and the execution of the works. The above mentioned activities were carried out with the scheme fund provided by the Government Departments.

Table 7.2: Availing of Schemes for Protecting and Managing Common Property Resources

Sl. No.	*Source*	*Fund Assistance (Total Rs.)*
1.	Social Forestry Scheme Fund	250 saplings—tree planting—eucalyptus and non-fruit bearing trees
2.	NGO contribution	Rs. 50,000 worth of food grain
3.	Community contribution—Namakku Naame Thittam	Rs. 50,000
4.	Community contribution	Rs. 30,000
5.	NAWAPRA (National Watershed Development Programme for Rainfed Areas)	Rs. 66,000
6.	Agricultural Engineering Department	Rs. 30,000
7.	Agricultural Engineering Department	Rs. 75,000
8.	Spl. SGRY Fund	Rs. 2.0 lakhs
9.	SGRY	Rs. 33,000
10.	SGRY	Rs. 50,000 (work in progress)

Source: Computed.

Village Economy

There are about 150 farmers. Most of the lands are rainfed and about 40 pumpsets are available in the village. Paddy, groundnut, black gram and sugarcane are the main crops. Sugarcane is profitable, as there is an assured price for the same, whereas the selling price of the other crops always fluctuates. The rain water stored in the PWD and the Union *kanmais* will be available only for three to four months. Moreover, the encroachment on the inlet channel is preventing the full flow of flood water. Due to lack of economic activities in the village, about 50 families as a whole and about 50 individual men and youths have migrated to other places. A number of youths are working in a cotton mill located at Pallathur, 10 km from the village. They go by bicycle for work. As the life style is very hard, the youths prefer to take rest rather than spare time for youth association activities.

Self-Help Groups

The concept of SHGs is only now picking up in the Panchayat. There are five groups and the group meetings are convened every week on Tuesdays at their respective places. Rani is also a member of a group. After the starting of SHGs the women are training their mind in social matters. They discuss the necessity of maintaining public hygiene and the personal cleanliness of their children. The SHG members attend the Gram Sabha meetings. After understanding the poor financial position of the panchayat and the availability of Government grant if the house tax is collected fully, the women are helping in the collection of house tax. Three SHGs have got bank loans. They planned a tour programme to get exposure to various self-employment opportunities along with visiting temples and

Fig. 7.5: SHG is in action

Fig. 7.6: Planning for Women Development

hill stations. Rani assisted in finalising the places in this regard. Due to the presence of SHGs they are witnessing changes in the perception of the menfolk too. They are now coming to realize the efficiency of womenfolk.

The SHG movement has not made any serious impact in K. Rayavaram. The non-governmental organizations serving in this area organize women into SHGs but the impact was not seriously felt. It was only after her exposure trip to Raligoah Village in Maharashtra that she realised the importance of women groups and, with the guidance of block officials she initiated the group formation activity. It was possible only after convincing the menfolk of concerned families. Now there are seven self-help groups and the membership altogether is 105.

Though the initiative of The Hunger Project, the Gandhigram Rural Institute concept of preparation of Development Plan was undertaken in the Village Panchayat. To attend an orientation programme, Rani along with the SHG leaders, visited Gandhigram, where they had an exposure to various khadi and village industries. Their SHG, after returning, asked her to help them in getting training from some association. She met the district officials and succeeded in getting permission for a number of SHG members to undergo training in paper bag production. The trained women, in turn, gave training to fellow members. They made an attempt, but did not succeed in this venture. In the mean time, credit with

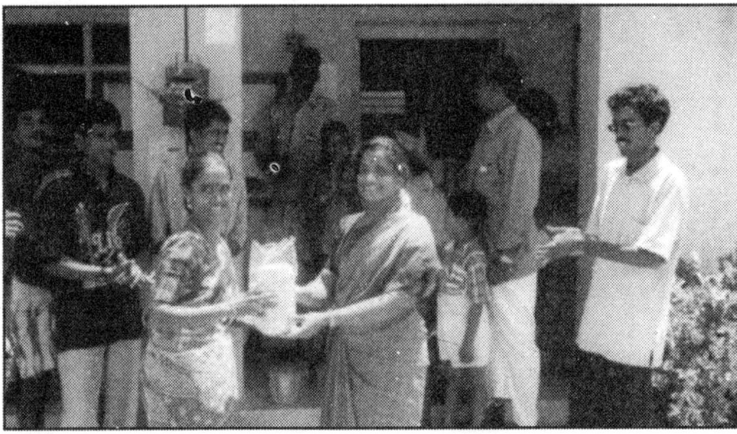

Fig. 7.7: Assistance provided to SHG women

subsidy was sanctioned to one group. Various trades were analysed. At last it was decided to engage in vessels/chair/furniture business, renting them out for social and home celebration. It is running at a profit as the group keeps three sets of vessels and other materials.

As the other group members were interested in some other activities, without waiting for government assistance, they themselves contributed to get training in the production of toilet soap, washing powder and cleaning powder. They produced toilet soaps and, during the Gram Sabha meeting

Fig. 7.8: Participating in Development Seminar

Fig. 7.9: Display for Awareness Creation

Fig. 7.10: SHG Meeting in Progress

they sold out. Raw materials were purchased from the Madurai wholesale market.

SHGs need professional guidance for its organizational as well as economic activities. At present she has equipped herself to fill the leadership gap. Through this exercise, she has more opportunities to move closely with the womenfolk. They used to share their family problems, personal problems as well as group issues. When she came to know that the literacy rate among the members was low, a non-formal education centre was organized by the group itself, engaging local educated young men and women. Now the SHG is her supporter. It has its impact on the village community also. If any woman President possesses determination to work with the SHGs, she can succeed, as in her case, Rani declared.

Educating the Masses

There are umpteen number of schemes available for the welfare of the marginalized sector, especially for women in the sectoral Department of Social Welfare. Even educated citizens cannot know all the details in this regard. So awareness has to be created among the public. But, creating mass awareness is not an easy task. Rani did an innovation in this regard. She met the district officials, NGOs and other concerned institutions and, with their guidance and assistance, she organized an exhibition in the village itself. Pictures, charts, photos, paintings, panels reporting the various schemes available in the Social Welfare and the Literacy Department were exhibited. The importance of women empowerment was explained with the help of field officials and educated youth volunteers. All the women in K. Rayavaram came in groups and spent a whole day there.

Performance

Rani was an ignorant women when she contested in the panchayat election. But, during the canvassing, she came to understand the public, their expectations, the issues and the official procedures. After assuming the position, her husband regularly briefed her on the details of various schemes in panchayat administration. He encouraged her independent leadership and so she used to meet officials without her husband. The vice-president is a public spirited person. He personally takes up several issues and tries to meet and explain to the officials. Because of this mutual cooperation and involvement they are able to run the administration smoothly. Once the water supply seemed to become an issue as there were a lot of illegal connections and extension of pipelines took place in a disorderly manner. This had happened before she assumed office under the Panchayati Raj System. They discussed this issue in the panchayat council meetings and decided to take necessary steps to disconnect all illegal connections. The block officials were properly told of this step. They reported the matter to the police station also. As requested, the BDO accompanied them during the operation for disconnection, which went on successfully.

For smooth distribution of water supply in an equitable way, they decided to provide 22 public taps. They gave the responsibility to select the suitable places to the concerned families which live on the street. Two to three days' time was given for finalising the site. After that Rani, the Vice-President and two Members went to the people and noted down the places selected by them. Accordingly, the public taps were provided. This exercise was smoothly carried out, as they entrusted the responsibility to the concerned street. And then it was decided to give individual tap connections. As per the government order, after verifying with the Tamil Nadu Water Supply and Drinage (TWAD) officials, they provided individual tap connections to 42 houses though they had been permitted to give 70 connections. They limited the number anticipating the future need for public taps.

Interfacing with Officials

In general, officials pose as authorities. They never patiently apply their mind to understand the explanations given by the president. The authorities, without verifying the facts with the panchayat, adjusted a portion of the State Finance Commission (SFC) for the payment of arrears to the Electricity Board. But, in fact, there was no arrears as the panchayat had properly paid the electricity bills. Rani met the concerned official, but he was not ready to give any serious attention. Rani took up the matter with the Collector and he called the concerned officer and ordered him to correct himself. Later it was done, but all this could be avoided if mutual understanding exists between officials and the president. Their mindset has to be changed.

She cited another issue as an example. It was said that a sum of Rs. 30,000 was due to the Union and they proposed to deduct the same. Rani opposed the decision and so they appointed a committee to verify the all earlier transactions of all the village panchayat. It was found that Rs. 30,000 was due to the panchayat from the Union. In spite of this the Union has not yet released the money to the panchayat.

The problem in the payment of electricity bills in Pudukottai is always an issue. This is due to the functioning of the Thirumayam Rural Electricity Cooperative Society, which is authorised to distribute electricity to villages and to collect the bill amount. There is no office of the Electricity Board with a good system of administration and adequate staff. The Society does not seem to be an able institution in this regard. It is reported that only in Pudukottai and Kumbakonam these types of societies are involved in the distribution of electricity.

If the officials properly guide the panchayat, they can avoid friction. During a Gram Sabha meeting, it was suggested to employ a watchman to safeguard the tree saplings planted in the *oorani* and the *kanmai.* Accordingly, a watchman was employed with a monthly honorarium of Rs. 150. But the expenses incurred on the honorarium for the watchman were objected to during the audit. The official pointed out only then that a mere resolution of the Gram Sabha is not sufficient, but that the Collector has to sanction the appointment. So, from the month of August 2000, the watchman was sent off and the Rs. 1,650 paid to him was objected to. The officer instructed the president to pay the amount.

A copy of the deliberations of each Gram Sabha meeting is submitted to the officials. But it is treated merely as a ceremony. The concerned officials do not give their time and mind to go through the reports and give their observations. For their failure the panchayat president is unnecessarily punished.

The panchayat president should be very keen and vigilant in availing of the schemes from the Government. Otherwise they will be lifted by some other panchayat. Due to difference of opinion between the president of one panchayat and a District Council Member who belongs to the same panchayat, a provision for group houses to six BC beneficiaries was cancelled. Rani heard of this incident and immediately met the project officer and succeeded in availing of the same. Getting group houses for BC is really a tough task. Only during the allocation to SC a few houses can be earmarked for BC. In Rani's village there is no SC family and so the allocation of group houses does not come to the Panchayat. At this juncture she came to know of the above incident and succeeded in getting 6 houses to the poor BC families in her village.

Maintaining linkage with the other elected representatives is essential to develop the village. In the present system of fund allocation under various schemes through different elected representatives, Rani realised the importance of each of them. She met them, shared her village's poor financial position and got allocations from those representatives. Under the allocation by the District Council, a Public Distribution System (PDS) shop, a kitchen shed and a BT road were provided at a total cost of Rs. 6.75 lakh. With the help of the Union Councillor and the Union Chairman, with whom she has a good rapport, additional school buildings, TV room and a BT road were provided at a total cost of Rs. 3.65 lakh. The MLA and the MP were also kind enough to her village. A library was constructed under the MP Fund scheme at a cost of Rs. 75,000. Construction of a bus shelter and a community hall, installation of a hand pump and black topping of a road were carried out under the MLA area development scheme. The total estimate for these works was Rs. 6.20 lakh. Under the TWAD assistance an OHT was constructed at a cost of Rs. 0.30 lakh. The panchayat is a weak one with regard to finance. By proper representation to the Collector they got sanction for provision of one hand pump in the village.

Mobilising Community Support

Desilting of the supply channel was referred to the Gram Sabha meeting. Rani suggested that the work could be taken up through the Namakku Naame Thittam (NNT) as there was no allocation for desilting work in the panchayat under any other head. She explained it to the farmers. Though there was no association among the farmers she met them in a group and it was decided to get contribution from each farmer. No amount was fixed in this regard but the estimate of the work and the quantum of peoples' contribution was explained. Rs. 12,500 was collected as people's contribution. Even a donation of rupees ten was accepted and accounted for. By using a JCB machine the desilting was done properly. Farmers participated in the work.

Overcoming an Attempt of Black Marking on the Village

The sales of illicit liquor was totally prevented through social control in the village panchayat jurisdiction. To ensure its sustainability the village panchayat council used to serve as a watchdog in this regard. Those individuals who had personal differences with the ward members schemed a plot against two ward members. They arranged false evidence of illicit distillation in the fields of two ward members and made a false complaint to the prohibition wing mobile police unit against the two ward members. The mobile police force entered the village and arrested the two members though it was a false complaint. The president was informed and immediately Rani came to the roadside and prevented the police van from moving on. The police official told her to come to police station for an enquiry and drove away the vehicle.

Rani made telephone calls to the local police officer and, as per his guidance, contacted the higher officials. Understanding the reality, they quickly moved into action. In the same night, along with the key persons of the village, she visited the mobile police unit and explained to them that it was a false case and revealed the names of those individuals who were involved in the arrangement of false evidence. The police brought those individuals and verified the truth. At last the issue was settled amicably.

Being a woman, it was an unusual to intervene in a police case, that too in a case of prohibition raid Rani felt. But to prevent a bad name for K. Rayavaram during her leadership, she stepped in boldly and succeeded in disproving the falsification attempt to file a false case.

Gender Sensitization

The Union Chairman is a woman. She encouraged the Panchayat to organise sports for women. They conducted competitions like running, musical chair, *rangoli* etc. Even elderly women took part in the running race. Women have also feelings and aspirations, which need an outlet. The SHG is successfully handling micro-credit activities. Milch animals have been purchased and the economic standard has improved. "If the talent of women is harvested, society will develop quickly" is the realisation of the public. The respect accorded to Rani by the public is a fitting example of women's empowerment. All these changes in the status of women have happened due to two main reasons, namely, the reservation for women in the Panchayati Raj System and the drive to organise SHGs by the government itself.

Panchayat Meeting

There are only two wards for which there are 6 members. Of them 4 are men and 2 are women. As all are living in the village, there is no absence. All attend the meetings regularly. There is no serious issue in general. All their interest is to improve the village. Rani used to explain the efforts initiated with various

Fig. 7.11: Gram Sabha Meeting

sectoral departments on which she requests their opinions and suggestions. On considering the poor financial status, they have all decided not to avail of the sitting fee permissible to them. The Travelling Allowance of Rs. 300 is not availed of by Rani. In this way the members are very cooperative.

Gram Sabha Meeting

The Gram Sabha meting is usually convened near the *oorani* which is near the panchayat office. It is the common place where the Village Committee also meets.

Proper intimation is given to the people and SHGs and so there is a good response. About 70 to 80 persons attend the meeting. They inform the people that TA and sitting fee are not availed of by the president and the members. The various details of fund allocation are explained. Income and expenditure are explained. The people do not appreciate the efforts in availing of funds from other sources, as they know of the MLA Fund, the MP Fund and the Councillors' Fund. But, a few others explain to them that even these allocations are not mandatory but it is only by the initiative of the president and the panchayat that they are availed of.

Rani explained the efforts of the panchayat in minimising the expenditure. Savings are ae made by proper planning and execution. Any repairs to the water supply system are attended to by local persons and there is no falsification in replacing the tube lights etc. All these are explained in the Gram Sabha meetings. There is no false voucher showing works like street maintenance or clearing of bushes. There are not many vouchers for incidental expenses in the accounts. All these details are properly explained in the Gram Sabha meeting. Due to this the panchayat is able to find funds from the panchayat account and the construction of three culverts and gravelling of road were carried out at a total cost of Rs. 1.17 lakh. After understanding these activities, the villagers have more respect for the panchayat.

Social Development

Additional building, water supply, toilet, kitchen shed are provided to the school. The District Primary Education Programme is implemented in the district and the panchayat school is also covered. Educational equipments are provided through this scheme. The Parent-Teachers Association is active. When out of three teachers one teacher was shifted to another school, the panchayat took up the issue and, with the help of the MLA, they met the District Education Officer (DEO) and succeeded in retaining the teacher. But, later in the year, due to poor strength, one teacher was shifted. About 20 to 25 children are going to a private English medium school. The panchayat was not able to prevent them. This was reflected in the primary school strength resulting in the shifting of one teacher. At this juncture, the Parent-Teachers Association came forward to employ one teacher locally and the payment of Rs. 250 to her was given by the Parent-Teachers Association.

Rani used to meet the Village Health Nurse (VHN) during her visits and discuss activities like immunization. The scheme benefiting girl children, insurance coverage to SHG members, insurance coverage to marginal farmers etc. are properly explained. Rani helps in these activities. About 30 farmers are covered so far. A common graveyard is provided. A *pucca* approach road is provided to the common graveyard. Under the Central Rural Sanitation Programme (CRSP) 39 toilets are provided and 50 additional toilets are going to be constructed; 18 new street lights and 6 sodium vapour lamps are also provided; and, 12 group houses are provided to poor BC people of all castes. The selection is done in the Gram Sabha meeting. The real poor, who live in huts, are identified from each community: 6 from the Vallambar and one each from Barber, Dhobi, Valayar, Kanakkar, Udayar and Vellalar communities. One Jeevandhara well was provided to a marginalised farmer. Health camp and veterinary camps were orgaised. 200 Recurring Deposites savings accounts were opened through a mobilization drive in the post office. Rani played a vital role in this achievement.

Rani herself explained the process by which she completely eradicated polythene from her village panchayat. It is now a plastics free village. She has become president for a second term and is continuing her activities. She became president of the Panchayat in the first period because of the reservation of seats for women. But now she has become president on her own by projecting her achievements in the first period and seeking the mandate of the people based on her performance. She scored a breakthrough in abolishing plastics and polythene in the panchayat because of an accident that took place in the village. Two milch animals died after swallowing polythene materials dumped in dust bins. Taking this tragedy to the Gram Sabha, she discussed this issue with

Fig. 7.12: Helping the Aged

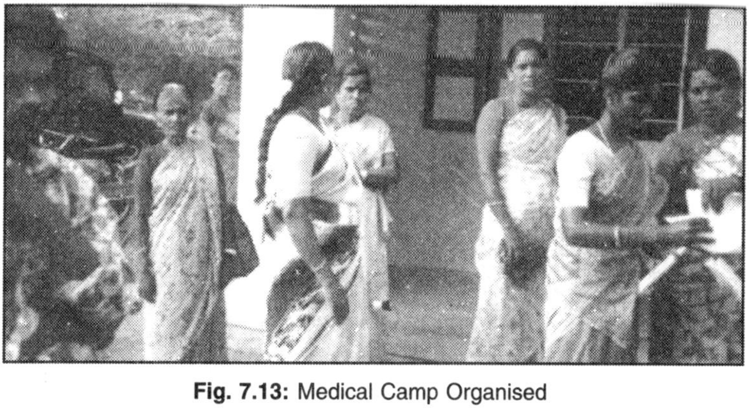

Fig. 7.13: Medical Camp Organised

the people. Having convinced the people, she evolved the norm that no one should use plastic articles in the panchayat area and that individuals who violated it would be penalized. The people consented and the entire village has been made plastics free. For this exercise she got needed support from the SHG women leaders.

Yet another breakthrough she has scored is establishing community action. There are two very big tanks in her panchayat area. Normally such tanks are desilted and renovated by the PWD. But the PWD did not take care of the two tanks. She sent petitions to the PWD. There was no response. She convened the Gram Sabha and discussed the issue with the members of the Gram Sabha. They passed a resolution that it should be reported to the District Collector for appropriate action. In the meanwhile, they decided to desilt the tank on their own because the monsoon was approaching and before that the tank had to be desilted. The entire tank was desilted with the help of the community. The SHG women provided lunch to the people who worked in the tank. Community power was demonstrated for which the panchayat president was responsible.

Execution of Contract Work

These works were executed by Rani's in-laws. There was no loss and, at the same time, they ensured quality. The officials, after inspection, certified the work as the best. A loss was incurred when a culvert was constructed. The tender works were carried out as per her huband's advice. His professional knowledge and experience are much helpful in these works.

Corruption

For the panchayat work the officials did not expect any bribe. But as per the vice-president's advice a small amount was given to the development department officials. Rani never got any favour from the contractors. And so the contractors showed preference to undertake works in this panchayat.

House Tax

When the Panchayat assumed power the house tax demand was Rs. 6,000 only. Hence they enhanced the house tax immediately from Rs. 6,000 to Rs. 10,120. After explaining the government instructions and the financial position of the panchayat to the people, there was no opposition to the proposal for enhancement of house tax. The whole demand is collected without any arrears.

Fig. 7.14: Receiving Awards

Fig. 7.15: Receiving Awards

Capacity Building Experience

Having attended the training programmes organised by the Department of Rural Development, SIRD (State Institute of Rural Development), RETC (Rural Extension Training Centre), NGO (Non Governmental Organisation) and GRI (Gandhigram Rural Institute), Rani's understanding of Panchayati Raj and its scope has improved. On 8.3.1999, when the world women's day was observed, an award was given to her as the best woman president at the district level. In the year 2000, she got the third position. After witnessing her hard work and independent nature, Rani was selected as the only president of village panchayats in a team to have an exposure to a village where the watershed related activities are carried out as a model. Rani learned accounts maintenance through a clerk there. The clerk was a young woman. Now only she is picking up. She got an award of Rs. one lakh for the best panchayat in the year 1999-2000. A shopping complex is now constructed at a cost of Rs. 1.50 lakh from the award fund, adding to the available panchayat fund. A doctor, a barber and a vendor have come forward to take the shops on rent.

Yet another milestone in her panchayat administration is settling a dispute over a tank. A tank which can store water for a year was under dispute. Nobody took responsibility and the government departments did not allow the panchayats to take over also. Water has to be stored in the tank during the rainy season. She appealed to the District Collector and he sanctioned Rs. 2 lakh for desilting the tank but she had to get the no objection certificate from the Public Works Department. She went back and forth to get the no objection certification. At last, with great difficulty, she got the letter and gave the entire money to a committee which has done the excellent work in the panchayat by desilting and deepening the tank. Further the committee has saved some amount and the panchayat has decided to utilize the money for constructing toilets for the ultra-poor families in this panchayat who are unable to give their share for the total sanitation programme. By keeping the village neat and clean she got an award from the District Collector. She received Rs. 50,000.

The Suffering

The responsibility of a village panchayat president is tough. It needs full time attention. Visiting various offices, meeting officials, revisiting for persuasion, interacting with villagers, overseeing the works and office administration and the lists are tedious. A woman who has dual responsibilities cannot find time for all these activities. Frequently, meetings are arranged in Pudukottai, the headquarters of the district. It is 40 km from the village. Sometimes, they have to contact the district officials. Due to this she is not able to look after her two sons and their studies. Her younger son's standard of education now-a-days is going down and she feels sorry for this. Her elder son is studying 7th standard and he openly criticises her functioning and he advises her to discontinue the services at least from the next time.

Her husband is very much attached to the village. He wishes to change the village into a developed one and asks for her support. He advises her to contest again, at least for another term, so that a minimum level of development is accomplished by them. In general, the officials are responsive only if the president meets them. She has to go over all the officials. The Village Committee favours her for a third term and she hopes that they will select her unopposed.

For an Effective Panchayati Raj System

Rani suggested the following points:

As the ward members' involvement and participation will strengthen the panchayat set-up, an orientation is needed for them. There is always fear in the minds of presidents when they are meeting or sharing with officials. This has to be dispelled by organising frequent interface between them. Enmity arises due to the election of the chairperson to the Union and the District Panchayat. After the election the councillor is neglected if he or she takes an opposition stand. In this dispute between the councillor and the chairperson, unnecessarily the village panchayat is also neglected. Hence the system of fund allocation should be streamlined and there should be direct election to the post of Union Chairman and District Chairman. Meetings with higher officials have to be arranged twice every month to avail of the benefit of the sectoral department schemes. The financial transactions in the village panchayat of K. Rayavarams are as follows.

In the Year 1997-1998

The major receipt was the SFC grant of Rs. 25,394. The stamp duty income was very meagre, i.e., Rs. 193 only. Altogether the total income was Rs. 36,971 only. On the expenses side the maintenance of street lights was high at Rs. 5,674. The salary to the staff was Rs. 3,350 and only nominal expenses were incurred on OHT maintenance and drinking water supply. The electricity bill was Rs. 2,100. Altogether the expenses were Rs. 12,846 only.

In the Year 1998-99

After enhancing the house tax, the income from the house tax was Rs. 13,795. Building plan approval licence fee income was Rs. 1,035. Stamp duty was a little more, i.e., Rs. 1,950. The major income was the house tax matching grant (Rs. 21,368) and the SFC (Rs. 24,994). Including the opening balance of Rs. 40,987, the total income was Rs. 96,727.

On the expenditure side it was found that electricity bill rose to Rs. 5,956 for street lights, Rs. 3,400 for motor pump and Rs. 1,882 for buildings. The maintenance of GLR and OHT cost Rs. 6,733. Street light maintenance cost Rs. 8,924 and panchayat building maintenance Rs. 7,796. Road improvement cost Rs. 2,400 and purchasing of new tools and furniture Rs. 4,570.

It is observed that the Panchayat, after saving a considerable amount during the previous year and improving the financial resources through house tax matching grant, was able to carry out a lot of works in the year 1998-99.

In the Year 1999-2000

The deposit collected for individual taps generated an income of Rs. 37,000 and the water tax collection was Rs. 3,510. Income by way of interests was Rs. 3,182 and the SFC was Rs. 49,154. From fines awarded, tree auction and other miscellaneous sources a sum of Rs. 1,000 and above was received. The total income was Rs. 1,16,639.

The total expenses in the year were Rs. 77,229. Rs. 37,000 was deposited separately as it was received as water supply deposit. The other expense was electricity bill. Altogether the bill was for Rs. 13,500, of which Rs. 3,095 was for OHT/GLR.

In the Year 2000-2001

Auction of trees (Rs. 16,950) generated an additional income along with the other routine income. Rs. 5,000 was received as donation. The house tax matching grant, including the previous year's balance, was Rs. 34,258. The SFC grant was Rs. 45,104. Rs. 4,450 was received as the equalization fund. The interest receipt was Rs. 2,923. The total income was Rs. 2,07,811.75.

On the expenditure side, the highest item was the payment of electricity bill: Rs. 10,567 for street lights and Rs. 24,080 for motor pump. The expenditure on the maintenance of street lights was Rs. 6,163. Laying of new road and improvement to old road was the main work, on which Rs. 53,722 was spent. There were other miscellaneous expenses. The total expenses were Rs. 1,30,842 and Rs. 76,794.75 was the closing balance.

The panchayat president's strategy of close monitoring of accounts and savings is understood from the above transactions.

In the Year 2002-2003

The house tax is Rs. 23,910 and a considerable amount of Rs. 10,104 has been collected from licence fee and house site plan approval. As stamp duty of Rs. 8,632 was received. The

SFC grant is Rs. 41,975. Altogether the income during the year 2002-2003 is Rs. 95,505. The unspent balance in the panchayat account is Rs. 67,954.

Under the scheme fund an SGRY allocation of Rs. 47,423 was received. Under CRSP, to construct household latrines, Rs. 18,000 was received.

In the water supply account the annual receipt was Rs. 32,409.

The main expenditures were construction of rainwater harvesting structure, environmental cleaning work to improve the green cover of the village, along with the routine establishment cost of salary, electricity bills, street light maintenance etc. It is Rs. 58,654 of expenditure in this year under the panchayat account. Under the scheme fund the renovation of Nambi *oorani* was taken up along with the construction of household latrines.

Observation

Rani is an educated, sincere and honest leader and, with her capacity, commitment and hard work, several tasks have been achieved. By her transparent activities she draws the support of the community. She gets the needed support from her husband and family for her panchayat works. She maintains a very good rapport with officials and this rapport helps her to achieve many things. Her vision, independent thinking, involvement of the community in panchayat work, honesty in her dealings have made the people respect her. She is a worthy model to be emulated by many women who are aspiring for power and position.

8

Crises Management

MR. V. CHANDRAN, KOTHATTAI VILLAGE PANCHAYAT

V. Chandran, president of Kothattai Gram Panchayat of Parangipettai Panchayat Union, Cuddalore District, has been hailed by many as he managed the crisis created by the *tsunami* in his panchayat area. Basically a marine engineer (38) hailing from the fisherfolk community he was in the Middle East for some time to earn his livelihood. He came back to his village and contested in the panchayat election and won. He carried out the panchayat activities very effectively with the participation of all despite the opposition from some of his own community men since the election. When he heard the news of *tsunami* he was in a bus. Pudukkuppam was the worst affected area. The total death toll came to 126. Only six persons stayed on in the village. Others totally vacated the village after the *tsunami* hit that area. The six were involved in removing dead bodies. In fact, people living in other villages had the courage to visit the seashore and involved themselves in the rescue operation. Fishermen who lived in Pudupattinam who saw the *tsunami* waves refused to go to the village again. They had such a kind of trauma after witnessing the *tsunami* waves. The rescue team saved twelve persons. Chandran went to village and bodies were removed and identified. The Jammath came to the rescue of the villagers. They provided food and first aid to the affected families.

When all the dead bodies were brought to one place, the villagers refused to bury the dead bodies. Finally, officials requested the panchayat leaders to accept the dead bodies. People were in an agitative mood and refused to accept the bodies. They refused to either burn or bury the dead bodies. Finally, Chandran convinced the people. Since he took the responsibility to bring more number of people from outside to help the victims, people started believing him. Before the government started the rescue operation, the panchayat president took the lead and, as a result, government officials followed the president and he was supported by the government in attending to the needs of the people. The panchayat president, with the help of the youth and the clerk, collected the data. While doing this exercise he consulted the traditional panchayat leader on every aspect of relief, rescue and rehabilitation. When he received relief material he openly maintained a note book and the entire responsibility was given to the traditional panchayat leader. In fact, the traditional panchayat leader was instrumental in opposing him in his panchayat area right from the days of his election.

When the data pertinent to the loss of life and property was consolidated, the Gram Sabha was asked to approve the same. As such there was no dispute over the data as a *pucca* record system was maintained. He created an information centre in the panchayat office to disseminate information relating to relief and rehabilitation works of the government and other donor agencies.

The panchayat leader identified the location for a temporary shelter. Necessary facilities were provided at the temporary shelter by the panchayat. Reboring was done by which good drinking water was supplied. Identity cards were prepared and issued to the affected 427 families. The panchayat never allowed any agency to deal with the affected persons directly and, in the same way, the panchayat never allowed the government officers to deal with the affected families directly. In all *tsunami* affected areas, data management became a big issue. In many of the panchayats every one was keeping a list of affected families and approached the donors and the government. But, in this panchayat, there was only one list which was approved by the Gram Sabha and endorsed by the traditional panchayat leader. Chandran maintained a very good relationship with the traditional panchayat leaders and he was always in consultation with the traditional panchayat leaders.

Collection of material, storing of material and distribution of material for relief were done in a scientific way. Chandran created a transparent system by which he distributed all the materials to the needy. He saw to it that nobody other than the affected families got any relief material. His involvement in all the activities was from day one. He formed many committees for all activities in order to involve more number of people. Every activity was carried out through a committee. Even in the Gram Sabha convened on 10th February, 2005 to approve the beneficiaries list, he allowed the people to examine each and every name included in the list. He invited higher officials including the District Collector. He carried out activities in a transparent way.

Chandran took special care of children and widows affected by the *tsunami.* Since affected persons were getting huge sums from the government, relatives showed keen interest in those individuals. To settle all the disputes in the best interests of the individuals, a lengthy dialogue was adopted with the involvement of the traditional panchayat. Safety measures were taken to save the money given by the government to the affected persons, especially widows and children. All the money which the government gave has been deposited safely.

Thus, Chandran established a good rapport with the people and won their confidence which enabled him to have a firm contact with the government officials and NGO representatives. NGOs played a key role in clearing the entire village and now they are providing permanent shelter. In his village all are poor fishermen. He demonstrated his leadership by maintaining his cordiality with the traditional panchayat leaders and all the other groups including his opponent who contested in the election. Further he proved his transparent administration by constituting a committee for relief and distribution of relief material by incorporating more number of individuals from the traditional panchayat leaders. On all occasions he went to the houses of others and never called anyone to his house. He was always responsive to the call of public, NGOs and government officials. He took responsibility in managing the affairs. He has been firm, though he has maintained transparency.

MR. R.V. SWAMINATHAN, PRATHAMARAPURAM VILLAGE PANCHAYAT

Prathamarapuram is a village panchayat located near the Velankanni Church. Seruthur is the fishermen community village under the jurisdiction of Prathamarapuram Village Panchayat. The president, Sri. R.V. Swaminathan, explained the details of the relief activities undertaken by his village panchayat administration.

The Day of Disaster

The president, hearing news of the *tsunami* from the local community, informed the Police, Fire station, RDO and the District Collector over the phone. Since he is a well informed person, he had all the phone numbers. He made arrangements to move the affected people to the hospitals. At the same time, all the families from the coastal area fled to safer places. The president helped them go to safer places, far away from the coastal area, by making arrangements with private transport companies, lorry and tractor owners. He found it very difficult to bring transport to this village. Most of them were put into the marriage hall and schools located in the village itself. The president arranged for preparing breakfast and lunch with the help of local community volunteers.

In the mean time, he made arrangements for visiting Seruthur village. A team of youths and other volunteers from the main village Prathamarapuram joined the youth and elders of the fishermen community, started the identification of dead bodies, and removed the same for burial. In the mean time government officials started to go over the affected area and collected various details and the president assisted them by providing the necessary details through verification and clarification from the concerned families and the community. The panchayat president established entire control over the activities and left no room for government officials to act on their own. In the beginning, he did not wait for the arrival of the officials.

Association with NGOs

The second and third day after the disaster, a number of NGOs came to the site and distributed various items of relief materials. The president helped them to identify the victim families and assisted in proper disposal of relief materials to the concerned families. By then, the Government formed a team of various sectoral officials and the relief work was systematized—removal of debris, restoration of electricity, drinking water supply, link road and connectivity to the affected area. The president joined the official team and assisted them. At the camp site, medical check-up and medicines were also provided by the team.

Various NGOs, volunteers and social institutions visited the area and a lot of activities were undertaken by them like counselling, distribution of provisions, play materials and other essential materials like blankets, buckets, vessels etc. to the affected families. In general, the NGOs used to meet the president and sought the help of the panchayat administration to contact the right persons or community leaders. The relief activities were carried out properly without any confusion. The president informed that some NGOs, when they directly contacted the affected families, faced a lot of problems in distributing the materials. The presence of the village panchayat president brought some order, Swaminathan claimed. Further, the president helped in identifying and establishing a temporary shelter with necessary facilities like drinking water supply, toilet and electricity.

When the Government arranged dole and other cash benefits to the affected families, the president assisted the Village Administrative Officer in listing the eligible families in this regard. He gave an impression to the officials as well as the members of the community that he is a person with leadership and sense of commitment. He maintained the exact data with regard to death and damage to properties. He did not permit any one to take advantage of the misery. He demonstrated his leadership in managing the situation very effectively. In many places the communities were divided on caste lines for distribution of relief material. But in his panchayat he maintained harmony among various segments of the society.

Role in the Drafting of Micro Level Plan

The president assisted the local NGO engaged by The Hunger Project, Gandhigram Rural Institute, to carry out the Micro Planning exercise. He assisted in identifying the local volunteers, farmer groups and SHG groups, helped in the baseline survey, focused group discussion, in conducting PRA (Participatory Rural Appraisal) exercise, and drafting the developmental plan for the village panchayat. Swaminathan explained that generally the fishermen community was very traditional in nature: they used to come to the village panchayat to stake their entitlements, namely, drinking water, road, street lights etc. For other needs, they used to seek the help of the traditional panchayat leaders. But, *tsunami* created a new atmosphere and interface with all sections of the community, Swaminathan said. It is a normal tendency among the poor, whether they are affected or not, where there is any opportunity to get any assistance from the government, they utilize it by any means. This is being exploited by all, from politicians to officials. This, in fact, created a lot of problems in the communities. But panchayat leaders, with their responsible action could avoid many of the unpleasant situations. The elected panchayat leaders have to act responsively with a sense of commitment.

Conclusion

It is a major complaint that in the *tsunami* relief and rehabilitation activities, panchayats were not involved and they were not consulted. The State government believed only the officials and not the panchayats. It is further argued that even the government officials established contact with traditional panchayat leaders and not with the constitutional panchayats. But the cases analysed in this study have amply established the fact that wherever the panchayat leaders took responsibility and responded to the situation without expecting direction from the government officials, they established control over the community. They did not allow the external agencies to divide the community. Panchayat leaders have established good rapport with traditional panchayat leaders. It is not the power and resources that matter it is only the leadership that matters.

9

Panchayat as an Instrument for Service

A.V. Nagarajan (42) is the president of the village panchayat, Varanavasi, in the Walajabad block of Kanchipuram district. It is a multicaste and multireligious village. Nagarajan, though, belongs to the *dalit* community, and contested in the general constituency in the panchayat elections held in the year 2006. He is married. His primary occupation is farming.

He has a rich orientation in public life. Earlier he was in the Janatha Dal Party. He was attracted towards the simple and plain leadership of Morarji Desai and V.P. Singh. In course of time, he was attracted towards the pro-poor, pro-marginalized and social justice activities of Pattali Makkal Katchi (PMK). Nagarajan opined that Dr. Ramdass has been fighting against the injustice done to socially weak and marginalized communities. For the past 9 years he participated actively in the activities of the PMK. For the past four years he has been the president of Kanchipuram West region of the PMK party. He is doing his best to fulfil the expectations of the founder leader of the PMK. When Dr. Ramdass advocated the importance of total prohibition and banning the use of tobacco in public places, Nagarajan swiftly acted. The distillation of illicit *arrack* was brought to the notice of the police then and there. Inspite of threat to his life, Nagarajan organized the villagers and demanded the arrest of hooch makers. Accordingly, the police arrested the hooligans and they were imprisoned. His association with the PMK helped him in all these activities.

When the government itself introduced TASMAC, a retail shop to sell Indian-made foreign liquor, Nagarajan in consultation with villagers passed a resolution in the Panchayat council and then in the gramsabha in order to prevent the opening of TASMAC shop at his village panchayat.

When the PMK leadership advocated strict prohibition, the State government acted strongly against smoking and the use of tobacco in public places. Nagarajan too made attempts in this regard. In general the community leaders used to advise the younger generation not to fall into the bad practice of smoking and alcoholism. There is a social control in many villages that youngsters should not smoke in public places, in front of elders and women. With regard to the consumption of liquor also there is a strict social control in many villages. In this context, the so-called welfare governments instead of recognizing the spirit of social control for bringing good behaviour, introduced schemes to break all the controls. Governments are not coming forward to prevent the sale of tobacco-based products inspite of heavy expenditure involved for treating diseases like cancer. In many villages, one could find a number of widows at the age of 30, 35 and 40 with three or four children. Their life is totally a struggle. The government has enacted and introduced a number of laws and programmes respectively. But they are not properly implemented. Hence, Nagarajan decided to implement the constitutional laws and programmes of the governments banning smoking and using of tobacco products in public.

Majority of elected representatives of the local bodies do not have the needed perception on the concept of decentralisation and good governance. Nagarajan is an exception. His leadership is unique. He perceived the power as an opportunity to transform the lives of the people in the rural areas. It is a not mere implementing agency. Power has to be assumed. When offices are created, the officials have to discharge certain earmarked responsibilities. In the same way the panchayat leaders have to assume responsibilities and act firmly. He passed a resolution in the village panchayat council that use of tobacco and cigarette smoking in public places should be banned. Actually, the provisions existing in the Tamil Nadu Panchayat Act 1994 have empowered the village panchayat to undertake preventive activities in this direction.

Reference

(i) **Chapter 3** of Tamil Nadu Panchayat Act 1994 section 6 sub section (3) reads,
"The village panchayat is empowered to do all necessary actions to accomplish the objectives for which it is formed."

(ii) **Chapter 8:** Section 111 sub section (5)
The power of village panchayat to fulfil other responsibilities:
"Construction of public buildings and establishment of other facilities for the inhabitants of the village, like protection, health, welfare, comfort, culture and recreation".

Nagarajan got the approval of the Gram Sabha for the resolution banning the smoking and the use of tobacco-based products in public places. The resolution was put into action. The constitutional law "The Act prohibiting of smoking and usage of tobacco products in public," was enacted in the year 2004, in the State of Tamil Nadu. Initially there was the enforcement of the Act. Later, due to the failure of police and lack of seriousness in the society, the Act became a failure. But in the village of Varanavasi, by the proactiveness of Nagarajan, and the social control exercised by the villagers one could see the synergy of constitutional law and the community law.

Civil society organizations like Church Axilary for Social Action (CASA), Ulhukadu Resource Centre Team and Social Education Trust of Chengelpet facilitated this uphill task.

The management of Cresent School of Tambaram extended its help to Nagarajan. They engaged their students to carry out a survey to find out the public opinion and support for the resolution of the village panchayat. It was a door to door survey. The finding is that 96 per cent of the respondents supported the resolution and expressed their cooperation for the continuity of the enforcement.

Varanavasi is the first village panchayat in the State of Tamil Nadu to have successfully implemented the Tobacco Control Act with the support of social control. Dr. Anbumani Ramdass the Central Minister of Health felicitated Nagarajan in a grand function at Chennai. The founder leader of the PMK party came down to visit the home of Nagarajan and felicitated him.

10

Work Hard and Earn Positions

Sitharevu is a big village panchayat, having a population of 20,000. There are 16 hamlets, including the main village, Sitharevu, in this village panchayat. It is a multi-caste and multi-religion village. Valayar, Muslim, Thevar and Naidú communities are numerically stronger than the other communities. They are numerically stronger than other communities namely, SC, Naicker, Boer, Gounder and Vellalar. There are five wards with 15 members, of whom 10 are men and five are women. The SC has a membership of two, one male and the other female.

The village economy of Sitharevu revolves around mainly agriculture and animal husbandry as in any other villages. But, there is a significant factor which contributes to the economy of the populace of Sitharevu village panchayat, i.e., labour employment opportunities in plantation estates which exist in the nearby Western Ghats area, namely, Panrimalai, Thandikudi and Adalur. Thousands of men and women have been employed in these estates where coffee, cardamom, and pepper are grown. The wages for the labourers is Rs. 45 for women and Rs. 80 for men. Some men, when they are engaged in wood cutting, earn more than rupees 100 per day as these types of work are for contract instead of on daily labour basis. In general, the landless labourers as well as small land holders in Sitharevu Village Panchayat have regular wage earning through labour employment opportunities available in the village itself as well as the plantations.

The Village Panchayat Council and its Pro-Poor Mindset

There are fifteen members in the Sitharevu village panchayat council whose main occupation is agriculture or manual labour. Hence, the village panchayat council itself is sensitive on the issues of the poor and they are serious in the successful implementation of programmes like Jawahar Rozgar Yojana. Further, the president, Mr.A. Selvam, a farmer, owning 5 acres of estate, is very conscious of protecting the Panchayat properties. He had encouragement from his grand father to involve himself in public activities as Selvam's grandfather was the first panchayat president of Sitharevu Village Panchayat. Mr. Selvam, though he had been defeated in the Panchayat elections held in 1996, without losing hope, entered again in 2001 and won. His first task immediately after assuming office was the removal of encroachments existing along the roadside as well as on panchayat *poramboke* near the main road. There were about twenty shops established illegally by individuals of different communities. Selvam succeeded in passing a resolution to evict those encroachments and seriously took the needed steps in this regard. Notice was served to all the encroachers, including a few inhabitants as a portion of their houses had extended into the rural highways. The president, Mr. Selvam, held consultations with all the officials concerned including police authorities and strictly stood by the decision for removal of encroachments. Due to the timely availability of both revenue and police officials, all the twenty encroachments were removed. Now two shelters for passengers have been provided in that area. And there is space sufficient for the parking of passenger buses and other vehicles. The village panchayat proposes to provide other amenities to the public in that area.

Yet another bold step of the village panchayat council was the redeeming of *poramboke* to the extent of an acre from the encroachment and the same was earmarked for the graveyard, in the hamlet named Kathirnaickanpatti. Earlier, the villagers had to take dead bodies along the *bunds* of fields as the encroacher illegally occupied the approach path to the graveyard and raised paddy crop. The issue of removal of encroachment was initiated through discussion with the encroacher by the village panchayat council, with the help of the Member of the Legislative Assembly Mr. I. Periyasamy. But as it was not seriously pursued by the then village panchayat council, Selvam waited. Then the issue was successfully tackled during the presidentship of Selvam with the timely help and support of police and revenue officials. Now with a width of 15 feet and a length of 200 feet a pucca approach path has been formed. Further, a handpump also has been erected at the graveyard, for public use.

Mr. Selvam's next task was the removal of a thirty-years old encroachment, along the approach path to the graveyard in another hamlet named Ottupatti. Selvam decided to stick to the decision inspite of the threat of the farmers who had encroached and were enjoying the common property. The Village Administrative Officer, with the reference village map, correctly identified the measurement with regard to the above said poramboke area and the higher officials stepped in to assist the village panchayat administration in the removal of the encroachments by about fifty farmers. With the help of a JCB machine about three hundred coconut trees and a vast extent of sorgham and paddy crops were uprooted and it took more than three days to clear everything. Now the village road has been improved as a metal road and a bridge has also been constructed to ensure the undisrupted use of the road even during the rainy season.

Public Participation in Educational Development

When the village panchayat attempted to get approval for upgrading the middle school into a high school, one local philanthropist named Nakulan Ambapithai came forward to donate Rs. 10 lakh to procure about 4 acres of land. During this period 2005-06, the then sitting MLA, Mr. Periasamy, extended his help in mobilizing funds from the SSA—Sarva Sikha Abhiyan Scheme—for the construction of the school buildings apart from his own contribution from the local area development scheme. The then sitting MP, Mr. Sithan also sanctioned from the Member of Parliament Local Area Development (MP LAD). The public came forward to volunteer themselves in the activities of planting tree saplings in the campus of the school. The village education committee has also been functioning well for the development of the school. There are other encroachments along the channel very near the school as well as on the banks of the channel. And so there is a threat of flood water entering into the school site. Hence, the Village Panchayat administration took steps to remove the encroachments and succeeded in its attempt. Further, under SGRY (Sampoorna Grama Rozgar Yojana), village labourers were engaged to desilt the channel during 2006-07. At this juncture, as a boon, the National Rural Employment Guarantee Act was enacted and in the State of Tamil Nadu, six districts were selected where the need for employment to the landless had been realized and Dindigul district was one among the districts chosen under this scheme.

The Implementation of National Rural Employment Scheme in Sitharevu Village Panchayat

As the implementation of the Drought Prone Area Development Programme (DPADP) commenced in the year 2005-06, the village farmers, cutting across castes and religions, came forward and sat together to discuss the various activities to be carried out through the DPADP. Three streams were identified to undertake maintenance work apart from land levelling, reclamation, bunding and construction of retaining wall to control flood water. These works could be successfully completed only by the availability of labourers to attend the work. As the labourers have regular employment opportunity in plantation estates, the turnout for other kind of manual work in the village is usually poor. But, considering the significance of the DPADP scheme, there was a good turn out for labour employment in DPADP scheme activities, the president explained. At this juncture, the NREGP was introduced in Sitharevu village panchayat. The President welcomed the programme but the rules and regulations prescribed in respect of quantum of work and distribution of wages were not easy to ahere to. Bankers were not showing real involvement in disbursement of money to labourers engaged in NREGA programmes, the president felt. Further, the public are not properly oriented in respect of the NREGA. The concepts of 100 days' employment to all the registered, and equal wages to men and women are projected by the government authorities. But the quantum of work to be carried out by each labourer and wage disbursement through bank is not properly explained to all. Hence the labourers perceived that this scheme was to help the people by giving money. At the same time they expect some work. People take it lightly. Further, even aged women reported for employment and demanded equal wages in spite of incompletion of the task assigned to each labourer. Moreover, the execution of the work had to be properly monitored and supervised. But the staff assigned for this task is the Makkal Nala Paniyalar, who has some other tasks of registering, work measurement, maintenance of registers and accounting, preparation for payment through banks etc. With all this handicaps, the NREGA has to be implemented, the president added.

There is yet another constraint. The district authorities instructed that each project activity under NREGA should be at a total cost of Rs. 3 lakh. Hence, the official of Athoor Union selected the Inichapuli Odai* at Sitharveu main village and the same was informed in the Gram Sabha meeting. During the implementation of this work the other villagers demanded to take up tank desilting and maintenance works, he added.

The Initial Phase of Implementation of NREGA

When the announcement of the NREGA programme was made in the panchayat, the villagers did not give much importance to that, according to Mr. Balasubramanian, aged 41, who is the District Secretary of the Congress Party, also a resident of Sitharevu village panchayat. Balasubramaniam had orientation since his youth through the local Community Based

Organisation named Ilaignar Narpani Iyakkam. He is assisting the poor families to avail themselves of their entitlements from the government schemes. His wife is a volunteer in the promotion of SHG activities and has herself formed three SHGs. He contested for the President's position in Sitharevu village panchayat during 2001 PRI election but he was defeated. Balasubramanian continues his service to the public in one way or the other. He shows more interest and involvement in the implementation of schemes promoted by the central government. Earlier, during the implementation of the SRGY, a bulldozer was hired instead of engaging labourers in the project. He objected to the work, contacted the Union and district authorities and demanded that the village panchayat council and the government officials should not use a bulldozer for labour work but to give encouragement and motivation to labourers so that they would report for labour employment under SGRY activities. In this context, when the NREGA is not properly taken into consideration in the village, Balasubramanian, with other village key leaders, met the district officials and informed them that they would prepare the people to enable them to fully participate in the NREGA programme activities. The District Collector, and the PO, DRDA, took necessary steps through the block officials for the initiation of necessary steps to undertake activities under NREGA in Sitharevu Village. Balasubramanian shared that villagers in general do not have faith in the village panchayat administration in respect of the distribution of wages. Hence, they do not come forward register their names, he observed.

Balasubramaniam and the other community leaders, along with the village panchayat administration, visited the streets in all hamlets including the main village Sitharevu, met the public and explained to them the salient features of the Act and the scope for getting continuous employment. They assured the public that the cash would be distributed through banks to all those who worked in the programme activities. The public were properly guided in all the processes—registration, photo for identity etc. in the initial phase of implementation. Everyday since the commencement of implementation of NREGA programme in Sitharevu village panchayat, Balasubramanian used to go over to the village panchayat office and the worksite, give encouragement to the labourers, and involved himself in the settlement of any dispute and in the disbursement of wages. He said that, to claim the wages, each labourer has to go over to the bank losing a day's employment. Further, there is a delay in the settlement of wages to the labourers from the bank due to heavy turn out for employment as well as for withdrawal of money from the account at a time. Further, Balasubramanian said that the labourers of Sitharevu had to travel seven to eight kilometres to report for employment, when the project activity was taken up in a hamlet located far away. They do not get any travel assistance even though they are entitled, Balasubramanian added. There was a suggestion to have work at each potential hamlet. But this is not easy to implement as there is lack of adequate staff to look into all these matters from registration, measurement, maintenance of register, supervision and wage disbursement by a single staff member from the village panchayat administration, Balasubramanian felt.

Mr. Balasubramanian further observed that the involvement of the village panchayat president and the block officials was not so serious though the NREGA targeted poor families. This might be due to the hardship in engaging labourers, but works carried out through bulldozer were easy and also from the contractor one could get personal favours, he added. In spite of all these hurdles, the NREGA programme implementation is seriously taken up through the involvement of public-oriented individuals like Balasubramanian and the concern shown by the district authorities. It was only after the assurance of the payment of wages every weekend that the villagers came forward to register their names, Balasubramanian pointed out.

Perception of Labourers involved in the Labour Employment under NREGA

A focus group discussion was conducted with 15 labourers to obtain their perception and experience in the project activities under NREGA. The following details have been shared :

1. The work is commenced at 8.30 a.m. and the lunch break is from 1 p.m. to 2 p.m. They have to work till 5 p.m.
2. As the employment is given by the government it is valuable and in future there might be some other concessions to the labourers who turn out for NREGA.
3. The work is within the village jurisdiction itself and so it is accessible.
4. Through the employment activities, in addition to the welfare of the poor labourers, common assets like tanks and channels are properly maintained and the usage of the same would be optimum by all.
5. The wage is equal for men and women.
6. The work is shared by a group of ten to fifteen labourers who, in general, hail from the same hamlet/streets/ families. Hence, their inter-personal relationship is strengthened.
7. There is no feeling of servitude when being engaged under NREGA.
8. The planters who regularly give employment now come forward to increase the wages to the labourers.
9. Generally more women turn out for NREGA than men as men usually join together for a task fixed on a piece rate or under contract. Such works are attended to by those men at their own convenient time.
10. Many men from the SC community used to engage themselves in contract labour in plantations or wet lands. And in these types of work, there is no suffering from direct sunlight. In plantations/wet lands there is always shade/coolness and so the working atmosphere is conducive to health whereas in the case of works like desilting of tank/channel it is not a contract work, it has to be attended to individually, and only at the time prescribed by the government. In contract work the work is completed in four and half hours, to five

hours, i.e., form 7.00 a.m. to 12.00 noon. Then the rest of the day, the labourer can take adequate rest or can attend to other personal work. Hence, most of the men labourers from SC as well as other castes prefer private works and they send their female counterparts to NREGA programme work.

11. There are a quite a number of couples who turn out for NREGA work as they prefer to work at a local site so that they can attend to the aged/sick/children in their families.
12. Among the labourers of NREGA, 80 per cent are women and 20 per cent are men.
13. Most of them bring their lunch and take rest under the shade of trees there or under the shade provided by the Panchayat administration.
14. During the employment under NREGA, about twenty five labourers contracted chickengunea fever and so discontinued their work.
15. The channel work is not a tough one whereas the tank work is a difficult one as the earth is hard, needing a crowbar to dig. Generally women are not used to do this job.

This is the Other Side of the Coin

1. The procedure like opening of a bank account, visiting the bank to withdraw the wages is a time consuming process as the bank is located in other villages/towns.
2. Once in a weak the disbursement of wages is done. Hence, for their daily expenses they have to depend on the others.
3. Many are illiterate and feel uneasy to keep the cheque leaf safe till it is surrendered to the bank. Three persons have lost/wasted their cheque leaves.
4. There is no adequate staff at the worksite to guide the workers.
5. Since a large number of labourers come to the bank at the same time, there is always a delay in getting money.

6. Initially the payment was proper. Later, in spite of three weeks' work, the payment is yet to be made and the work was stopped though the villagers were ready to work.
7. Many a time the Union officials, after measuring the quantum of work, were instructed to give extra labour to complete the task as prescribed but were not ready to consider aspects like hard soil.
8. There were many items of work in each hamlet which could be taken up under NREGA instead of a big work at one place which demanded mobilization of many workers from various hamlets. Some villagers had to travel by bus to reach the work sites. Their travel cost was not reimbursed by the Union administration.
9. The disbursement of wages through bank is the right procedure. Some of the labourers prefer to get cash directly from the village panchayat administration which cannot be worked out well—as there is a chance of misappropriation.
10. Men labourers have to do extra work as in a group of labourers engaged in a task under NREGA, the women are not able to use crowbars or spades. The women outnumber men in a group. The women prefer to shift earth to working with crowbars and spades.
11. Men's wages for works in agriculture activities is generally Rs. 100. But in NREGA the wage is only Rs. 80. Hence men do not prefer to work though they have registered their names.
12. Since the commencement of the NREGA programme in Sitheruvu (i.e. from the month of May 2006 till date—September 2006) so far employment for 38 days only had been provided though labourers regularly reported for work.
13. The planning was not proper with regard to identification of activities. This was due to lack of effective cooperation among the stakeholders, namely, the officials, the village panchayat administration and the general community.

14. Earlier the bank identified for the transaction of finance under NREGA for Sitharevu village was IOB, Sithayankottai. They did not show proper concern in the assignment when a large number of labourers turned up for the withdrawal of their wage amount. And the decision taken to change the banker was delayed unduly. Now the changed banker is SBI, Pattiveeranpatti.

The observations made by village panchayat staff : (the clerk and the Makkal Nala Paniyalar).

1. The government has made general propaganda about the NREGA; but the details regarding the tasks, quantum of work per labourer have not been properly disseminated to the public.
2. Public are of the opinion that if they report for the employment it is the duty of the village panchayat to give employment/wages. "The fund is given by the government and so the village panchayat should not prescribe unnecessary conditions", is the feeling of the public.
3. As large number of workers turn up for employment, taking attendance, allocation of work and monitoring are very difficult. In the mean time, mothers who bring their children used to leave the worksite, informing that they had to feed their children and returned to the site a little bit late by which the task assigned to that group was left incomplete, which resulted in disbursement of less wages to all.
4. When the labourers fail to adhere to quality, it is difficult to scold them as they claim that the wage was given by the government not by the panchayat administration.
5. The village panchayat president himself did not have the guts to correct the labourers as he felt that that would create unnecessary political differences among the village panchayat council members and the local political leaders.

6. Sometimes aged persons who could not do the hard labour required in NREGA programme used to turn out for employment. Only by persuasion the very old among them were sent back.
7. At Chellampatti hamlet, the villagers demanded desilting/maintenance works. But when the work was commenced on 23.08.2006, only 8 persons turned out for work from Chellampatti. The staff of the village panchayat administration visited each family and explained the details of the scheme. Almost all families in Chellampatti belong to the SC community. Only on the second day the number of labourers increased to 21, then to 30. As the work had to be completed, labourers from Sitharevu main village were mobilized. About one hundred labourers were brought from Sitharevu. A few more women came to work from Chellampatti. The work taken up under NREGA should be discussed in detail at each hamlet. Otherwise the execution be delayed.

First Spell of Employment

Total No. of Workers	*Wages earned per worker (Rs.)*
164	240
184	160
111	80

Second Spell of Employment

Total No. of Workers	*Wages earned per worker (Rs.)*
174	640
91	560
84	480
51	400
36	320
27	240
61	160
53	80

Details of NREGA—Projects Carried Out in Sitharevu Village

Sl. No.	Name of the work and place when work was undertaken and duration of the work	Programme Allocation Amount Rs.	Finance Actual Utilization Rs.	Total Man-days Employment provided	SC labourers Male	SC labourers Female	Non-SC labourers Male	Non-SC labourers Female	Total labourers Male	Total labourers Female	Income per worker Male	Income per worker Female
1.	Inichipuli Odai-main Sitharevu village 22.05.06 to 24.05.06	1,50,000	77,360	967	1	—	173	285	174	285	240	80
2.	Vendodai maintenance Sitharevu village 26.05.06 to 06.06.06	3,00,000	2,59,600	3245	1	—	185	394	186	394	640	80
3.	Chellampatti tank maintenance Chellampatti village 23.08.06 to 25.08.06, 26.08.06 to 01.09.06	3,20,000	1,57,670	2082	41	161	101	388	142	549	690	75
4.	Rengasamuthiram tank, Reganrajapuram Colony, 2.09.06 to 8.09.06, 11.09.206 to	7,30,000		3520	178	767	643	1932	821	2699	480	80
	15.09.06			2701	154	530	492	1525	646	2055	400	80
		—	—	12,515	—	—	—	—	—	—	—	—

Third Spell of Employment

Total No. of Workers	*Wages earned per worker (Rs.)*
18	240
84	160
84	80

Impact of the NREGA Programme

1. As the incoming channel maintenance was properly done at the main *odai,* namely, Inichapuli *odai,* the excess rainwater would be properly drained into water bodies like tanks and *ooranies.*
2. The main tank, Chellampatti tank, is desilted and the bund is strengthened, and repair work at the Kalingu (opening device to let out the storage water for irrigation), there would be storage of more water and so the farmers could successfully undertake agriculture activities.
3. The wells located around the tank would get more water due to percolation when the tank is filled with water.
4. About 12,500 mandays employment was generated; about 800 males and 2700 females were engaged in the labour employment; for about 37 days, in four spells, employment was provided.

Issues/Constraints

1. Registration/other follow-up, like identification photo.
2. Quantum of work-fixing.
3. Quality of the work.
4. Inadequate number of staff.
5. Lack of full involvement of the village panchayat council.
6. No turn out from many hamlets/villages.
7. More women labourers.
8. Delay in the disbursement of wages.

9. Lactating mothers, aged and sick also report for employment; but are not fully fit to work.
10. Preference for labour-intensive work only.

Conclusion

The NREGA project is the right step in the economic empowerment of the poor. The district authorities need special orientation in programme planning involving the village community. Though there is a reference to the constitution of the committees in this regard, it is not yet seriously attempted. Involvement of SHGs, youths, farmers would enhance the quality of work and benefit all concerned. There should be a year plan and a five year plan. Then only poor families will sustain their income and might come out from the clutches of poverty and underemployment/unemployment. Activities like afforestation and land development activities in the lands of small/marginal farmers should be planned under NREGA. This will improve the capital amount of the poor/marginal farmers. Activities like brick making by the poor and construction of simple houses for the poor can be attempted under NREGA. Instead of allocation of funds to all village panchayats, demand driven approach would bring a new mindset among the poor as well as the bureaucracy. A sharing workshop at union level as well as district level should be organized to understand the overall impact of the programme by which the future plan could be redesigned by the villages through the guidance of the officials concerned.

11

The Inevitable Force called Voluntarism

Introduction

We are in a historic juncture where everything is decided by the market forces. Market values are the guiding values for life and profession. Mortality, ethics, human values are made irrelevant. The whole humanity is regulated thus. Serving the people, caring for others are no more relevant. 'Serve and prosper' is the new *mantra*. In this context, serving the poor without expecting any return is a rare thing. Here is an example of a youth who created an organization and associated himself with other such volunteers and served the poor. *Manitham* an association functioning in the Dindigul District of Tamilnadu, is a model in involving volunteers to perform social service in a secular way successfully at the local level.

Founder-Leader

Mr. J. Suresh, aged 36 is the founder President of *Manitham*. It is not a registered body like a non governmental organization or cooperative society. Though it is an informal body it has a nomenclature, and it has its own style of functioning. It has an office building, volunteers as staff, conceptualized aims/ objectives, well chalked out programmes and activities and it has established branches in villages across the district.

Profile of Suresh

Suresh is the son of an ex-serviceman, who lived in a hamlet village of Maduvur gram panchayat, namely, Pugayilaipatti in Sanarpatti block of Dindigul District in Tamilnadu. After the completion of his schooling, he did not opt to continue his study. Later he graduated in Political Science through distance education. Now he is studying for the Post Graduate Diploma in 'Youth in Development' from Annamalai University. Still his thirst to acquire knowledge from a different arena remained unquenched. He used to purchase a number of books and magazines related to community organsiation and community development, laws, women's empowerment, youth and child rights. He is a married person having a daughter. His wife is an active volunteer in the consumer federation and now an active volunteer and a member in the core team of *Manitham*. Suresh and his wife belong to the same caste—Christian, Vanniar. Though they mutually fell in love, their marriage was an arranged one. His father-in-law is a retired teacher. His cousin is a student of law who is also seriously involved in the activities of *Manitham*.

Social Orientation of Suresh

One's parents and teachers are equated with God in the Indian society. The personality of the parents has its own impact on the socialization process of the children. Suresh was moulded by his parents. His father used to encourage the participation of Suresh in all the extra curricular activities at school. Suresh was the pupil leader and he was one of the key students of the student's cultural committee and a good stage artist. His confident and fearless voice gave him the opportunity to take up heroic roles in dramas staged during the cultural programmes.

Next to the parents, the teachers played a significant role in moulding the personality of students. Suresh narrated that from his first standard to fifth standard one of his teachers used to come to the school well ahead of school time and volunteered herself in cleaning the school premises. Suresh's house is located very near the school. Hence, he himself volunteered and joined the teacher in her voluntary work by which he learned a lot from that teacher, he added. And after the completion of the school final examination he showed interest in the social affairs in his village alongwith the members of his peer group.

The Village and its Social System

In Pugayilaipatti village, Christian Vanniar is the dominant caste, numerically as well as socially. There are three Churches. There are other castes but they are very few in number. The public affairs of the village committee in which the key positions are held by Nallanmani, the Maniakaran and the Servai. They are hereditarily leaders. These three persons alongwith a few key community leaders, handle the activities like, organizing temple festivals, fixation and collection of Thalakkattu Vari (cash contribution per family), settlement of disputes among the villagers, organising cultural and sports events and undertaking repair and maintenance works in village temples and village commons.

Voice against Unfairness of Traditional Committee

Suresh opined that as the traditional system of village administration was an age old one, in the context of democracy it has to be redesigned. Further, he observed that on several occasions the judgment of the committee was not fair. Prejudice and favouritism were exercised by the traditional team. Lack of gender sensitivity and social justice were found in the functioning of the traditional team, he added. In general, villagers used to feel that the system of hereditary position should be done away with. But none of them came openly to encounter the traditional leaders. The youths of Pugayilaipatti used to raise their voices but the voice was suppressed.

Since an unfair verdict was given in a scheme involving poor widow with personal motive by the traditional leader, the youths raised their voice and demanded to withdraw the verdict as the women was really innocent. The traditional leaders as usual shouted at the youth members and refused to yield to their pressure. The traditional leaders even went to the police and lodged a false complaint against the youths. The police and revenue officials visited the village and threatened the youths not to get involved in the affairs of the village committee. Suresh took a leading role in the argument without fear. His boldness and his articulation of the arguments attracted the others. Many villagers suggested holding a village meeting exclusively to discuss the particular issue. The government officials agreed with the suggestion and accordingly a separate meeting was conducted. In that meeting, it was realized that the women was not a culprit. Several villagers came forward fearlessly to share their information/ situations, related to the issue. The officials understood the situation and endorsed the view of the villagers. At last, the villagers succeeded in making a change in the traditional leadership. Out of three key positions, the second position—Maniakarar from a traditional family was done away with and a retired teacher from an ordinary family was selected as the Maniakarar. This was the first successful step in democratizing the traditional committee through the initiatives of the youth group, Suresh claimed.

Filling the Gap in the Leadership by Youths

The traditional head "Nattanmai" started to neglect the common people who sided with the youth group. The Nattanmai used to influence the local field level government officials for obtaining welfare entitlements to the villagers. Due to his attitudinal change in respect of extending assistance to the needy poor, the villagers felt desperate. Suresh and his youth team realized the importance of filling the gap and stepped into hectic activities related to improve the socio-economic status of those who approached them. He established rapport with the staff of police, revenue, health and educational departments and helped the eligible poor to avail the benefit of government schemes like pension to old age persons, widow and orphans, financial and other material assistance to physically handicapped, obtaining ration cards to the needy families, and IAY housing and economic loans with subsidy to the eligible poor. The youth team even organised a demonstration when there was unusual delay in taking action against their petitions in respect of provision of safe drinking water and transport facilities. Villagers, after witnessing the performance of the youth team appreciated them. The youth team got popularity among the villagers and the faith reposed on them by the villagers grew strong day by day. The youth team of Pugayilaipatti visited the other villages of Madur village panchayat and took initiatives to organize all the youths at the village panchayat level. In the mean time, Suresh had an opportunity to get into contact with FEDCOT—Consumer Movement of Tamilnadu and built up his leadership by qualifying through various capacity building exercises given by FEDCOT. And with the guidance of the office bearers of Dindigul district of the Consumer Movement, Suresh established Madur village Panchayat Consumers Right Protection Movement during the year 1991-92. Suresh became a very active volunteer of FEDCOT, engaged as a resource person, handled many classes in training sessions related to the empowerment of the consumers. He made use of all the opportunities to strengthen his contacts with common villagers especially of the youths in many villages of Dindigul district. In the course of time, he made contact with the "Peoples' Watch" an association working for the promotion and protection of human rights in the State of Tamilnadu and Pondicherry. After undergoing necessary training and orientation he served as a field staff of People's Watch during 1997-98 for monitoring and conducting field study on the violations of human rights. Major issues like custodial death, sexual harassment at police stations, and abuses meted out to tribal families of Sathiamangalam Forest area by the Task Force during the period of their operation to nab the notorious sandalwood smuggler Veerappan. Suresh did his field work in respect of communal riots erupted in the district of

Ramanathapuram and violence during general election to the Assembly and Parliament as well as in the issue of non-conducting of election in four village panchayats of Tamilnadu due to reservation of seats for the scheduled castes. During his involvement in various assignments as referred above, Suresh gained knowledge and in dealing with field officials as well as higher level officials, comprehended their attitudes and perceptions, the functioning of the government machinery and the plight of the poor and the marginalized. Suresh sharpened his vision in respect of politics through his involvement in public affairs. At least he had an insight into the methods of organizing youth volunteers and other adult volunteers from the farming community, unorganised labourers and women who were not conventional in serving the community but functioned as an alternative force to transform the society. And during the year 2001 *Manitham* came into existence by the efforts of Suresh, with a handful of volunteers.

Membership in *Manitham*

Enlistment as a member in *Manitham* is not entertained to every volunteer, Suresh told. Volunteers who come forward to join *Manitham* have to possess the following characteristics :

- should not get involved in casteism;
- should not get involved in religion;
- should not get involved in party politics;
- should not react to criticism;
- should not show any favoritism to any one during the activities of *Manitham*; and
- should have courage and should revere and respect their parents and women.

About 175 active volunteers were identified, Suresh claimed. Among these 175 volunteers a core group of about 35 was finalized based on their potentials, their time available and for the public service commitment to the organsiation. Suresh collected from the writings of justice V.R. Krishnannayar that it is the "humane quality which make individuals as perfect human beings". This motivated him to establish a people's movement with human touch—*Manitham.*

Strengthening the Activities of *Manitham*

The enlisted volunteers were oriented in the activities of the *Manitham*. They were told that they should conduct themselves as role models in reflecting the ideologies of *Manitham*. As true volunteers they should not expect anything from others. The core team members were divided into groups, visited colleges and higher secondary schools, interacted with the students and involved them in social welfare activities. After assessing their interests, follow up activities were initiated at their villages. Many youth volunteers stayed over during the night and discussed issues with the village youths. They were motivated to have higher aims and objectives instead of wasting their energy and time meaninglessly in cricket and activities of fans associations of cine stars. All the youths were organized and an orientation programme was conducted at the campus of the International Christian Movement—ICM Dindigul. About 170 persons attended the training programme.

Based on the discussion with the members, activities to be carried out through *Manitham* were classified into (i) service centre, (ii) cultural centre, (iii) extension of *Manitham*. The volunteers, after their orientation, were involved in the organisation according to their wishes. The service centre activities focused on the empowerment of very poor through campaigning for enrolment and retention of all school age children and facilitating the youths to avail the benefits of socio-economic welfare measures provided by the government. Further, the legal aid awareness and assistance were ensured to the needy ones. No fee was collected from the public who approached *Manitham* for help. The cultural centre trained the youth volunteers in the folk and village traditional arts. The volunteers conducted several cultural programmes.

Public meetings and cycle rallies to explain the aims/ objectives of *Manitham* were conducted. Suresh told that there were hundreds of thousands of villagers who came to know about it and committed themselves to work for social justice. A public meeting was organized to uphold social justice and without any expectations more than thousand villagers enthusiastically participated in the procession conducted before the commitment of the meeting. The participants showed their solidarity in the protection of the marginalized. The participants themselves met the expenditure of these public programmes organized during 2003-04 to sensitise the public. And in the year 2004-05 a procession was organized, demanding the implementation of Employment Guarantee Act and House Guarantee Act all over the district. Funds were not collected from the members/public to organise these types of programmes. These programmes were planned in a participatory manner. The participants themselves realized the worthiness of voluntarism and helped in finding sponsors. Further they themselves contributed to meet out the expenditure in respect of demonstrations, rallies etc. organized by *Manitham*. Expenditure in respect of transportation, food packets, rent of the audio system, conference hall rent, caps to all participants was met by the different individuals/sponsors. Suresh explained that donations used were received only from the members of *Manitham* and those who recognized the activities of *Manitham* and did not expect any favours in return. *Manitham* took precautions in maintaining its identity—secular and apolitical, Suresh emphasized. There were plots to lure him and *Manitham* by selfish individuals/organizations, Suresh told. Hence donations and other assistances were not collected from non-members/institutions which were selfish, he added. Cutting across castes and religions, youth, women and unorganized labourers were enlisted as members of *Manitham*. In this context, more care was given to maintain the secular nature of the organization, Suresh stressed.

Organization of Self Help Groups among Youths

A majority of women members of *Manitham* is marginalized labourers. To consolidate their efforts and force, they were organized into groups of 25 members each. Of course men were also organized into groups. Rs. 15 per member was collected as membership fee and the same was spent on the day of establishment of the branch of *Manitham* in the concerned village or area. Inauguration of the branch of *Manitham* was performed in a splendid manner. Cultural shows, children's activities, and activities for the adults were conducted during the inaugural ceremony. The membership fee collected was refunded to them to meet out the expenses.

Members-cum-volunteers of *Manitham* are availing services through the guidance of the core team/office bearers of *Manitham*.

Ecolf India, an NGO functioning at the national level came forward to implement its micro-finance activities for the benefit of members of *Manitham*. The management of Ecolf appointed its own staff and initiated the micro-finance activities among the Self Help Groups of *Manitham*. *Manitham* does not receive any financial assistance in these transactions. The office bearers of *Manitham* render assistance in the effective implementation of the micro-finance activities.

The members of SHG movement are encouraged to learn and practice the concept of thrift and saving. Now, there are 120 SHG groups. Ecolf releases credit amount four times, more than the savings amount of each group. The repayment is made by groups through ICICI Bank. The women members of the SHGs are oriented in social issues and are shaped as volunteers as well as good citizens. They participate in the activities of *Manitham*.

Demonstration demanding the Right of Livelihood

During the year 2007, *Manitham* organized a procession-cum-conference demanding that the government ensures the right of livelihood for poor and the marginalized. Issues like educational expenditure, minimum support price to paddy, prevalence of corruption and anti-people mindset of the bureaucracy were discussed in the conference. About 5000 people participated in the procession and the conference followed. Witnessing the discipline and the force of the volunteers who mobilized themselves, raised their voice in respect of practical issues affecting the unorganized and poor families, the political leaders of the various political parties of the local units were astonished, Suresh pointed.

Vigilance in upholding Social Justice

The volunteers of *Manitham* especially the office bearers of *Manitham* have been properly oriented in the activities of handling the issues in respect of upholding social justice and the right to claim entitlement for the poor. *Manitham* closely associated itself with the Free Legal Aid Society of Dindigul District, Human Right Forum and other rights-based organizations.

PRI—A Scope for Effective Voluntarism

Manitham envisaged PRIs as a scope for effective utilisation of voluntarism. Suresh encouraged his colleagues who had better chances to contest in the PRIs election in the year 2006. Suresh and his volunteers in the village panchayat of Pugaiyilaipatti contested in all nine wards in addition to the position of the president by Suresh. Though Suresh was defeated, out of nine ward members eight ward members had won in the election. The one who had been defeated was a young man who belonged to the scheduled caste community but he fielded his candidature in a common ward. Villagers overwhelmingly extended their support to the volunteers of *Manitham* and at the same time, in one ward the electorate did not have maturity to accept the SC candidate in a common ward. Hence voters of that ward supported the candidate who belonged to the Vanniar majority caste. The reasons for the defeat of Suresh were that if Suresh won, he would seriously take action against the encroachers, and wouldn't allow anybody to escape from payment dues like house tax and water tax to the panchayat. Further, the elders who are traditional in outlook and uphold the supremacy of casteism syndicated themselves and influenced voters belonging to Vanniars. The opponents spent money lavishly during the election, donated money to renovate the temples in all hamlets and thereby influenced the villagers. Though Suresh was also Vanniar, he never showed any inclination to casteism. Suresh asserted that he had learnt a lesson from the local body election, that honesty is not sufficient and it is only those who have the capacity to counter evil forces could succeed.

Calling a Spade a Spade

As volunteers of *Manitham* won in the PRI election, it is a majority force in the council of Pugaiyilaipatti village panchayat, one of them became the vice-president. All the eight members stood firmly against the wrong doings of the president. The malpractices of the president in the implementation of programmes under National Rural Employment Guarantee Act were exposed to the public by *Manitham*. But due to the connivance of the officials the president was saved, Suresh explained. *Manitham* went to the High Court Bench at Madurai, and filed a complaint against the malpractices of the president. The court rejected the practice at the admission stage but directed *Manitham* to make a complaint to the District Collector. But the district administration has not yet initiated any enquiry against the president, Suresh added. The villagers after witnessing the misdeeds of the panchayat president regretted to casting votes in favour of the president.

Manitham's Successful Entry in Ponnimanthurai Village Panchayat

During the election to the local bodies in the year 2006, in the village panchayat of Ponnimanthurai of Reddiarchatram block, Mr. Kamaraj, the office bearer of the branch of *Manitham* in Ponnimanthurai contested for the position of the president. He belonged to a community which is numerically weak. The opponent is an active youth of the DMK party. The village elders and the DMK party men met Suresh and asked him to advise the candidate of *Manitham* to withdraw his candidature. Suresh stood firm on the decision of fielding the representative of *Manitham*. At last the candidature of the DMK party was defeated. The young president who was oriented through *Manitham* movement functions effectively as the president and the villagers cutting across castes extended their support to his leadership. Suresh envisaged that before the end of the year 2010, *Manitham* would be branched off into each village panchayat and steadily make inroads into the local bodies. He further remarked that PRIs are the best place to strengthen the *Manitham* movement and to attain the goals of the organization.

Suresh's Involvement in Lok Adalat

To speed up the settlement of pending cases especially civil disputes, the Lok Adalat is in operation. In the district of Dindigul, the Lok Adalat consists of three members—the district judge, the senior advocate and a social worker. Cases related to civil disputes pending a long period and cases in respect of money lenders are being settled through peaceful negotiations by the Lok Adalat. Suresh served as one of the panel members. In the category of social worker, Suresh actively involved himself in the settlement of disputes. About 305 cases have been settled in the district of Dindigul alone, he claimed. He had an opportunity to serve as a panel member when a mega Lok Adalat was convened in Madurai covering 15 districts of Tamilnadu. The judges and magistrates praised his voluntarism and officially supported his representations.

The cultural team of *Manitham* staged dramas/cultural programmes in New Delhi, Mumbai and over AIR Madurai. The programmes staged by *Manitham* in respect of the right of prisoners is very popular, Suresh remarked.

Information Empowerment and the Community Role of *Manitham*

The volunteers of *Manitham* give much importance to empower the community of especially rural poor by disseminating a number of developmental issues through their cultural team. Social issues like female infanticide, child labour, human rights violation issues faced by the labourers of spinning mills in and around Dindigul, ecology and environmental issues, and issues in availing bank loans to the really poor students have been focused by *Manitham*.

Suresh opined that due to the good and yeoman services rendered to the poor families without any expectation/ favouritism , the villagers encouraged their youths to join in the activities of *Manitham*. These youths, coming with a feeling of dedication have contributed a lot. In course of time they move out of voluntarism and engage themselves in the self/ labour/government employment and so they found no time to devote to the activities of *Manitham*. The orientation and training input given to them wouldn't be a waste, but they are not directly beneficial to *Manitham*. Again *Manitham* enlists youths/students and the newly enlisted youths have to develop their personality and leadership quality through training and practical exposure. Suresh and his core team used to directly orient the newly enlisted volunteers. Suresh told that the most urgent task of *Manitham* is to establish a training centre with full-fledged facilities like audio-visual aids/ equipments and facilitating boarding and lodging etc. Suresh admits that sustaining voluntarism for the cause of human society is a challenging task, and as of now majority of the youths do not come for voluntarism. Instead, they used to spend their time/energy for their own individual development or the welfare of their castes/religion. *Manitham*, being secular in its approach, makes the youngsters acquire a true sense and spirit of voluntarism. It is a victory, Suresh claimed.

Democratisation of Traditional Committee

Suresh and *Manitham* or *Manitham* Suresh is a striking phrase in the town of Dindigul. *Manitham* facilitates the enolment of about 4,000 unorganised workers into the government sponsored welfare programmes meant for unorganized labour. It has dealt successfully with various issues related to the enlistments/settlement of dues owed to poor and the marginalised; assisted all those eligible to avail government schemes/programmes without any corrupt practice. His leadership has become a significant one in his village. During the year 2006, the villagers succeeded in their attempt to transform and democratize the years-old traditional committee. The three key positions in the committee namely the Nattanmai, the Maniakarar and the Servai have been changed from traditional familial system to democratic system of election/selection of the best. Accordingly, the villagers have unanimously elected Suresh an Nattanmai and in respect of other two key positions, new individuals have been selected. The transformation was a smooth one, Suresh claimed.

Upholding the Democratic Values

The new committee under the leadership of Suresh has organized festivals and Jallikattu, the traditional sport of taming the bulls. The whole affair of the festival lasted for a period of one month—during the month of February 2006. On 1st February the new committee assumed office. There are about 750 families living in the village Pugaiyilaipatti. Each family contributed Rs. 150 to meet the expenditure. Apart from this, donations were collected. Altogether it was Rs. 3.16 lakh, Suresh claimed. After meeting out all expenditure, there was a saving of Rs. 1.37 lakh which was properly submitted to the villagers, during the social audit. The new committee showed utmost care and attention in spending public money. All procurements were directly done by the sub-committees exclusively formed to avoid any middlemen. Further, during these festival days, many individuals who claimed to be involved in temple affairs frequently visited the local hotels for refreshment to eat in the account of the village committee. The amount in this respect was a huge one during earlier periods, Suresh told. This practice was not allowed by Suresh. Hence a considerable amount was saved. Further, by proper planning of activities, Suresh was able to limit expenses. During the event of Jallikattu, as per the direction of court/police department, barricades had to be provided to ensure the safety of public who gathered in large numbers for Jallikattu. Long casuarina tree poles were purchased in this respect. Generally, after the completion of the Jallikattu, the committee used to collect the wooden poles and allowed their favourites to take for themselves. Suresh plugged this loophole. He properly collected back all these casuarina poles and auctioned the same in public. To ensure a good return, he himself fixed the auction price of each bundle of poles. The others were compelled to purchase the remaining timbers. This money spent for the purchase of casuarina poles was refunded through this auction. Villagers witnessed the potential in the leadership of Suresh and his committee. He properly accounted all transactions and with necessary vouchers and bills submitted the bills within a week. Villagers approved the same and the social audit system was practiced in a true sense. After this meeting, Suresh announced that he had proposed to resign from the position of Nattanmai as he could not find time to manage the organization *Manitham*. But the villagers requested him to continue in the position of Nattanmai and permitted him to come weekly once to the village and so that he could conduct the affairs of the committee.

Prevention of the Illegal Sale of Liquour

The TASMAC liquor shop run by the government of Tamilnadu has been operating in a nearby village of Pugaiyilaipatti. The local politicians of the popular political parties engaged themselves in the illegal sale of liquor procured from the TASMAC shop. The village committee under the leadership of Suresh stepped in quickly and the illegal sale was prevented. The politicians who belonged to the ruling party influenced the government officials to help them continue their business. But the villagers stood very firmly and requested the officials not to yield to the proceedings of the politicians.

Application of Right to Information Act

Manitham in associating with the other rights-based organizations like Consumer Forum, has organized campaigns and training camps on the merits of Right to Information Act.

Issues in delaying the distribution of ration cards, employment registration of a physically handicapped person under special category, requesting to permit the inspection of NREGP works by an Enquiry Commission constituted by the public, availing electricity line connection by a small farmer, sexual abuse of a staff in the school, and delay in sanctioning educational loan to the eligible students were the major issues raised through the Right to Information Act. In all cases, *Manitham* succeeded in claiming the right of its client, Suresh pointed out.

Manitham brings Social Harmony

Ayyakuttiayapatti is a small hamlet in Siluvathur village panchayat of Sanarpatti Block. It is a monocaste village—Vanniars of Hindu religion are the inhabitants of this village. Due to differences of opinion among the existing families, the common affairs like celebration of village temple festivals etc. are not carried out in Ayyakuttiapatti. A few families whose members are the volunteers of *Manitham* brought up this issue of social disharmony existing in their village. Suresh initiated peace talks with the various groups and elders of the community. He succeeded in bringing them all together and their enmity was removed. After a gap of twenty-eight years, the celebration of village temple festival was conducted with the involvement of all success of the people and successfully executed to the satisfaction of all. *Mantiham's* potential as a secular movement has been proved in this case, Suresh claimed.

In strengthening the Voluntarism of the Youth

Manitham is now attracting new youths. The youths once deeply involved in the centre-based organizations have shown interest in joining *Manitham*. They envisage that *Manitham* is the right organization to serve people and prosper. The volunteers of *Manitham* get respect and recognition in public. Moreover, due to their secular outlook and simplicity, the government officials especially in revenue department, police and judiciary extend their cooperation to them. Disciplining and shaping the youths is the first and foremost task of *Manitham* and then social transformation is the ultimate goal, Suresh remarked. The youth when oriented in public affairs came to understand the society and its dynamism, the various social problems and their causes, and steadily equipped themselves to work in the transformation of their society.

A Systematic Approach

Manitham facilitates the sufferers to equip themselves in dealing with their problems. Here is an example. Soundaraja Spinning Mill is a reputed firm functioning in the town of Dindigul. A scheme called "Sumangali" is in operation in many spinning mills functioning in the State of Tamilnadu. Under this scheme, young women are admitted as contract labourers who have been exploited by the management. As no case of complaint has been registered with the police, the issues related to 'Sumangali' scheme have not come to the notice of the people. In the case of Soundaraja Mill, it was told that the management compelled the workers of Sumangali scheme to work for a minimum 26 days in a month and if a worker was absent one day, at the rate of fifteen rupees per day was deducted for all the twenty five days. Further the management did not distribute the incentives and other financial assistances as assured to each of the workers. Some of the workers brought this to the notice of *Manitham* and requested *Manitham* to organize a meeting in this regard for which they could mobilize all the workers who had signed the contract.

Suresh and his team separately discussed the merits and demerits of the case, and then informed the workers that *Manitham* wouldn't represent their case but was ready to empower and enlighten them to lobby for themselves with the management. One of the loyal workers of the management who had secretly recorded the proceedings of the meeting organized by *Manitham* informed the management, Suresh told. The management immediately contacted Suresh through the influence of the village elders to come for negotiation. Suresh refused to oblige but demanded that the management must talk to the workers. Accordingly, all the issues were discussed and after five days of negotiations a settlement was reached. The management announced that the minimum days for the worker to report for work was 22 and for the days on which they are absent the wages would be cut. Earlier these issues were brought to the notice of the labour commissioner and for about five days the workers struck their work. Inspite of their direct action the issue was not settled. But *Manitham* succeeded in solving the issue and workers got their entitlements, Suresh told.

Manitham did not instigate the workers. It facilitated them and enlightened them. Volunteers of *Manitham* initially thought that the success was their personal victory. After proper orientation, they came to understand and practice the concept of empowerment of the poor/volunteers. *Manitham* as an organization-cum-movement and its volunteers are now getting maturity to weigh both the successes and failures as equal. Suresh declared that the success of voluntarism is in understanding one's own life. Simple and humble life is the secret to sustain the spirit of voluntarism, he added.

Miles to Go

Manitham continues its journey in shaping the youths as good citizens who know the socio-political contexts and equipping them for transforming the society. It empowers the poor and the marginalized. Many volunteers, who received their orientation through *Manitham* have migrated to other neighbouring towns and cities of Tamil Nadu, they seek the assistance of Suresh to organize *Manitham* movement in their respective areas. Suresh has decided to do more work in the district of Dindigul as there are a number of issues to be settled at the local level. He aims at thinking globally and acting locally. He has proposed to take the *Manitham* movement to all the village panchayats of Dindigul during the coming years.

We are in a historic juncture where everything is decided by the market. Market values are the guiding values for life and profession. Morality, ethics, human values have become irrelevant. This is how the whole of humanity operates. Serving the people, caring for the others are no more relevant.* Serve and prosper' is the new *mantra*. In this context, the person who serves the poor without expecting anything in return, is a legend by himself. In this context a youth has created an organization and associated himself with other volunteers and has served the poor. He deserves the attention of everyone.

12

Synergy between the Potentials of the Panchayats and Youths

The aspiration to achieve economic prosperity, social justice and to democratize institutions, organizations and society is increasing among the people in general and the marginalized and the deprived in particular.[1] Nearly half of the world is in the grip of the authoritarian form of government. Societies which have liberated themselves from the colonial yoke could not sustain the democratic structure which had been created at the dawn of Independence. Yet aspirations to democracy and development are growing. To realize such aspirations an enabling environment is an imperative need. Government policies, institutional structures, programmes are the vehicles by which the needed environmental conditions can be created.[2] At present, in India, such a kind of enabling environment has been created through a series of actions namely reform in governance, reform in economy, enunciation of new programmes such as National Rural Employment Guarantee Scheme, Backward Area Development Grant, National Rural Health Mission, Sarva Siksha Abhiyan, Bharat Nirman Rural Infrastructure Scheme and Decentralization of Powers. To get the maximum benefits from the above reforms and schemes a governance structure has been created through enacting the 73rd Amendment to the Constitution of India and the Right to Information Act. If all the above schemes and programmes are translated into action in letter and spirit, the problems which we face namely anemia, malnutrition, illiteracy, insanitation, pollution, environmental degradation, unemployment, abject poverty, people living in sub-human living conditions, poor drinking water supply, unmanageability of waste, poor health facilities in India can be solved very easily and for which what is needed is commitment and professionalism for action at every level down to grassroots. Our government system is known for its professionalism in enacting laws, evolving schemes and developing programmes but the same system does not have the capacity to translate the same into action and to produce the expected outcome. Many failures are assessed and realistically evaluated.[3] At all levels one issue has being found missing in the process of development, namely 'people-centric activity' and the absence of 'outcome' evaluation. Whenever, programmes and schemes are implemented on supply-driven framework and while evaluating the same outcome was never concentrated seriously but output is always reported.[4] Government and other allied institutions gradually expanded in an unlimited fashion and started working for the uplift of the people. As a result, government machinery became bigger and bigger and the heavy weight of the government punished the people by sitting on the shoulders of the people.[5] People became inactive in governance and started believing that they have no role in development and they have only the responsibility of putting demands to the government for services and benefits through petitions. For even a small activity government has created offices and positions. It is strange that all are attached with offices not with people. Accountability is fixed but it is always serving the masters not the real masters (people) in democracy. While exhibiting the upward accountability, it is always for output and not for outcome. Despite all those efforts, conditions have not improved the life of the poor as expected.

Yet the state claims its ownership of development which ultimately results in the reduction of citizens to beneficiaries and petitioners. This kind of activity makes the people develop a dependency syndrome. To reverse the paradigm of development and governance from a supply driven to a demand driven one and from government centric to people centric, a new institutional mechanism was introduced through the 73rd Amendment to the Constitution of India. This new dispensation and institutional mechanism is aimed at creating an enabling environment for people's participation.[6] How this new dispensation is being used is the major question and concern of all. All innovative activities are no doubt the creations of the creative minority in any society. To realize the full potential of such innovative activities, the stakeholders should have skill and capacity to make proper use of the innovative initiatives.

The 73rd Amendment to the Constitution is one such initiative which has come with a potential to transform the power relations among the social collectivities. It can effect economic development also. How to make use of the potentials is a major problem in India. Since decentralization is a centralized drive, every one expects that pressure has to come from the Central government to the State government for proper devolution of powers. For the first time in independent India democratic governance is established at the grassroots with the participation of the people, including the hitherto marginalized groups. The groups which were hitherto marginalized have to organize themselves to take power into their hands and to determine their destiny.[7]

When governance is established at the grassroots, Constitutional provisions are in interaction with community practices. India is known for strong community practices and hence while operating the constitutional provision one has to expect strong protest from the communities when constitutional provision removes the community practices in the name of democratic principles. Thus, devolution of powers becomes a major concern full of challenges and opportunities. This transformation has to cross a series of barriers and obstacles. One cannot expect this transformation to take place smoothly as the society has an entrenched inequality in the economy and discrimination in social practices.

On many occasions people want to find solutions administratively or managerially to the issue of devolution of powers. Issues and problems related to power transfer can be achieved only through a prolonged struggle of the people and that cannot be done through a simple administrative decision.

It has been noticed in India how the marginalized are struggling to claim the basic entitlements guaranteed by the Constitution. It is always a tussle between the provisions of the Constitution and the practices and procedures of the community. Since Indian polity is mediated through middlemen, many of the Constitutional provisions are not invoked. The Constitution always grants but the community always rejects.[8] In many areas, positions in panchayats are controlled by the traditional panchayat leaders. We have noticed when panchayat president positions are reserved for *dalits,* the community leaders belonging to the caste Hindus act negatively and *dalits* are not allowed to contest in the election in four Gram Panchayats in Tamil Nadu namely Pappapatti, Keeripatti, Nattarmangalam and Kottakatchienthal. This challenge has been responded to by many of the youths belonging to the left parties and now elections have been conducted. It is an open violation of a constitutional provision. In other areas the same thing happens in subtle ways. How are we to overcome this problem? This type of problems could be solved through an organised way by the youths. It is a country known for unevenness, disparities and discrimination on many fronts.

In our six decades of democracy we have seen transformation only in a few segments of the society. Though democracy provides the scope for people to solve their problems and achieve development through representative institutions, people cannot raise their voice on the failures of the representatives and even if they raise their voice they are not heard and even if they are heard, they are not heeded. The voiceless people are brought to the election scenario as voters through mediation through the local mediators belonging to dominant castes and communities. The 73rd Amendment breaks the brokerage. This amendment provides opportunity to develop a plan for *dalit* development, women development, child development. Likewise sectoral plans can be evolved for health, natural resources, education, and so on. It needs only vision and commitment and understanding of the available opportunities.

Many of the fine provisions of the Indian Constitution are inoperative and ineffective as they are not claimed intensively. It is obvious from our experience that people who are losing their power and privileges by the provisions of the Constitution are aware of the full implications of the provisions. But the people who are going to gain power and advantage from the provisions are neither aware nor are in a position to claim their dues. Those people who are going to lose power will find a strategy to retain it by hook or by crook.

Against this background, one has to look at the 73rd Amendment to the Constitution of India. The amendment has enough potential to alter the nature of governance and power relations among the unequals. It has got tremendous potential to solve the problem of exclusion. It is unfortunate that these potentials are not known to the people who are going to gain power. People who are in power and who are going to lose power have understood thoroughly the full implications of the amendment. Having understood the implications, they have devised a subtle mechanism to retain the power with them through new devices. The wife or the daughter is being sponsored for local body elections when the seat is reserved for women. A farm labourer is being sponsored by the landlord if the seat is reserved for *dalits.* These are all the new strategies evolved by the community to retain power with them.

Even twelve years after the enactment of the amendments to the Constitution, people are not aware of the full implications of the amendments. A lot of confusion prevails in the process of implementing the amendments in letter and spirit. Sometimes confusion is created deliberately with the objective of delaying the process. One major confusion is over whether the panchayat is a state subject or not. Some are arguing that it is a state subject and that the centre cannot do anything against the state in the process of implementation. Officials in the central government and state governments, legal luminaries, NGOs and activists are giving different versions of the same amendments. L.C. Jain, an expert on this subject, who has headed many committees and is a person of such eminence and erudition advanced a logical and theoretical argument that after passing the 73rd Amendment, there is no reason to view Panchayati Raj as a state subject. The 73rd Amendment is the outcome of the failure of the States to make the panchayat institutions of self governance. The 73rd Amendment has gone through a process and two-third members of the National Parliament have approved and more than 50 per cent of the State governments have accepted this new dispensation. In essence, it is a new governance structure and it has its own legitimacy for governance. To give clarity to this issue Rajiv Gandhi developed and projected the framework for creating the New Panchayati Raj System in India. The speeches delivered by Rajiv Gandhi in Parliament while piloting the 64th Amendment Bill and concluding the debate on the bill are historic and path-breaking. These classic speeches have to be considered the basic framework for decentralization of power in India. It is unfortunate that many have forgotten them.[9]

Even to enact a conformity legislation, the central government had to intervene. After the enactment, pressure had to be exerted on the State governments to conduct elections. After conducting elections, for proper devolution of powers, finance and functionaries, once again pressure had to be exerted by the central government. Till date there are many provisions in the 73rd Constitutional Amendment which have not been operationalized. These violations are justified under the plea that Panchayati Raj is a state subject. The creation of a weak Panchayati Raj system is due to the unwillingness on the part of the State governments to create a power structure at the grassroots.[10] Against this background many seek an administrative solution to the issue of the Panchayati Raj system. To make the Panchayati Raj system realistic, a massive peoples' movement at the grassroots is required. A movement has to emerge from the grassroots.[11] It is not a concession one has to extend to the *dalits*, women and people in general. It is a reasonable claim and a legitimate right of the people. It has to be claimed. To claim a provision people have to understand what benefits they are going to gain and in the same way what benefits the *dalits* are going to gain. Respective segments should know the potentials and for which they have to fight and claim their rights.[12] One should not expect charity from the State government. State governments are not submitting petitions to the UN to claim their rights and share of power from the central government. In the same way, the local bodies have to claim their rights and power for which women and *dalits* have to extend support. To create such an environment, organisations and institutions have to work. All those who are working in the panchayats as supporting structures now are working in the rural areas in a project mode but are not mobilizing a mass movement. People who are spearheading micro and macro movements for socio-economic transformation of the *dalits*, tribals and women have to see the true potential of the new dispensation. If panchayats are strengthened their share of resources and services will be secured safe and delivered effectively and efficiently. When *dalits*, women and *adivasis* are in position in the respective grassroots institutions with power and authority and with a sense of commitment, many of their problems will be solved very easily. Not only will their problems be solved, but they will also be empowered.

Despite all the drawbacks, the panchayats have started transforming the living conditions of the poor.[13] Arguments are projected based on the experience of the process of decentralization that takes place in the world. Decentralization will work effectively if (a) there is a strong presence of a middle class, (b) land reform is carried out successfully, (c) there is a larger presence of civil society organisations, (d) the society has a high literacy rate, and (e) adequate powers and finances are with grassroots institutions.

In India a new proposition is emerging. Wherever committed leadership with vision and capability is emerging, decentralization works effectively. A large number of leaders at the grassroots have struggled to transform the life of struggling collectivities and masses. The leaders who are in position have to demonstrate that they are more efficient, humane, responsive and responsible in delivering the services to the people and more particularly to the poor, *dalit* and women.[14]

But the positive achievements are not highlighted. Very poor attention was given by the researchers on these areas and the research institutions have also not noticed the crucial changes taking place at the grassroots. As a result well researched documents are not adequately available. The media projects only the federal and State governments' performance and not the local governments'. Barring a few, newspapers and television networks are not collecting reports from the grassroots. It needs more specialists to cover stories of decentralized governance at the grassroots.

It is unfortunate that in India, the media is not sensitized on this issue of decentralization. A new transformative leadership is emerging but it is not captured and disseminated. In Tamil Nadu an experiment was conducted by organizing a media workshop on the implications of decentralized governance which brought about tremendous results. By capturing very good stories, struggles and successes of the women leaders in delivering services with the help of the media, they got national awards. A vernacular daily by issuing a weekly supplement exclusively for local bodies created awareness among the people about the new dispensation.[15] At present the media involvement is very little, especially, at the national level. As the media involved itself in the freedom struggle, it has to engage itself in the decentralization process also. It is indeed the second freedom struggle to achieve Gram Swaraj. Our Swaraj has come up to the districts but not down below.

Capacity-building is yet another major step in this direction. In the absence of a capacity-building policy, the capacity-building exercises undertaken by different agencies are conducted with different perspectives. Moreover, at present, the coverage is not even one-third of the leaders who are recruited for local bodies. Our training institutions, barring a few, are the asylums for unwanted and incapable officials. Unwanted officials are put in training institutions. In this scenario, one finds the level of the commitment on the part of State government and capability of the trainers working in training institutions to be very poor. Training is to be conducted massively and a support structure has to be created to support leaders who are engaged in struggles in the field. The training should aim at improving the capacity of the leaders in governance.[16] In many places and training institutions, panchayat leaders are being trained to carry out the schemes and programmes of the Central and State governments. As a result the panchayat leaders emerge as contractors rather than as leaders for governance. Along with the training institutions a large number of trainers are not necessarily attached. The training institutions can involve themselves in conducting training and extend handhold support to panchayat leaders to fulfil their duties and responsibilities. They are barefoot trainers. Many of the training institutions give training. But they are not extending handhold support to the leaders who are facing problems in the field.

In many donor-driven programmes and government schemes, creation of stakeholder groups is an imperative. There is no connection between Statutory Committees of the panchayats and the Stakeholder Committees. When the project is over the Stakeholder Committees wither away. Some of the donor agencies provide funds for both strengthening local bodies and sectoral programmes with two different stipulations. For strengthening local bodies, the donor agencies advise that the programme coordinator should ensure that there won't be any parallel body in the panchayat area. By the same agency for a sectoral programme, the coordinator is instructed to see that the Stakeholder Committee should not be disturbed by the Panchayat Statutory Committee. In such a way donor agencies impose their will in development activities by providing financial support. A careful reading of the Panchayat Act one can help the panchayat to bring any scheme under its fold through Gram Sabha. In such a way, the panchayat leaders and Gram Sabha members have to be oriented and trained.

On the ground, every gram panchayat should have an administrative unit not only to administer development but also to manage data. At present all confusion in administration, allocation and management are due to the absence of a sound data base at the grassroots. Only at the district level, we have a data base, below the district level there is no strong scientific data base. The data base which is available in the district level are not scientific. In the absence of scientific data base, we have no alternative and hence we are forced to use the district level data base. For the effective management of issues and problems, a scientific data base should be created. Even after establishing governing units, a data base has not been created in each Gram Panchayat, each Block Panchayat, and each District Panchayat. So yet another major step is that of creating a scientific data base. To create a data base, huge manpower is needed. This can be done by the youth groups and educated unemployed in the rural areas. By doing this, management of issues can be handled effectively.

Yet another issue is planning from below. It is still only on paper barring Kerala. There are sporadic experiments in many States. Panchayats can at least prepare a wish list and ask the government departments to work on that list. This kind of pressure alone will alter the existing scenario of work on supply to work on demand. It is remarkable on the part of the Ministry of Panchayati Raj, Government of India, that it has stipulated that unless the district plan is prepared, Backward Area Grant Fund will not be released. All the flagship programmes of the central government, be it National Rural Employment Scheme or National Rural Health Mission, all are to be carried through the involvement of the panchayats. Thus panchayats have a definite role. The stakeholders have to assume the roles and discharge their responsibilities.

In India the local bodies are confronting a very serious problem. Even after the departure of the British, though we proclaim ourselves a representative democracy, the democratic elements have not taken deep roots in the society as a culture. Our democracy is always equated with elections. An election is one of the aspects of a democracy. Even the election is seen as only for the National Parliament and State Legislatures. Elections should form a part of all organizations and institutions which are governed democratically. In local body elections, violation of Constitutional provisions is common. In the name of consensus, many segments of the society are not allowed to participate in the election and contest in the election. In some places positions are auctioned. In some places individuals are nominated by the traditional panchayat leaders. Still, traditional panchayat leaders have control over the commons. In the context of poor financial devolution to the panchayats, traditional panchayats, by their strong resource base, control the constitutional panchayats.

Though we are in a democracy, our leaders have learnt the art of ruling the masses from the British. As a result, our representatives have acquired the qualities of rulers not leaders. One finds a lot of domination in every aspect of life. Actually they are not really true leaders leading the masses and yet they are ruling the masses. This ruler culture has to be changed and hence the grassroots leaders should not follow the model of our regional and national leaders and they have to set examples and they should not become rulers. A new democratic culture could be created through the Gram Sabha. First, people have to be mobilized especially from the women and *dalit* segments. Next, they are to be organised and make them sit together on equal footing and make them speak. Opportunity should be given to all segments to speak. Their voices have to be heard and to be responded. It requires skill and understanding on the part of the leaders and for this exercise a large number of support volunteers are needed. This could be effectively done with the support of the youth and SHG members. By doing this exercise effectively the Panchayat leaders should really be leaders and they should become the role models for the regional and national leaders. Hence, many leadership schools have to be created to train the panchayat leaders. A large number of leadership schools are needed for this country.

Primarily devolution has to start from the central government. The Centre should devolve some of its powers which are demanded by the State sovernments. The central government should give up the practice of centralizing powers. Secondly, it has to reduce its size and then only it can give responsibility to State governments. Thirdly, the central government has got a responsibility to oversee the devolution process and work for devolving powers from the State governments to local governments. The central government has enacted a legislation and it is mandatory to devolve powers. The central government cannot say that local bodies are a State subject. When it was a State subject, local bodies were not strong. To change the scenario, a Constitutional Amendment was brought in. After the amendment it cannot be treated as a state subject. A new interpretation has to be given. Otherwise a new list, namely, the fourth list has to be created. Political party leaders are making such demands anew.

Fourthly, compelling conditions have to be created at the State level to devolve powers. Many of the State governments have come to the stage of managing the government in terms of finance and the local governments do not have the privilege of concentrating on development activities with their resources. They have to rely on the resources of the central government through schemes and programmes. The central government which finances development activities should decide and devolve financial resources to development activities through the local bodies. Now this has been taken care of by the Central Planning Commission and the Ministry of Panchayati Raj, Government of India. State government cannot divert the funds and it cannot withhold the amount more than a month and if it keeps the amount the State government has to pay an interest to the amount when it is given to the local bodies. The amount received by every district for rural development activities through schemes and programmes should be known to the leaders and the people. This information has to reach the Gram Sabha. Who will do it? An informed youth can do this exercise.

Fifthly, the State government has to downsize the government and the responsibilities have to be handed over to the local bodies as per the framework of the 73rd Amendment to the Constitution of India. Below the district level, it was only bureaucratic raj. The bureaucracy had developed a practice of establishing dominance over the community and it had developed a mindset to subordinate the citizens. Citizens have been reduced to subjects. People have been kept away from the orbit of governance. The bureaucracy has established a strong linkage with the representatives of political parties that too the ruling party or parties. Rajiv Gandhi branded such officials *development brokers,* who took 85 per cent of the resources meant for development. The bureaucracy has to change its attitude and behaviour and they have to work with the representatives of the people. Still the development brokers are having linkages with the offices and continuing their practices. To avoid such brokerage and brokers, Panchayat leaders, SHG leaders and youth groups have to be on the job in getting all the details of the development schemes and programmes and disseminate them in Gram Sabha meetings. They have to work with the panchayat leaders.

Sixthly, people have to be sensitized on the new responsibilities of the citizens. Developing citizenry is a new task to be performed by the civil society organizations. Transforming the petitioners, voters, and beneficiaries into informed citizenry is the responsibility of the civil society. Civic engagement has to be evolved by the civil society organisations.

The survival of our democracy relies on the votes of the poor. The poors are drawn towards the political parties through doles. Political parties have developed an art of introducing populism to attract the poor for their own electoral victories. As a result, political parties perpetuate competitive populism. The main casualty of populism is the self-dignity of the citizens. But the 73rd Amendment envisages citizen development and citizens empowerment. As a dependency syndrome has crept into every aspect of life in the society, even for devolution of powers every one expects that some drive from above is needed. Here it is necessary to quote the sayings of Rajiv Gandhi to underline the direction in which the decentralization drive has to take place.

> *"We trust the people, we have faith in the people. It is the people who must determine their own destinies and the destiny of the nation. To the people of India, let us ensure maximum democracy and maximum devolution. Let the people be empowered".*

Understanding the process of devolution and development at the grassroots is an imperative need. Initiatives have to be taken from below and above for devolution of powers. People should be sensitized on the new opportunities for prosperity. People and the leaders at the grassroots have to make use of the instruments such as the Right to Information Act to bring the governing institutions under the fold of the people. The new schemes and programmes are aiming at improving the infrastructure facilities at the grassroots, providing employment opportunity to increase the purchasing power of the people, and improving the delivery of services. In the same way the proposal for the establishment of a business hub at panchayat level has to be utilized by the panchayat for the advantage of the people. Opportunities created from above have to be used by the stakeholders by building up their skills, capability and capacity. All this requires a movement from below. This movement can be initiated by the youth. Youth club members can be resource persons for training and they can become support structure. They can assist the panchayats to develop a plan for the Gram Panchayat. They can help mobilize the people for Gram Sabha. Make the Gram Sabha a dissemination centre, discourse centre, guidance centre, counselling centre, and information centre. People have to be engaged, informed, initiated and enlightened. The Gram Sabha, is a strong space, which is unattended. Youth can play a very effective role provided they are equipped. Cent per cent school enrolment, cent per cent immunization, cent percent institutional delivery, cent per cent sanitation, zero dropout rate, child-labour-free, anemia-free, malnutrition-free villages can be developed. In every village if one youth is trained fully in Panchayati Raj, he will train others in the village. The youth groups can work for removing the barriers for smooth functioning of Gram Panchayat. They can mobilize the people for development initiative. To perform the above function, the youth should have needed capacity, skill and capability. If the schemes and programmes are implemented properly and they are monitored properly many of the development works will be completed efficiently and effectively. Thus a movement can be created from below to fully harness the potentials of the new dispensation and for which youth can play a vital role.

Sl.No.	*Youth Activities in Panchayat*
1.	Mobilizing students for enrolment
2.	Taking steps to stop school dropouts
3.	Helping the school to create toilet culture
4.	Mobilizing the people for Gram Sabha meeting and train them for dialogue
5.	Helping Panchayats to create a data base at Panchayat office
6.	Helping the Panchayats to evolve micro plan
7.	Training the Panchayat leaders in Panchayat governance
8.	Youth can help the statutory committees of the Panchayat functioning
9.	Youth can collect all the details of the government schemes and disseminate them in Gram Sabha meeting
10.	Youth can use the computer of the Gram Panchayat and take information from the net and disseminate it to the needy
11.	Youth can create a resource centre to help the Panchayats
12.	Youth can organise school functions
13.	Youth can monitor the scheme implementations by the officials
14.	Engaging the school children
15.	Conducting fast literacy for non-literates
16.	Helping the Panchayats for resource mobilization
17.	Create awareness among the *dalit* youth about employment opportunities
18.	Helping the Panchayats to keep the village clean
19.	Help Panchayats to protect and manage natural resources
20.	Help Panchayats to remove untouchability—Help the Panchayats to identify the evil practices such as—Two-tumbler system

Note: These are possible provided youth groups are trained seriously for this purpose. Sivagangai District is a model. This youth group should have all documents such as Panchayat Act, Rules, Government Orders, Schemes, scheme procedures. They should be in the document form and available on the internet.

NOTES AND REFERENCES

1. International Commission on Peace and Food, *Developing Human Resourcefulness: Strategies to Eradicate Poverty*, California, ICPF, 1990, p. 2.
2. For prosperity and economic development a new opportunity is created to utilize the full potentials of technology, capital and human capability in a new framework called globalization of

economy. To avoid threats and ill effects of such new ventures and to make use of the profit for the poor, decentralization of power is designed. This new decentralization is further designed to deepen democracy.

3. Review Committees and Reform Committees are appointed. The recommendations of these committees are religiously protected in the libraries for reference rather acting on them.
4. Robert Chambers, *Rural Development: Putting the Last First*, Harlow: Longman Scientific and Technical, 1983.
5. Hari Mohan Mathur, *Administering Development in the Third World Constraints and Choices*, New Delhi: Sage Publications, 1986.
6. T.K. Oommen, "Changing Paradigms of Development: The Evolving Participatory Society" *Journal of Social and Economic Development*, 1:1 (Jan-Jun, 1998).
7. K.C., Sivaramakrishnan, *Power to the People? The Politics and Progress of Decentralization*, New Delhi: Konark Publishers Private Ltd, 2000.
8. D. Bandyopadhyay, "Panchayats and Democracy: Elites *versus* Dalits" in D. Bandyopadhyay and Amitava Mukherjee (Eds) *New Issues in Panchayati Raj*, New Delhi: Concept Publishing Company, 2004.
9. G. Palanithurai, *A Framework for Devolution of Powers for Democracy and Development* (Monograph), Gandhigram: Rajiv Gandhi Chair for Panchayati Raj Studies, 2006.
10. G. Palanithurai, *New Panchayati Raj System in Tamil Nadu* (Monograph), Gandhigram: Rajiv Gandhi Chair for Panchayati Raj Studies, 2005.
11. George Mathew, *Panchayati Raj from Legislation to Movement*, New Delhi: Concept Publishing Company, 1994.
12. G. Palanithurai, *Dalit Leadership in Panchayats* (Monograph), Gandhigram: Rajiv Gandhi Chair for Panchayati Raj Studies, 2003.
13. Suresh Misra and Rajvir S. Dhaka, *Grassroots Democracy in Action*, New Delhi: Concept Publishing Company, 2004; The Hunger Project, *Thus Spoke the Press: Select Articles on Elected Women Leaders in Village Panchayats*, New Delhi: The Hunger Project, 2006.
14. G. Palanithurai, *Leadership Matters Much in Governance at Grassroots*, New Delhi: Concept Publishing Company, 2006.
15. G. Palanithurai, *Media and Grassroots Governance* (Monograph), Gandhigram: Rajiv Gandhi Chair for Panchayati Raj Studies, 2004.
16. G. Palanithurai, *Capacity Building for Local Body Leaders*, New Delhi: Concept Publishing Company, 2004.

13

Youth at the Grassroots Governance

Introduction

It is axiomatic and obvious that people in the developing countries, especially the poors are far away from the orbit of governance and deprived of their entitlements and as a result, they are powerless and they are not able to secure their livelihood despite the fact that there are variety of schemes and programmes evolved by the central and State governments to reduce poverty and empower the poor[1]. The present gap between the people and the government is wide[2] which needs strong intervention to make the people move closer to governance and vice-versa. It is not only the reduction of gap between the people and the government but also to restore the self-respect of the people[3]. To perform the above task a strategy as well as a mechanism is needed. In the name of administration, management and governance a heavy battalion of personnel are functioning at the top either in the country capital or in the State capital or in the district headquarters or at least in the Block Development offices. We have more number of personnel for transaction and processing files but less number of people for carrying out development activities. But the critical problems and issues are at the grassroots level which need more personnel with a sense of commitment to tackle the problems. But there is no personnel at that level for development work. We need to have more people to carry out development schemes, programmes and works.

Millions of people are affected by poverty, disease and hunger. Even after five decades of democratic governance, planned development activities, governments both at the Centre and the State are not in a position to declare that conditions have been created to all the people especially the poor to lead a honourable and decent human life. To alleviate poverty, end hunger, cure diseases, and to create conditions to enable the people to lead a honourable and decent human living, there are umpteen schemes and programmes. But these programmes and schemes even after implementation have not produced the results as expected[4]. There have been discussions on the reasons for the poor performance of the government through the schemes and programmes. One major reason attributed among others is lack of participation of people in the process of decision-making and development[5]. There are development schemes and allocation of resources for the schemes annually and for every five years based on the Five Year Plan proposals. But the information relating to all those schemes and allocation of resources are not reaching the people and especially the needy. In the fast changing global scenario, every hamlet or village should have connectivity to get needed information from outside world because global changes are having deeper impact on the lives of the people at the grassroots. Moreover, people at the grassroots have to change their mode of activities commensurate with the changes taking place. To make every village a knowledge society, a linkage organization is needed which would create connectivity[6]. In order to attack the major problems in the developing countries and especially the poor nations yet another lofty goal has been fixed by the UN which is called Millennium Development Goal. To achieve Millennium Development Goal, in every village, health governance, education governance, development management, gender governance have to be done with the participation of people through Panchayati Institutions. Even for those exercises panchayats need manpower. And the whole process has to be through participatory mode.

A New Dispensation

In order to reverse the process of development from supply driven to demand driven, from non-participatory to participatory, and from top down planning to bottom up planning a new dispensation was introduced in governance through 73rd and 74th Amendments to the Constitution of India. It provides opportunity to the people of all sections to participate in decision-making and planning for their development. A totally new paradigm of governance has come in vogue and in which women and *dalits* are provided opportunity to participate legitimately not as onlookers but as participants[7]. Untold and undiscussed problems of the *dalits* and women could be discussed at the grassroots. The unleashed potentials could be tapped for the advantage of the poor, women and *dalits*. In the new dispensation, people have to be mobilized for community action. It is not so easy to mobilize people as they have been driven away from the public domain for social action by taking up all responsibilities by the government over decades. People have been reduced to the level of petitioners and beneficiaries. People have been made to contend with the status accorded to them and as a result they are in a state of powerlessness[8]. Hence a vast gap has been created between the people and the government. People have to be sensitized on the roles and responsibilities to be discharged under new dispensation as citizens. Preparing the people for development action is a highly complicated and stupendous task. Because, in the fifty years of democratic governance people have learnt many lessons in development and delivery of services. They have set notions and rigid mindset. They have to delearn for the new exercise. It could be done only through active intervention constantly by the groups who are nearer to them. To perform the above task, the groups have to be trained adequately[9]. A heavy volume of works have to be carried out at the ground as twenty-nine statutory responsibilities have to be borne by the panchayats with the active participation of the people. At the lowest level the staff attached with Gram Panchayat is very limited not to the extent of the requirement[10]. In this context the role of youth in an organized way can help the panchayats to ensure development and social justice through planning and execution of the same at the micro level. Generally, people use to ask, without money how can panchayats achieve development? To achieve social development, social justice and to educate people about the responsibilities of the citizens, money is not required. Enlightened citizens and eternal vigilance are the prices of democracy. In our democracy both are missing and as a result people are deprived of many of their entitlements. What is needed is the commitment and owning responsibility of development activities on the part of the citizens. To make any big success, micro models of success are necessary.

An Experiment for Emulation

For this exercise, I draw inspiration from the micro plan exercises done in 54 Gram Panchayats in four districts of Tamil Nadu by the people with the active support of the district administration. The whole exercise of micro planning was done with the participation of the people. In all the 54 Gram Panchayats The Hunger Project of New Delhi and Gandhigram Rural Institute have helped the people of the respective panchayats prepare a perspective plan for their development. In the preparation of the plan, panchayat leaders with the support of The Hunger Project staff mobilized the people and sensitized the community to look at the conditions in which they live and the new opportunities coming through decentralization. Further, the plans were developed on the basis of the data generated and confirmed by the people. Priorities of activities have been decided through the Participatory Rural Appraisal (PRA) exercises. The needs of the people have been integrated with the existing schemes of rural development. The whole document was approved in the Gram Sabha. Now it became a valid blueprint which is endorsed by the district administration. All the sectoral departments have to carry out the activities in accordance with the priorities made by the people through the plan. In the plan document people have declared that the people of the villages have committed themselves to achieve the following :

- Enrolling all the children who have completed five years of age in school.
- Ensuring that the enrolled children continue their studies without dropping out.
- Conducting school annual day celebration to enable the students to display their creative potential.
- Providing basic amenities like drinking water, toilet, playing ground and vegetable garden in the school.
- Creating a sanitation and toilet culture among the students.
- Establishing reading rooms to encourage the desire to learn among the villagers and putting to use the Ayyan Thiruvalluvar Library.
- Providing toilet facility and play-things for children in the *anganwadi* and trimming their nails to ensure hygiene.
- Enrolling all the children who have completed two and a half years of age in the *anganwadi* and helping them to learn the habit of attending to their personal cleanliness.
- Ensuring the age-specific weight and the general health of children by providing them with appropriate balanced nutritious meal and ensuring the proper conduct of activities such as providing nutritious flour and noon meal under the integrated child welfare scheme.
- Preventing female infanticide by creating awareness among the villagers.
- Ensuring that all the children receive fully and properly the benefits of the immunization programme.
- Creating an environment free of child labour.
- Adopting measures to prevent child mortality.
- Creating awareness among the people about gender equality.
- Ensuring that all deliveries take place only in hospitals.

- Creating awareness among women about prenatal and postnatal care.
- Helping women to fully receive the benefits of the activities under the postnatal child welfare schemes.
- Helping pregnant women to properly receive benefits such as prenatal care, medical examination, immunization vaccines, nutritious flour and pregnancy assistance money.
- Providing the required minimum basic facilities in the sub-health centre.
- Helping the village health nurse to discharge her welfare functions well.
- Taking steps to ensure optimum utilization of the women's sanitary complexes.
- Ensuring that all the people get safe drinking water.
- Completely eradicating open air defecation.
- Arranging for common public toilets and their proper use.
- Removing waste in order to create a sanitary village.
- Creating awareness among the people about the dangers to the village from non-degradable substances like plastics and polythene and taking steps for their prohibition.
- Augmenting finances by converting public wastes into manure.
- Planting, rearing and protecting saplings in public places to transform the village into a green village.
- Ensuring minimum basic amenities to all the habitations in the village.
- Installing solar lights on streets.
- Ensuring that all eligible families get ration cards.
- Arranging to issue *pattas* to those who own no house sites.
- Ensuring that essential commodities are properly available under the public distribution system.
- Building houses for houseless people.
- Eradicating untouchability, two-tumbler system and creating social harmony.

- Ensuring that the Adi Dravidar community gets all the benefits it is eligible for.
- Organizing poor women into self-help groups and helping them to achieve social and economic upliftment.
- Making all the arrangements required to enable the self help groups to produce articles and to market them.
- Bringing together the village artisans into a federation, enhancing their manual skills and arranging for employment opportunities for them.
- Creating awareness to ensure that girls are married only after they complete twenty-one years of age.
- Observing the families of weak, destitute, elderly people, poor widows, poverty-stricken artisans and guaranteeing their livelihood.
- Identifying the disabled and reaching to them benefits that ought to reach them.
- Showing the way for male as well as female self help groups to function robustly.
- Motivating and guiding self help groups participating fully in public welfare activities and in Gram Sabha meetings.
- Repairing and maintaining water sources such as ponds, tanks, *ooranis* and *kanmois,* collecting rainwater in them and using them properly.
- Creating the right perspective among the people regarding the importance of water, water management and utilization of water.
- Developing natural resources and protecting them from damage and degradation.
- Creating awareness among the people to cultivate medicinal plans in public places in the village and in habitations and to use them.
- Creating awareness among the people to effect changes in agriculture to suit circumstances.
- Reclaiming common property resources from encroachment.
- Regulating common property resources and taking steps to augment the panchayat income through them.

- Reorienting the panchayat activities to a people-centred mode and carrying them out with people's participation.
- Transforming the panchayat into an arena for people's action.
- Transforming the people into social citizens and making them participate in all panchayat activities.
- Transforming the Gram Sabha into a forum for social upliftment instead of a forum for collecting grievances.
- Involving women and *dalits* in a big way in all the activities of the village.
- Synergising the different organizations functioning in the village for development activities[11].

Many of the activities mentioned above need no schemes and money from government. For cutting the nails of the school going children, a very big scheme is not required. To educate the school going children especially from the poor families on the implication of washing their hands before taking food, we don't require a 'hand wash' scheme. What we need is a committed group of volunteers in each and every village. The Gram Panchayats which have embarked on the planning exercise at micro level have done the exercise seriously.

After preparing the plan, the Gram Sabha in the respective panchayats decided to carry out the activities with the help of different groups of people from among the members of Gram Sabha. The prepared plan document has been submitted to all the sectoral departments to carry out activities on the priorities identified by the people in the plan. Further they have not only given responsibility to sectoral departments but they have also taken up major responsibilities. They have formed different groups to do the follow-up activities. A set of groups follow the sectoral departments and another set of groups have to take initiative on their own to carry out the activities in the panchayats by mobilizing the people. In all the villages, major responsibilities have been given to youth groups. The following table will amply illustrate how for each of the village activities, Gram Sabha members rely on the youth.

Village Development Plan—Activities for People's Participation

Sl. No.	*Activity*	*Responsibility*	*Methodology*
1.	School enrolment	Youth Associations, self-help groups, Ward Members	Wardwise verification and identification of school age children; contact the parents and ensure 100% enrolment.
2.	Conducting School Annual Day Celebration	Parents Teachers Association, Youth and SHGs, Village Panchayat	Plan to identify the hidden talents among school children, arrange for necessary orientation to improve their skills and talents; assist in conducting the Annual Day celebration, prize distribution
3.	Establishing garden at school; tree planting	PTA, Youth Associations	Join hands with school students, assist in establishing a garden and tree planting in school campus. Assist in availing of subsidy/free of cost tree saplings from the government.
4.	Implementing adult literacy/ Neo literacy programme	Youth Associations, SHGs, Village Panchayat	In association with staff of literacy programme, identify the individuals who need literacy; assist in the implementation of the literacy programme.
5.	Bringing the reading centre into utility	Youth, SHGs	In consultation with the Village Panchayat, the volunteers can look after the reading centre; can collect books from donors.
6.	Enrolment of dropouts	Youth, SHGs, Village Panchayat	Through VEC the youths and SHG volunteers can assist in counselling the parents of concerned school dropouts and help the dropouts to join the formal school or special school. The Village Panchayat can give special consideration to those families who are very poor. Whose dropout wards have been enrolled by extending socio-economic welfare programmes.
7.	Immunization Programme—Implementation	Youth Associations, SHGs, Ward Members	Through the VHN and *anganwadi* workers, children can be listed for immunization; the concerned parents can be contacted for timely attendance to receive immunization due to their ward. Any left out children can be further identified by proper follow up. In this way 100% immunization can be achieved.

Sl. No.	Activity	Responsibility	Methodology
8.	Enrolment of children in *anganwadi*	Youth Association, SHG, Ward Members	Those children who have completed two and a half years can be identified and their parents contacted. The significance of child care through *anganwadi* can be shared with them and the eligible children enrolled in the *anganwadi.* In habitants at a distance can be persuaded to engage volunteers to look after children in the village itself
9.	In *anganwadi*—maintaining the cleanliness of children—periodical trimming of nails of children	Youth Associations, SHGs	Nail cutter can be purchased by the volunteers, periodically they can visit and trim the nails of children.
10.	Establishment of garden at *anganwadi*	Youth Associations, SHGs	Garden can be formed; papaya, drumstick saplings, greens, creepers can be planted. The vegetables and fruits produced can enrich the nutritional status of children.
11.	Supervision of distribution of free noon meal, nutritional powder	Youths Associations, SHGs, Village Panchayat	Ensure the distribution to all eligible children, cleanliness in the kitchen and proper intake of the food, and porridge powder by the beneficiaries. Prevention of misuse and wastage.
12.	Proper delivery of RCH services	Youth Associations, SHGs, Village Panchayat	Assist in the prompt and timely registration of all pregnancies, ensure proper checkup and follow-up of referral services; assist in availing cash incentive to eligible pregnant women Counselling on small family norm.
13.	Utility and maintenance of women sanitary complex	SHG, women Ward Members	Counselling of nearby families, forming of users' group, collecting of maintenance fee, maintenance of the complex, awareness building on personal hygiene and environmental sanitation, development of garden in the yard of the complex.
14.	Prevention of water wastage, misuse, and	Youth Associations, SHGs, VWSC	Monitoring of pipeline burst, leakage and promptly reporting to the village panchayat, assisting in the repair work;

Sl. No.	*Activity*	*Responsibility*	*Methodology*
	proper water supply management system and its delivery		monitoring the supply of water wastage, misuse during the time of scarcity, assist in the regularization of supply equally to all—assisting in simple maintenance by encouraging voluntary contribution construction of RWH structures near the hand pumps.
15.	Maintenance of streets	VWSC, Youths and SHGs	Awareness generation in sorting of bio-degradable and non-bio-degradable wastes by the householders and traders and vendors, with the guidance of NGOs, maintaining the manure yard, installation of soak pits, cleaning campaign at public places periodically through *shramdan.*
16.	Greening of the village	Youth Associations, SHGs, Village Panchayat	Availing of the subsidized tree saplings from the government, encourage householders to plant tree saplings at public places, undertake planting of avenue trees, fruit bearing trees, assisting in social control of felling trees in common lands.
17.	Proper delivery of Gram services	Youth Associations, SHGs, Village Panchayat	Assist in ensuring of family cards to all eligible householders, monitoring of distribution of essential commodities quality and quantity, prevention of pilferage and theft, if necessary, come forward to independently manage the Gram by an SHG.
18.	Welfare service for the marginalized sector	Youth Associations, SHGs, Village Panchayat	Listing poor widows, old age persons, and assisting to avail of welfare, identification of poor who do not possess house site, patta and bring housing scheme to them, identification of physically/mentally disabled and assist to avail of medical checkup for the measurement of the percentage of the disability, assist in availing of eligible rehabilitation services from government and donor agencies, identification of poor women who are not enrolled in SHGs and help them to become SHG members.

Sl. No.	*Activity*	*Responsibility*	*Methodology*
19.	Eradication of untouch-ability	Youth Asso-ciations, SHGs, Village Panchayat	Mass awareness programme, procession, cultural programmes, in case untouchability exists, undertaking counselling and peace making initiatives; if necessary, initiate legal action against the culprits; organizing social programmes to enable all sections of the community to mingle and understand one another.
20.	Promotion of SHG activities	Youth Asso-ciations, SHGs, Village Panchayat	Establishing good rapport with the concerned NGOs; assisting SHGs to get proper link with various departments and avail of welfare services from the same; assisting to get adequate skills development; assist in the maintenance of SHG building; encourage them to participate in the Gram Sabha; providing opportunity to the members in Standing Committees. Involving the SHG members in common activities related to provision of drinking water supply, environmental protection and other social development activities.
21.	Upliftment of poor traditional artisans	Youth Asso-ciations, SHGs, Village Panchayat	Assisting to an SHG to update their skills and technology; to protect the CPR from which they get raw materials; assist to avail of welfare schemes pertaining to them; to improve their market by buying their products; to enable them to understand the market system and trend.
22.	Welfare of Adolescent Girls	SHGs, Village Panchayat	Assist in awareness programme on personal hygiene, anemia, AIDS awareness, prevention of child labour, availing of vocational training, counseling them to be cautious against exploitation in their work place.
23.	Management of common property resources	Youth Asso-ciations, SHGs, Village Panchayat	Identification of village commons and verification of its status; removal of encroachment through persuasion and, if necessary, through legal action; protection by natural fencing; protection of water sources from pollution through social control; undertake social forestry;

Sl. No.	Activity	Responsibility	Methodology
			plan for fuel, raw materials for village artisans, and fodder and medicinal plants.
24.	Augmentation of resources of Village Panchayat and improving of people's participation in Gram Sabha	Youth Associations, SHGs, Farmers Committee, other CBOs	Mass awareness on the income and expenditure of Village Panchayats; details of fixation of various taxes; dues in the demand; necessary revision; promotion of remunerative social forestry; village based management system for the distribution of water supply and providing opportunity to discuss the above issues in the Gram Sabha; efforts to activate the Standing Committees; the significance of self-sufficiency and self-governance[12].

The above activities are going on in 54 Gram Panchayats in Tamil Nadu. They are the role models.

In Tamil Nadu we have roughly 10,000 youth clubs and 2,800 mahila mandals. In each club, one would find minimum of 40 to 50 members. Nearly 6,40,000 people are ready on the ground for any community action. By following the model of 54 Gram Panchayats who have developed micro plans, in all the Gram Panchayats in Tamil Nadu, similar plan can be developed with the active support and participation of the youth groups available in every village. Now the initiative has come from the government of Tamil Nadu through a new scheme. Government of Tamil Nadu has announced a new scheme which is called 'Namadhu Gramam' (our village). The main aim of the scheme is to prepare a plan for every village to achieve social development and by which Tamil Nadu will attain number one rank in Human Development. Once a plan is prepared, all the existing rural development schemes of the Government of India and government of Tamil Nadu would be dovetailed towards the micro plan. What is needed is a working force with a sense of commitment and knowledge on governance at micro level to act as a link between the people and the institutions of governance to achieve development. Youth clubs created by the NYK can act as a link agency.

Before embarking upon this exercise, the youth club members, mahila madal members and NYK volunteers have to be trained in panchayat management and micro plan preparation. Even for mobilizing the people for community action and prepare the micro plan, the panchayats can make use of the resources available at their disposal from the Namathu Gramam scheme. The youth groups, both men and women, will act as catalysts and ultimately people will gain benefits, panchayat will be strengthened and government departments can achieve the targets and youth will become inevitable change agents. Youth also will enhance their capacity and capability. While preparing micro plan for the whole village, youth can prepare sectoral plan for the benefit of youths. Thus the youth both men and women stand to gain economic benefits also. To train this village volunteers, training programme is available in the 'Namathu Gramam' scheme which can be used profitably.

Conclusion

The youth clubs and mahila mandals are the vital social capital which can work effectively with panchayats in mobilizing people for plan preparation and collecting needed data from the people and other organizations. The youth clubs have to work further with the panchayats to implement the plan. For social development activities, people have to be mobilized frequently. In the whole process all Millennium Development Goals could be achieved by utilizing the existing schemes and programmes of the government with the active participation of people. All government programmes and schemes can be monitored, supervised and evaluated by the youth groups with the support of the panchayats. For many of the works, people have to be mobilized and sensitized and the same could be done by the youth clubs and mahila mandals. Governance of education and health at the grassroots with the active involvement of the youth clubs and mahila mandals through the panchayats could be achieved. By performing this task Millennium Development Goals can be achieved. Panchayats can be transformed into a citizens centre which can provide information to the citizens. By doing so the Mission 2007 Goals of creating every village a 'Knowledge Centre' can be achieved. It will become dialogue centre, discourse centre and discussion centre. By involving the youth club and mahila mandal members in the panchayat activities panchayat will become a strong and vibrant citizens' centre. This mission is achievable in Tamil Nadu, as we have seen the works in 54 Gram Panchayats.

NOTES AND REFERENCES

1. Nearly two hundred and fifty six programmes have evolved over a period of time for rural development by the State and the Centre. For more details about the schemes refer to G. Palanithurai, *New Panchayati Raj System in Tamil Nadu: Act, Rules and Schemes* (Tamil), Chennai: South Vision, 2003.
2. G. Palanithurai, "Women Governance for Development at Grassroots", *The Indian Journal of Public Administration*, Jan-Mar, 2004, Vol. 1, p. 349.
3. G. Palanithurai, *Towards Decentralization of Power* (Monograph), Gandhigram, Rajiv Gandhi Chair for Panchayati Raj Studies, 2002, p. 7.
4. Sometimes, people are facing problems because of the development programmes implemented in their areas. For more details see N. Vittal, "Governance for Development" *The Indian Journal of Public Administration*, Vol. 1, Jan-March 2004, p. 32.
5. Hari Mohan Mathur, *Administering Development in the Third World: Constraints and Choices*, New Delhi: Sage Publications, 1986, pp. 14-21.
6. In order to bring knowledge connectivity which is so fundamental to bridge the urban-rural divide, rich-poor divide and global-local divide in human well being a movement has been initiated in India under Mission 2007 with an alliance of 150 organizations. The main objective of the mission is to create 'Every Village a Knowledge Centre'. For more details see. M.S. Swaminathan Foundation, *Mission 2007: Every Village A Knowledge Centre*, Chennai: MSSRF, 2005, www.mission2007.org.
7. How women and *dalits* are participating in the process of governance and achieving development has been captured through a documentation process. For more details see, G. Palanithurai,

Process and Performance of Women and Dalit Gram Panchayat Presidents, New Delhi: Concept Publishing Company, 2005.

8. A study was conducted for Second State Finance Commission on the issue of mobilization of people for Gram Sabha and the report of study provides details about the process refer to G. Palanithurai and V. Ragupathy, *Functional Efficiency of Gram Sabha*, New Delhi: Concept Publishing Company, 2005.
9. For more details see, S.C. Dube, *Modernization and Development: The Search for Alternative Paradigms*, New Delhi, Vistaar Publications, 1988, p. 93.
10. G. Palanithurai, *Problems Faced by the Gram Panchayats of Tamil Nadu in Managing Development*, Gandhigram, Rajiv Gandhi Chair for Panchayati Raj Studies, 2002.
11. The above action points are taken from the plan document of a Gram Panchayat, refer to Meenaveli Gram Panchayat, *Village Development Plan*, (the translated version of the plan document is published by The Hunger Project, New Delhi).
12. *Ibid.*

ANNEXURE-I

Youth Clubs/Mahila Mandals in Tamil Nadu at a Glance

(As on June 2000)

Sl. No.	*Name of the NYK (Nehru Yuva Kendra)*	*Existing No. of Youth Clubs as on 30th June 2000*	*Existing No. of Mahila Mandals as on 30th June 2000*
1.	Chennai-Rural	100	15
2.	Coimbatore	390	86
3.	Cuddalore	302	58
4.	Dharmapuri	315	60
5.	Dindigul	622	121
6.	Erode	598	75
7.	Karur	130	5
8.	Madurai	685	147
9.	Nagapattinam	420	100
10.	Nagarkoil	467	204
11.	Namakkal	60	15
12.	Nilgiris	324	24
13.	Perambalur	140	15
14.	Pudukkottai	358	54
15.	Ramanathapuram	324	122
16.	Salem	376	142
17.	Sivagangai	98	43
18.	Sriperumpudur	213	46
19.	Tanjore	297	154
20.	Theni	57	24
21.	Thiruvallur	275	75
22.	Thiruvannamalai	801	352
23.	Thiruvarur	196	40
24.	Tirunelveli	480	381
25.	Trichy	367	60
26.	Tuticorin	45	56
27.	Vellore	505	54
28.	Villupuram	191	10
29.	Virudhunagar	412	202
	Total	**9,548**	**2,740**

ANNEXURE-II

List of Panchayat Developed Micro Plan with the Participation of People

Sivagangai District

Sl. No.	Panchayat	Union
1.	Veppangulam	Kallal
2.	Nerpugapatti	Kallal
3.	Kalipuli	Kallal
4.	Velangudi	Tirupathoor
5.	Vaduvanpatti	Singampunari
6.	Sevalpatti	Singampunari
7.	Kozhikudipatti	Singampunari
8.	Urathupatti	S.Pudur
9.	Manaloor	S.Pudur
10.	Keelavayal	S.Pudur

Pudukkottai District

Sl. No.	Name of the Village	Block
11.	Parambur	Annavasal
12.	Melapudhuvayal	Gunnandarkoil
13.	Neunjikudi	Ponnamaravathi
14.	Mookkampatti	Pudukkottai
15.	Veerasilai	Thirumayam
16.	Meenaveli	Viralimalai
17.	Merpanaikadu	Aranthangi
18.	Poovalur	Avudaiyarkoil
19.	Pudhukulam	Kandarvakottai
20.	Izhakadividuthi	Karambakudi
21.	Idayathimangalam	Manamelkudi
22.	Melathur	Thiruvarankulam
23.	K. Rayavaram	Arimalam

Dindigul District

Sl. No.	Panchayat	Panchayat Union
24.	Sithargalnatham	Nilakkottai
25.	Kodanginaickenpatti	Nilakkottai
26.	Noothulapuram	Nilakkottai
27.	Karisalpatti	Reddiarchatram
28.	Pannaipatti	Reddiarchatram
29.	Kamatchipuram	Reddiarchatram
30.	Silvarpatti	Reddiarchatram
31.	Athoor	Athoor
32.	N. Panjampatty	Athoor
33.	Thevarappanpatty	Athoor
34.	Kallikkampatty	Athoor
35.	Anaipatty	Dindigul
36.	M.M. Koviloor	Dindigul
37.	Balakrishnapuram	Dindigul
38.	Mullipadi	Dindigul
39.	Thottanoothu	Dindigul

Tuticorin District

Sl. No.	Panchayat	Panchayat Union
40.	Ottanatham	Ottapidaram
41.	Puthiamputhur	Ottapidaram
42.	Kodiyankulam	Ottapidaram
43.	Pattinamaruthur	Ottapidaram
44.	Tharuvaikulam	Ottapidaram
45.	Sriparangusanallur	Srivaikundam
46.	Siruthondanallur	Srivaikundam
47.	Thirupani Chettikulam	Srivaikundam
48.	Parakiramapandi	Srivaikundam
49.	Mukkani	Srivaikundam
50.	Mettilpatti	Puthur
51.	Mathalapuram	Puthur
52.	Kadalkudi	Puthur
53.	Thappathy	Puthur
54.	Iyanrajapatti	Puthur

14

Youth Movement for Strengthening the Panchayats

Vision Statement

The vision of the Panchayat Yuva Shakti Abhiyan is to ensure maximum participation of people, more specifically from the marginalized segments, in the process of development and democracy for which people have to be mobilized with the active and vibrant involvement of the youth and the panchayat constantly and continuously as a mass movement.

Mission Statement

- To make our grassroots democracy a truly participatory and inclusive one.
- To change the mindset of the people from the notion of beneficiaries and petitioners to one of participants in the process of development as citizens.
- To make the grassroots a space for development, more particularly of social and economic development of the marginalized segments of the society.
- To engage the communities in development activities through a dialogue with the active participation of the youth (men and women) with a sense of commitment and rectitude.
- To equip the youth by building their skills, capacity and capability in managing development and governance, to build the capacity of the Panchayat

representatives so that, in turn, both will build the capacity of the citizens to manage the affairs of the community on their own.

Background

Global, national, regional, socio political, economic and environmental conditions bring both opportunities and threats. Opportunities have to be used very effectively and threats have to be avoided.

For this the people have to be prepared and equipped. Globalization and decentralization are implemented in varied phases. Tamil Nadu is one of the progressive States in India in terms of social development and equity along with economic progress. It has impressive track record of social movement and political movement with the active participation of all segments of the society right from the freedom struggle.

At present the full potential of the New Panchayati Raj System has not been utilized in Tamil Nadu as it is not known to the people. Further, in Tamil Nadu, given the power resources, and the functionaries, a large number of panchayat leaders have registered significant achievements by building up their skill, capacity and capability and by building up a vision with a sense of commitment. Tamil Nadu is the second State in getting national awards for excellent work done by panchayats on sanitation.

But the youth power has not been utilized fully in the activities of the panchayats. To some extent women power has been utilized by the panchayats, as a large number of SHG women participate in Gram Sabha meetings. The vibrancy of the SHG women can be effectively utilized if the youth involve themselves in panchayat activities in a meaningful way.

The existing pace of social and economic development can be accelerated and the desire for more democracy and development of the communities can be achieved by building up a movement.

By creating a proper synergy between the panchayats and the youth force in the State of Tamil Nadu, the State can be made number one in human development and gender development with equity and social justice. It will be a model to other States.

What We Propose through this Movement

- Make the governance at grassroots participatory.
- Proper and effective implementation of all the historic, innovative, rural development programmes like NREGA, Bharat Nirman, National Rural Health Mission, Sarvasiksha Abhiyan, Backward Area Development Programme, Anaithu Grama Anna Marumalarchi Thittam, Varumun Kappom with the active participation of the youth and panchayat representatives.
- Evolving micro plan in every Gram Panchayat based on the vision of the people by integrating the government schemes and the needs of the community.

Proposed Activities

For Village Development Plan Strategies for Youth's Participation

Sl. No.	*Activity*	*Responsibility*	*Methodology*
1.	School enrolment and ensure continuity without dropout	Youth Associations, self-help groups, Ward Members	Wardwise verification and identification of school age children; contact the parents and ensure 100% enrolment. Through VEC the youths and SHG volunteers can assist in counselling the parents of concerned school dropouts and help the dropouts to join the formal school or special school. The Village Panchayat can give special consideration to those families who are very poor, whose dropout wards have been enrolled by extending socio-economic welfare programmes.
2.	Conducting School Annual Day	Parent Teachers Association, Youth	Plan to identify the hidden talents among school children, arrange for necessary orientation to improve

Sl. No.	*Activity*	*Responsibility*	*Methodology*
	Celebration	and SHGs, Village Panchayat	their skills and talents; assist in conducting the Annual Day celebration, prize distribution
3.	Establishing garden at school; tree planting	PTA, Youth Associations	Join hands with school students, assist in establishing a garden and tree planting in school campus. Assist in availing of subsidy/free of cost tree saplings from the government.
4.	Providing basic amenities like drinking water, toilet, play ground and vegetable garden in the school	PTA and youth club, SHG and Village Education Committee	Mobilizing public contribution—cash/kind/free labour to improve the infrastructure facilities in schools.
5.	Creating sanitation and toilet culture among the students	PTA and youth club, SHG and Village Education Committee	Organizing awareness/education programmes; conducting moral and counselling classes in schools; follow-up with the parents of children.
6.	Implementing adult literacy/ Neo literacy programme	Youth Associations, SHGs, Village Panchayat	In association with staff of literacy programme, identify the individuals who need literacy; assist in the implementation of the literacy programme.
7.	Bringing the reading centre into utility	Youth, SHGs	In consultation with the Village Panchayat, the volunteers can look after the reading centre; can collect books from donors.
8.	Eradication of child labour practice	SHG, youth club, PTA, VEC, Village Panchayat, NGO	Conducting household survey—identification of child labour-counselling to the concerned parents—under Sarva Siksha Abhiyan enrolment of redeemed child labour in to formal school or special school; help the concerned parents to get needed assistance to reduce their poverty; assist the statutory authorities in monitoring activities in respect of elimination of child labour.
9.	Immunization Programme—implementation	Youth Associations, SHGs, Ward Members	Through the VHN and anganwadi workers, children can be listed for immunization; the concerned parents can be contacted for timely attendance

Sl. No.	*Activity*	*Responsibility*	*Methodology*
			to receive immunization due to their ward. Any left out children can be further identified by proper follow up. In this way 100% immunization can be achieved.
10.	Enrolment of children in *anganwadi*	Youth Association, SHG, Ward Members	Those children who have completed two and a half years can be identified and their parents contacted. The significance of child care through *anganwadi* can be shared with them and the eligible children enrolled in the *anganwadi*. Inhabitants at a distance can be persuaded to engage volunteers to look after children in the village itself
11.	In *anganwadi*—maintaining the cleanliness of children—periodical trimming of nails of children	Youth Associations, SHGs	Nail cutter can be purchased by the volunteers, periodically they can visit and trim the nails of children.
12.	Establishment of garden at *anganwadi*	Youth Associations, SHGs	Garden can be formed; papaya, drumstick saplings, greens, creepers can be planted. The vegetables and fruits produced can enrich the nutritional status of children.
13.	Supervision of distribution of free noon meal, nutritional powder, ensuring the age specific weight and general health of children	Youth Associations, SHGs, Village Panchayat	Ensure the distribution to all eligible children, cleanliness in the kitchen and proper intake of the food, and porridge powder by the beneficiaries. Prevention of misuse and wastage. Follow-up with mothers of malnutritious children to get improvement in the health status of children.
14.	Improving the infrastructure facilities in sub-health centres; helping the village	SHG, Youth Club and Village Panchayat, VWSC	Mobilizing public contribution and provide needed materials to improve the functions of the health staff; assist in data collection; assist in public propagation in respect of control of water borne/communicable diseases.

Sl. No.	*Activity*	*Responsibility*	*Methodology*
	health nurse to discharge her function more effectively		
15.	Creating awareness on gender equality	SHG, Youth club, PTA, VEC, Village Panchayat, NGO	Organizing public awareness activities in this regard; ensuring adequate representation to women in statutory committees formed by PRIs; ensuring the implementation of equal wage to men and women; assisting to affected women to get way from any misdeed committees among them; organizing free legal aid etc.
16.	Proper delivery of RCH services	Youth Associations, SHGs, Village Panchayat	Assist in the prompt and timely registration of all pregnancies, ensure proper checkup and follow-up of referral services; assist in availing cash incentive to eligible pregnant women Counselling on small family norm.
17.	Utility and maintenance of women sanitary complex	SHG, women Ward Members	Counselling of nearby families, forming of users' group, collecting of maintenance fee, maintenance of the complex, awareness building on personal hygiene and environmental sanitation, development of garden in the yard of the complex.
18.	Prevention of water wastage, misuse, and proper water supply management system and its delivery	Youth Associations, SHGs, VWSC	Monitoring of pipeline burst, leakage and promptly reporting to the Village Panchayat, assisting in the repair work; monitoring the supply of water-wastage, misuse during the time of scarcity, assist in the regularization of supply equally to all—assisting in simple maintenance by encouraging voluntary contribution construction of RWH structures near the hand pumps.
19.	Maintenance of streets	VWSC, Youths and SHGs	Awareness generation in sorting of bio-degradable and non-biodegradable wastes by the householders and traders and vendors; with the guidance of NGOs; maintaining the manureyard, installation of soak pits; cleaning campaign at public places periodically through *shramdan*.

Sl. No.	*Activity*	*Responsibility*	*Methodology*
20.	Ensuring minimum basic facilities in each habitation	SHG and youth club, Panchayat Ward Members, Village Panchayat	Conducting survey to identify the gaps in the availability of minimum basic facilities, prepare the list of priorities; draft plan to augment resources to fulfil the same; mobilize public contribution.
21.	Greening of the village	Youth Associations, SHGs, Village Panchayat	Availing of the subsidized tree saplings from the government; encourage householders to plant tree saplings at public places; undertake planting of avenue trees, fruit bearing trees; assisting in social control of felling trees in common lands.
22.	Proper delivery of public distribution services	Youth Associations, SHGs, Village Panchayat	Assist in ensuring of family cards to all eligible householders; monitoring of distribution of essential commodities quality and quantity; prevention of pilferage and theft; if necessary, come forward to independently manage the PDS by an SHG.
23.	Welfare service for the marginalized sector	Youth Associations, SHGs, Village Panchayat	Listing poor widows, old age persons, and assisting to avail of welfare; identification of poor who do not possess house site, *patta* and bring housing scheme to them; identification of physically/mentally disabled and assist to avail of medical checkup for the measurement of the percentage of the disability; assist in availing of eligible rehabilitation services from government and donor agencies; identification of poor women who are not enrolled in SHGs and help them to become SHG members
24.	Ensuring house site to eligible poor and construction of houses to poor	SHG and youth club, Village Panchayat	Conducting household survey, identification of poor who need free house patta, interface with the appropriate authorities to avail their entitlements/ various schemes meant for construction of houses to poor.
25.	Eradication of untouchability	Youth Associations, SHGs, Village Panchayat	Mass awareness programme, procession, cultural programmes; in case untouchability exists, undertaking counselling and peace making initiatives; if necessary, initiate legal action

Sl. No.	*Activity*	*Responsibility*	*Methodology*
			against the culprits; organizing social programmes to enable all sections of the community to mingle and understand one another.
26.	Promotion of SHG activities	Youth Associations, SHGs, Village Panchayat	Establishing good rapport with the concerned NGOs; assisting SHGs to get proper link with various departments and avail of welfare services from the same; assisting to get adequate skills development; assist in the maintenance of SHG building; encourage them to participate in the Gram Sabha; providing opportunity to be members in Standing Committees. Involving the SHG members in common activities related to provision of drinking water supply, environmental protection and other social development activities.
27.	Upliftment of poor traditional artisans	Youth Associations, SHGs, Village Panchayat	Assisting to an SHG; to update their skills and technology; to protect the CPR from which they get raw materials; assist to avail of welfare schemes pertaining to them; to improve their market by buying their products; to enable them to understand the market system and trend.
28.	Welfare of Adolescent Girls	SHGs, Village Panchayat	Assist in awareness programme on personal hygiene, anemia, AIDS awareness, prevention of child labour, availing of vocational training, counselling them to cautious against exploitation in their workspot; awareness on proper age for marriage.
29.	Prevention of female infanticide	SHGs and Youth Club Village Panchayat	Organizing individual counselling with the target pregnant women and ensure the benefit of entitlements earmarked to poor parents with two female children e.g. cash deposit on the name of female children, school scholarship, etc.
30.	Management of common property resources	Youth Associations, SHGs, Village Panchayat	Identification of village commons and verification of its status; removal of encroachment through persuasion and, if necessary, through legal action; protection by natural fencing; protection

Sl. No.	*Activity*	*Responsibility*	*Methodology*
			of water sources from pollution through social control; undertake social forestry; plan for fuel, raw materials for village artisans, and fodder and medicinal plants.
31.	Augmentation of resources of Village Panchayat and improving of people's participation in Gram Sabha	Youth Associations, SHGs, Farmers Committee, other CBOs	Mass awareness on the income and expenditure of Village Panchayats; details of fixation of various taxes; dues in the demand; necessary revision; promotion of remunerative social forestry; village based management system for the distribution of water supply and providing opportunity to discuss the above issues in the Gram Sabha; efforts to activate the Standing Committees; the significance of self-sufficiency and self-governance.
32.	Reorienting the Panchayat activities to people-centered mode and participatory approach	SHGs, youth clubs and other CBOs	Conducting mass awareness on the concept of decentralization. Identification of suitable representatives to enlist in the statutory committees. Sensitizing the community on the significance of Gram Sabha, social auditing, people's planning.
33.	Synergizing different stakeholders and their activities for village development	SHG and youth clubs and Village Panchayat	List of various sectoral department's schemes and programmes with all details. Disseminate the same for public awareness. Assist in household survey to identify eligible family to avail schemes to concerned civil departments. Assist the Village Panchayat to have a plan for establishing proper linkages/joint activities for the development of villages.

Proposed Methodology

To work with panchayat leaders the youth should acquire necessary skills and capacity in panchayat management. They have to be trained. The youth groups have to be trained professionally to equip them with the nuances of panchayat and development management.

Further they should be provided with adequate reference material on the tasks to be performed by the youth groups at the grassroots through the panchayats. In Tamil Nadu the Rajiv Gandhi Institute of Youth and Development has to take up this responsibility of training the youth leaders.

In every district a youth group will be marked as the resource team and training team and located at the district headquarters with all necessary connectivity to help panchayat functionaries and youth groups.

By issuing a guideline by the State government, the youth groups can legitimately involve themselves in awareness creation, training and social mobilization for governance and development work at the grassroots. The Ministry of Youth, Government of India, and the Government of Tamil Nadu have to allocate resources to train the youth in governance and development at the grassroots.

To monitor and facilitate the whole exercise, a State level committee has to be constituted.

Chairperson	:	Secretary, Rural Development and Panchayati Raj
Convener	:	Zonal Director, NYK (Nehru Yuva Kendra)
Members	:	District NYK Coordinators

Yet another committee has to be constituted at the district level

Chairperson	:	District Collector
Convener	:	NYK Coordinator
Members	:	District Panchayat President
		Block Panchayat Presidents
		NYK Volunteers (5)
		Panchayat Presidents (5)

Every four months activities have to be reviewed.

Expected Outcome

Governance Monitored to Check if

- Gram Sabha meeting was conducted
- Quorum was maintained and deliberations took place
- Women participated
- *Dalits* participated
- Statutory committees were constituted
- Statutory committees functioned
- Committee reports were discussed
- Committees actively engaged in panchayat activities
- Transparency was maintained in panchayat administration
- Planning was done at Gram Panchayat level
- Panchayat meets were held regularly
- Women and *Dalit* ward members participated
- Panchayat budget was prepared seriously
- Panchayat presented the budget in the Gram Sabha
- Panchayat mobilised resources internally and effectively.

Development Monitored to Check if

- School enrolment increased
- Dropouts declined
- Malnutrition affected children declined
- Anemia affected women declined
- Child labour eradicated
- Female infanticide eradicated
- Child mortality declined
- Gender equality promoted
- Institutional delivery ensured
- Pre-natal care and post-natal care for women given
- Requirement of basic facilities in the sub-health centre fulfilled
- Women's sanitary complexes utilized

- Safe drinking water provided
- Open air defecation eradicated
- Public toilets utilized
- Clean village environment created
- Use of plastics and polythene stopped
- Waste converted into wealth
- Afforestation measures undertaken
- Basic amenities to all the habitations ensured
- Solar lights installed
- Pattas issued to poor pattaless families
- Essential commodities under PDS distributed to all the needy
- Untouchability eradicated
- Adi Dravidar Community benefits ensured
- Poor women SHG organised
- Income generation activity for SHG arranged
- Village artisans federated
- Early marriage of girls stopped
- Livelihood opportunities provided for marginalized and deprived
- Participation of SHG members in public welfare activities and Gram Sabha ensured
- Water resources protected
- Natural resources protected
- Medicinal plants cultivated
- Encroachment removed
- Common property resources utilized properly to generate income
- Transformed panchayat into an arena for people's action
- People transformed into social citizens
- Gram Sabha transformed into a forum for social upliftment
- Women and *dalits* involved in the activities of the village
- Different organisations synergized for development activities.

APPENDICES

APPENDIX-I

National Youth Policy 2003

Preamble

The National Youth Policy, 2003 reiterates the commitment of the entire nation to the composite and all-round development of the young sons and daughters of India and seeks to establish an all-India perspective to fulfil their legitimate aspirations so that they are all strong of heart, body and mind in successfully accomplishing the challenging tasks of national reconstruction and social changes that lie ahead.

The earlier National Youth Policy was formulated in 1988. The socio-economic conditions in the country have since undergone a significant change and have been shaped by wide-ranging technological advancement. The National Youth Policy-2003 is designed to galvanize the youth to rise up to the new challenges, keeping in view the global scenario, and aims at motivating them to be active and committed participants in the exciting task of national development.

The policy is based on recognition of the contribution that the youth can, and should, make to the growth and well-being of the community and endeavours to ensure effective co-ordination between the policies, programmes and delivery systems of the various ministries, departments and other agencies. The thrust of the policy centres around "Youth Empowerment" in different spheres of national life.

For India to occupy her rightful place in the comity of nations and to meaningfully discharge the manifold obligations thereto, it would be imperative to ensure the effective pursuit of youth development programmes which promote personality development and qualities of citizenship and enhance commitment to community service, social justice, self-reliance, national integration and humanism, an inclusive view of the entire universe as enshrined in our ancient scriptures. The policy, therefore, recognizes these inter-related values and principles as its basic premise.

Rationale

Since our national progress depends, crucially, on the ways and means through which the youth are encouraged and nurtured as a positive force for national progress and are enabled to contribute to socio-economic development, it is essential for an appropriate policy framework to be in place to harness the energies of the youth in this task.

Recognizing, further, that youth development is a multi-faceted concept, it is equally necessary that all the relevant agencies, including the ministries and departments of the Central and State governments, and local self government bodies and Panchayati Raj institutions devise their plans and programmes bearing these aspects and features in mind. The policy will facilitate a multi-dimensional and integrated approach in this behalf, with the State agencies striving to accelerate the formulation and implementation of programmes.

An important indicator of the success of such programmes being the stake of the beneficiaries in the results of the same, this policy also stresses that the youth of the country should enjoy greater participation in the processes of decision-making and execution at local and higher levels. Such participation would be facilitated by identifiable structures, transparent procedures and wider representation of the youth in appropriate bodies, with the emphasis being more on working with the youth than for the youth.

The Definition of Youth

This policy will cover all the youth in the country in the age group of 13 to 35 years. It is acknowledged that since all the persons within this age group are unlikely to be one homogeneous group, but rather a conglomeration of sub-groups with differing social roles and requirements, the age group may, therefore, be divided into two broad sub-groups viz. 13-19 years and 20-35 years. The youth belonging to the age group 13-19, which is a major part of the adolescent age group, will be regarded as a separate constituency.

The number of youth in the age group of 13-35 years, as per the 1991 Census, was estimated at about 34 crore or 38 crore in 1997, which is anticipated to increase to about 51 crore by the year 2016. The percentage of youth in the total population, which, according to the 1996 Census projections, is estimated to be about 37 per cent in 1997, is also likely to increase to about 40 per cent by the year 2016. The availability of a human resource of such magnitude for achieving socio-economic change and technological excellence needs commensurate infrastructure and suitable priorities to maximize its contribution to national development.

Objectives of the National Youth Policy

The objectives of the National Youth Policy are :

— to instil in the youth, at large, an abiding awareness of, and adherence to, the secular principles and values enshrined in the Constitution of India, with unswerving commitment to Patriotism, National Security, National Integration, Non-violence and Social Justice;
— to develop Qualities of Citizenship and dedication to Community Service amongst all sections of the youth;
— to promote awareness, amongst the youth, in the fields of Indian history and heritage, arts and culture;
— to provide the youth with proper educational and training opportunities and to facilitate access to information in respect of employment opportunities and to other services, including entrepreneurial guidance and financial credit;
— to facilitate access, for all sections of the youth, to health information and services and to promote a social

environment which strongly inhibits the use of drugs and other forms of substance abuse, wards off disease (like HIV/AIDS), ensures measures for deaddiction and mainstreaming of the affected persons and enhances the availability of sports and recreational facilities as constructive outlets for the abundant energy of the youth;

— to sustain and reinforce the spirit of volunteerism amongst the youth in order to build up individual character and generate a sense of commitment to the goals of developmental programmes;

— to create an international perspective in the youth and to involve them in promoting peace and understanding and the establishment of a just global economic order;

— to develop youth leadership in various socio-economic and cultural spheres and to encourage the involvement of Non-Governmental Organizations, Co-operatives and Non-formal groups of young people; and

— to promote a major participatory role for the youth in the protection and preservation of nature, including natural resources, to channelise their abundant energies in community service so as to improve the environment and foster a scientific, inquisitive reasoning and rational attitude in the younger generation and to encourage the youth to undertake such travel excursions as would better acquaint them with cultural harmony, amidst diversity, in India, and overseas.

Thrust Areas of the Policy

Youth empowerment: The Policy recognizes that in order for the youth to effectively participate in decision making processes, it is essential that they are better equipped with requisite knowledge, skills and capabilities. Towards this end, the Policy envisions the following :

Attainment of higher educational levels and expertise by the youth, in line with their abilities and aptitudes, and access to employment opportunities accordingly;

Adequate nutrition for the full development of physical and mental potential and the creation of an environment which promotes good health, and ensures protection from disease and unwholesome habits;

Development of youth leadership and its involvement in programmes and activities pertaining to National Development;

Equality of opportunity and respect for Human and Fundamental Rights without distinction of race, caste, creed, sex, language, religion or geographic location and access to facilities relating to Sports, Cultural, Recreational and Adventure activities.

Gender Justice: The Policy recognizes the prevailing gender bias to be the main factor responsible for the poor status of health and economic well-being of women in our society and that any discrimination on grounds of sex violates the basic rights of the individual concerned and it, therefore, stands for the elimination of gender discrimination in every sphere. The Policy enunciates that :

(a) Every girl child and young woman will have access to education and would also be a primary target of efforts to spread literacy.

(b) Women will have access to adequate health services (including reproductive health programmes) and will have full say in defining the size of the family.

(c) Domestic violence will be viewed not only as violation of women's freedom but also as that of human rights.

(d) All necessary steps should be taken for women's access to the decision-making process, to professional positions and to productive resources and economic opportunities.

(e) Young men, particularly the male adolescents shall be properly oriented, through education and counselling to respect the status and rights of women.

The Policy Further Enunciates that

(a) Action would be pursued to eliminate all forms of discrimination in respect of the girl child, negative cultural attitudes and practices against women, discrimination against women in education, skill development and training, and the socio-economic exploitation of women, particularly young women;

(b) Concerted efforts will be made to promote a family value system that nurtures a closer bond between men and women, and ensures equality, mutual respect and sharing of responsibility between the sexes.

Inter-Sectoral Approach : The policy recognizes that an inter-sectoral approach is a pre-requisite for dealing with youth-related issues. It, therefore, advocates the establishment of a coordinating mechanism among the various central government ministries and departments and between the Central and State governments, and the community based organisations and youth bodies for facilitating convergence in youth related schemes, developing integrated policy initiatives for youth programmes and for reviewing on-going activities/ schemes to fill in gaps and remove unnecessary duplication and overlap.

Information and Research Network: Youth development efforts in India have been hampered by lack of adequate information and research base. The policy, therefore, suggests the establishment of a well organized information and research network in regard to various areas of concern to the youth to facilitate the formulation of focused youth development schemes and programmes. The Rajiv Gandhi National Institute of Youth Development (RGNIYD) will serve as the apex Information and Research Centre on youth development issues. The National Youth Centre and the State Youth Centres will also serve as store houses of information for the youth. At the micro level, the Youth Development Centres under the NYKs will be equipped to serve as information centres for the local youth.

Privileges of Youth

The Policy acknowledges that the youth of the country should be assured of the following :

Appropriate education and training which enables them to render themselves socially useful and economically productive;

Gainful employment and adequate opportunities for personal development and advancement for those not currently in employment;

Requisite shelter and a clean environment, as also basic health services of quality;

Social defence and protection from all manner of exploitation;

Suitable participation in decision-making bodies which are concerned with issues relating to the youth and with socio-economic and cultural matters;

Sufficient allocation of public funds for youth development;

Access to Sports, Physical Education, Adventure and Recreational opportunities.

Responsibilities of Youth

The policy exhorts the youth to fulfil their responsibilities, as are enumerated below :

— to contribute to sectoral, family and self development and to promote social and inter-generation understanding and gender equality;
— to extend respect to teachers and elders, parents and the family, in consonance with our cultural norms and traditions;
— to uphold the unity and integrity of the nation, maintain peace and harmony, observe Fundamental Duties and respect the Fundamental Rights and Freedoms guaranteed under the Constitution to all sections of the people;

— to respect others' faiths and beliefs in the religious, cultural and social spheres and to different schools of thought and to neither exploit nor be instrumental in the exploitation of fellow citizens and other persons, especially women;
— to promote appropriate standards of ethical conduct in individual and social life, to maintain honesty and integrity of character and be committed to fight against all forms of corruption, social evils and practices;
— to preserve and protect the environment; and
— to commit themselves to create a discrimination and exploitation free environment and to devote their time and energy in nation building activities.

Key Sectors of Youth Concern

The Policy recognizes the following areas as key sectors of concern for the youth :

(i) Education;
(ii) Training and Employment;
(iii) Health and Family welfare;
(iv) Preservation of Environment, Ecology and Wild Life;
(v) Recreation and Sports;
(vi) Arts and Culture;
(vii) Science and Technology; and
(viii) Civics and good Citizenship.

Education

- The Policy acknowledges that the objective of providing appropriate education, which enables the youth to develop into good citizens of the country, should also suitably influence relevant actions of the Government and public behaviour.
- It is recognized that the need of the educational system to instil, in the youth, an abiding sense of patriotism and in values oriented towards the unity and integrity of the country, equally calls for the elimination of violence in all forms, adherence to good moral and

ethical values and respect and reverence for India's composite culture and national heritage.

- This policy emphasizes that the learning process should minimise the stress and strain, which the system may exert on students, especially in the early years. The thrust of the educational system, particularly in the early years, ought to be on learning, rather than on merely qualifying in examinations and memory-based tests. The policy lays emphasis on outdoor learning as an integral part of the educational process and on Physical Education, Sports, Games and Adventure activities.
- Academic institutions should be equipped with adequate sports and recreational facilities.
- Education, above the secondary level should have a high degree of vocationalisation so as to enable the youth to acquire such requisite skills as would augment avenues of employment for them; technical institutions need to be strengthened and their number increased keeping an eye on our country's emergence as a major force in information technology.
- There needs to be greater uniformity in the educational system and standards in various parts of the country.
- Closer links should be developed between the educational system and prospective employers, on an institutional basis and career counselling should be a part of the educational system, from the secondary level onwards. Programmes need to be undertaken for proper dissemination of information, amongst young men and women, in respect of career options.
- Programmes should be undertaken to upgrade the existing skills of young artisans of traditional handicrafts and other products and for those who may wish to take up the same as a vocation. Education system should also have a rural orientation to address the varied needs of agriculture, agro-processing and other areas of rural economy.

- Educational curriculum in schools should include information on health issues, including reproductive health, HIV-AIDS and also on population issues.
- Youth clubs and Mahila Mandals should be encouraged to involve their members in programmes like "Sarva Shiksha Abhiyan" and Total Literacy Campaign for universalisation of primary education, and spread of literacy and to organize activities to promote book reading habits among the youth.

Training and Employment

- This policy recognizes that the question of employment is, at present, of very serious concern for the Indian youth and that several social issues arise out of widespread unemployment and under-employment of the youth.
- This policy further acknowledges that the incidence of unemployment is more pronounced in the rural areas and in urban slums and calls for appropriate strategies and commensurate efforts to deal with it.
- The current trends suggest that the growth rate of the labour force has been higher than the growth rate of population and that the growth rate of employment has not been in proportion to GDP growth.
- The critical issues in this area include a mis-match between skills-requirement and employment opportunities, low technology levels, low wages and low productivity, occupational shifts in employment, under-employment owing to seasonal factors, excess labour supply in relation to demand, migration of the labour force from the rural to urban areas and limited participation of women in the work force, especially in the organized sector.
- The incidence of unemployment has been accentuated by advances in technology and communications, to tackle which, opportunities for self-employment need to be created. Schemes to provide "seed money" to

assist viable enterprises initiated by the youth need to be drawn up. A network of youth skill training centres would be needed to establish and build up the capacities of the young people for income generation activities.

- Adequate funding for both pre-job and on-the-job training for youth by government as well as other stake holders should be ensured. For proper vocational guidance and career counselling, schools and colleges should pay adequate attention to this aspect as part of their co-curricular activities.
- Government, in conjunction with youth organisations, will develop training programmes for young people in the rural areas, based on their needs. Special schemes would also be developed for young women, youth with disabilities and for young people returning from the urban to the rural areas, alongside flexibility in training systems and collaboration between training institutions and potential employers.
- Co-operative schemes involving Self Help Groups of young people in the production and marketing of goods and services would be encouraged and strengthened, with government support. Banks and Co-operatives would be advised to make identifiable allocations of soft credit to young people and their Self Help Groups and micro-credit adopted as a strategy to enable young women and men, in the rural areas, to undertake fruitful economic ventures.
- A data bank will be created to keep abreast of the employment opportunities being generated, as also the availability of young people, with the requisite skills, for the same.

Health

- The policy recognises that a holistic approach towards health, mental, physical and spiritual, needs to be adopted after careful assessment of the health needs of the youth.

- As per the youth population projections (based on the 1991 Census), about 21.4% of the total population in 1996 was estimated to be in the age group of 10-19 years; of these, about 78.4% lived in the rural and the remaining (21.6%) in the urban areas. The mean age of marriage in the rural areas was 21.56 years for males and 16.67 years for females. In the urban areas, the mean age for marriage was 24.32 years for males and 19.92 years for females. In other words, most women in India are married during the age of adolescence.
- The areas of focus of this Policy, in so far as health of the youth is concerned, are:
  (a) General Health;
  (b) Mental Health;
  (c) Spiritual Health;
  (d) AIDS, Sexually Transmitted Diseases, Substance Abuse; and
  (e) Population Education.

(a) General Health

- **Nutrition :** The policy recognises an urgent need for greater concentration on nutritional studies on the youth—particularly the young women and the adolescents and advocates all measures to lessen the differences between their daily average intake of energy and proteins and the recommended daily intake allowances (RDA). The policy particularly emphasises on reduction of this gap, which is wider among the children of growing age as per Indian National Nutritional Profile, 1998.
- The growth rate standard of Indian adolescents, measured in terms of Body Mass Index (BMI) viz. ratio between weight and height, is lower in India than in most of the industrialised nations. Iron deficiency and anemia are common, especially in girls. The growth-related requirements of adolescents often continue beyond the teenage years and overlap with the

nutritional needs of early pregnancy, which has an impact on the health of new-born children, in addition to the mothers. Discriminatory practices in respect of girls also lead to lack of adequate nutritional intake, which results in malnutrition, anaemia and other micro-nutrient deficiencies in young girls which are more noticeable in the rural areas. These concerns need to be effectively tackled through appropriate measures, including awareness-generation programmes.

- The policy lays emphasis on the importance of hygiene and sanitation in promoting a healthy society. All efforts should be made to inculcate in the youth a sense of hygiene and sanitation right from early education. The youth on their part should be encouraged to organise mass awareness campaigns in their neighbourhood to promote better hygiene and sanitation. Their services should also be utilised in creating better sanitation facilities for the community, both in rural areas and urban slums.
- **Health education and health consciousness:** This Policy strongly recommends introduction of health education in the curricula of regular/formal education in higher classes of schools and colleges, in non-formal education centres and in every other organised interaction with the youth. The policy advocates that every youth of India should clearly understand the what, why and how of good health within his or her socio-economic parameters. A policy of minimum physical exercise for all should be propagated.

(b) Mental Health

- Lack of proper education often leads to mental depression. In an environment that is becoming complex and competitive by the day, the chances of young minds being afflicted with depression are ever rising. This is particularly so, among adolescents who are showing higher incidence of suicidal traits than ever before. Against this background, this policy advocates a system of education which teaches the youth to fight back rather than give in. It also recommends establishment of State sponsored and free counselling services for the youth, particularly the adolescents.

- Adolescence is a period of change and, consequently, one of stress, characterized by uncertainties in regard to identity and position in the peer group, in society at large and in the context of one's own responsibilities as an adult. The compulsions of parental approval often encounter the emerging aspirations of independence. Adolescents exhibit mood-swings and might even indulge in self-destructive activities, such as use of alcohol, drugs and violence; they need, therefore, to be treated with openness, understanding and sympathy and offered creative channels to harness their energies. This would necessitate training and capacity building of all professional groups including NGOs working with the youth belonging to this age group.

(c) Spiritual Health

- Health of the mind should be coupled with the health of the spirit. Towards this, yoga and meditation should be propagated widely among the youth. Yoga, in particular, should be taught in the schools.

(d) HIV/AIDS, Sexually Transmitted Diseases and Substance Abuse

- The Policy recognizes that the percentage of young people falling prey to substance abuse, STDs and HIV/AIDS being relatively higher, these issues need be tackled as, primarily, confronting the younger generation, particularly the adolescents who are most affected. Being highly impressionable, and, therefore, prone to high risk behaviour, they require proper education and awareness about reproductive health issues, including safe sexual behaviour. The Policy, therefore, advocates a two-pronged approach of education and awareness for prevention and proper treatment and counselling for cure and rehabilitation. It further enjoins that information in respect of the reproductive health system should form part of the educational curriculum. The Policy also stresses the need for establishment of adolescent clinics in large hospitals and similar projects in rural areas to address the health needs of the young adults.

(e) Population Education

- The Policy recognises that a growing population is a serious national problem that has negated many of our achievements in the field of development. The youth have an important role to play in this sphere and can create greater awareness in this regard through community programmes.
- Responsible sexual behaviour can be promoted through education in family-life issues and control of population. Pregnancy and childbirth, in the adolescent period, particularly for young women below 17 years of age who are living in unhealthy conditions and without adequate access to health services, has been a serious bio-medical hazard. The adolescent age-group has to be sensitised in regard to the correct age for marriage and for the first pregnancy, sufficient spacing between births and limiting the size of the family. It is conceded that in spite of several initiatives taken by the Government, the social climate enjoins the young couple to produce their first child soon after marriage. This scenario is unlikely to change in the near or medium term. Entering into matrimony at the right age assumes critical importance in this context, apart from its healthy impact in checking the high rate of population growth. It is equally imperative that young adults be sensitised to their role and responsibilities as

responsible parents. Ante-natal, natal and post-natal services of quality are also necessary for young women.

- The following strategies should be adopted to provide better health services to the youth :

  (a) Government , in co-operation with the Youth Organisations and NGOs, would promote the establishment of Youth Health Associations, at the grass-root level, to ensure proper sanitation, health and hygiene and would, in cooperation with Youth Organisations, develop Family Welfare Services for young people and provide counselling services;
  (b) Programmes would be instituted, with the support of Youth Organisations and NGOs, to sensitise medical and para-medical students on the issues of health and hygiene and also in the IEC component of various disease control programmes; and
  (c) Young people will be recognised as "Health Promoters".

- The youth will also be involved in a structured manner in the following health-related activities :

  (a) Construction of lavatories, water points, dispensaries and wells; cleaning of public places and related environment protection activities; community surveys and research on health-related matters;
  (b) Safe blood donation, nutrition and food production projects;
  (c) Information, education and prevention campaigns in respect of health concerns, such as malaria, malnutrition, STD (including HIV/AIDS), teenage pregnancy and abuse of alcohol and other harmful substances;
  (d) "Peer Education" will be an important element in promoting health services.

- This Policy urges upon universal accessibility of an acceptable, affordable and quality health care service to the youth throughout the length and breadth of this country to be made available in close proximity to their places of residence. The youth should have this accessibility for themselves as well as for other vulnerable age groups whom they could help out.

Environment

- The Policy recognises that children and young people are particularly vulnerable to the ill effects of environmental degradation. Unplanned industrialisation, which leads to pollution and to degradation of rivers, forests and land, adversely affects the young who have a vital stake in a healthy environment.
- Considering the importance of community involvement in preservation of the environment, the Policy exhorts young people to play an increasingly significant role in mobilising the public, at large, in this national endeavour. The Policy also advocates motivating the youth to develop respect for Nature and to lead lifestyle which are less resource consumptive and more source conservationist.
- The Policy recognises that women are seriously affected by environmental degradation resulting, *inter alia,* in lack of potable water and scarcity of fuel wood. The migration of men to cities to seek employment often isolates the womenfolk who are left to fend for themselves.
- Having regard to the above, the Policy highlights the following lines of concrete action :

  (a) Greater emphasis should be placed on environmental education in school curricula and training programmes should be arranged to inform teachers on environmental issues so as to enable them to instruct the youth suitably. Environmental education should also be a part of the outdoor learning process;

(b) The participation of Youth Organisations in gathering environmental data and in understanding environmental issues would be encouraged as a means of improving their knowledge of immediate surroundings and accentuating personal concern towards proper environmental management;

(c) Motivating the youth to establish nature and adventure clubs in villages and towns with a view to creating mass awareness towards protection of the country's bio-diversity, and to work with local bodies and NGOs in planning and management of our forests, rural water bodies, common land and natural resources through active local participation.

(d) Vocational training, in recycling of materials and managing waste materials, would be promoted so as to ensure that more young people may find a local source of livelihood and, at the same time, arrest degradation of the environment; and

(e) Youth organisations, at the grass root level, would be assisted in provision of training in agro-forestry, agriculture and traditional agricultural practices.

(f) Promotion of both traditional and alternative technologies for water conservation and water harvesting through Youth organisations.

Sports and Recreation

- Having recognised that the overall objective of the Policy is the all-round development of personality of the youth and noting that sports, physical education, adventure, recreation and related activities might often be overlooked, this Policy strongly supports these activities as important areas of human resource development. No system of education could be considered successful, unless it addresses the urges and aspirations of the youth to be creative and appreciative of the manifold facets of nature and of social life.

- The Policy, accordingly, enunciates that :

(a) Sports and games be promoted as a mass movement by making it a way of life;

(b) Sports, games and physical education including Yoga, should be compulsory in all educational institutions;

(c) Every educational institution should have adequate facilities for recreation, adventure and sports activities, including playgrounds;

(d) Provision be made for common play grounds in the master plans of all civic and municipal areas;

(e) At least one-fifth of the time spent by a student in an educational institution should be earmarked for outdoor activities;

(f) Geographically disadvantaged areas would be extended additional support for the promotion of sports and games;

(g) Rural, traditional and indigenous sports would be accorded special attention and it would be the responsibility of the Panchayat Institutions with the help of local youth organisations to develop and maintain infrastructure for this purpose. The involvement of organised youth bodies such as youth clubs under the NYKS (Nehru Yuva Kendra Sangathan), the volunteers of the NSS and the Scouts and Guides in the creation and maintenance of sports infrastructure will go a long way in reducing the high cost of such infrastructure;

(h) A National Youth Festival will be held each year, starting at the Block level and culminating at the National Level;

(i) Youth Hostels would be constructed in as many places of historical and cultural interest as possible, to promote youth tourism;

(j) Youth organizations devoted to such activities will be encouraged; and
(k) Adventure activities among the youth be promoted to inculcate qualities of leadership, resilience, courage, discipline and love for nature and the environment.

Arts and Culture

- Activities connected with arts and culture provide recreation to individuals, sharpen their sensitivities and afford a vehicle to inculcate desirable ideals and values. The Policy recognizes the importance of arts and culture in a holistic approach to youth development and that Young People need to be sensitised to the great heritage of our country and provided with opportunities to understand and follow pluralistic forms of culture.
- This Policy, therefore, enunciates the following :

(a) The youth should be better enabled to imbibe the rich traditions and culture of India and sensitised to the need to preserve and enrich this extraordinary heritage. This will be sought to be achieved *inter alia* through

(i) inclusion of learning and appreciation of the country's rich heritage in art, architecture, music and dance etc. in the educational curricula at the school level;
(ii) encouraging and facilitating through financial assistance in association with concerned State Government/PRIs etc., visits to ancient monuments/heritage sites during which attempt would be made to impress upon the young people the need for preservation of our ancient heritage by involving them in voluntary work for cleaning up the sites and

surroundings and educating and motivating the local youth to protect such monuments against vandalism etc. The Ministry of Railways and State STUs will be persuded to offer concessional fares for such organised educational trips and for organising special services to such places, particularly during holidays;

(iii) encouraging and facilitating the visits of well known artists to educational institutions to impart lessons in appreciation through demonstrations/workshops/performances;

(iv) encouraging and facilitating in association with State Governments/PRIs/NGOs attendance of young persons at performances by well known artistes in their respective areas.

(b) A National Youth Centre would be established to provide young people with a common platform where they can express their opinions and views on various issues concerning them. Such a Youth Centre will also provide them with ample scope to give exposure to their creative genius and abilities in the fields of various cultural expressions like fine arts, music, theatre, film etc. State Youth Centres would be established, on similar lines, in the various States.

Science and Technology

- As the adaptation of scientific and technological principles and developments, to maximise the use of local resources, are central to empowerment in the quality of life, the Policy recognises the importance of emerging, modern technologies, particularly in the field of information technology and electronic media, in enabling the youth to perform and achieve in all sectors of their interest.

- The Policy also recognises that young scientists and technologists should be extended adequate facilities for research and that the contribution of the private sector in this field should be encouraged.
- The National Youth Policy, therefore, provides for :

  (a) Review of policies in respect of the School Curriculum and the non-formal education sector so that Science may be popularised amongst all sections of the youth;
  (b) Support to providing exposure to the youth to the scientific temper and way of life;
  (c) Development of mechanisms within the system to identify and train gifted youth, as early as possible, in the fields of science and technology;
  (d) The best and the most positive use of information and communications technology, as well as all forms of media, including the electronic media, for youth development as well as for promoting and protecting the richness of our culture;
  (e) Promoting a multi-sectoral approach involving, *inter alia*, the private sector and NGOs, to orient the youth towards scientific and technological studies and research;
  (f) Ensuring co-ordination between the various Government Ministries/Departments and Scientific Organisations/Institutions dealing with youth development programmes;
  (g) Upgrading science curricula in institutions of learning to inculcate the scientific approach amongst all sections of the younger generation;
  (h) Linking the projects of the young scientists to the problems of the people and ensuring better interaction between labs and the industry;
  (i) Documentation of the large repository of physical and knowledge based resources within the country to prevent their piracy by vested interests.

Civics and Citizenship

- Human behaviour is significantly shaped by norms and values, which are a basis for attitudinal growth. The dominant features in the Indian society, which impinge on the cultural and other values of young people, include areas such as family life, education, work and occupational activities, gender, class and ethnic relations, religion, mass communication, artistic and creative expression, sports, recreation, politics and the economic environment.
- Anti-social behaviour is a manifestation of the absence of well-accepted values, attitudes and norms in the individual and in society which can reflect itself in crime, violent action, breakdown of parental authority in family life, corruption in public life, obscenity in the media, indiscipline in schools and in sporting activities and low productivity at the workplace.
- The Policy, therefore, envisages the following strategies :

  (a) Embodying instruction in the values like respect for teachers and parents, adolescent and the aged besides religious tolerance, and compassion towards the poor and the needy. The concept of family as the basic and most important asset of Indian society will be strengthened.

  (b) To motivate the youth to resist fragmentation of society on the basis of caste, religion, language and ethnicity and for promotion of democratic values enshrined in our Constitution.

  (c) To mobilise the youth to create local pressure groups within the community to fight corruption at all levels and to ensure that the benefits of development reach those for whom they are intended and are not siphoned off by middlemen and the powerful.

(d) Laying emphasis on the economic and social security of the youth belonging to underprivileged sections of our society and those who are mentally and physically challenged.

Priority Target Groups

This Policy will accord priority to the following groups of young people :

(a) Rural and Tribal Youth;
(b) Out-of-school Youth;
(c) Adolescents particularly female adolescents;
(d) Youth with disabilities;
(e) Youth under specially difficult circumstances like victims of trafficking; orphans and street children.

Implementation Mechanism

The Policy envisions the following implementation mechanisms :

(a) All Ministries/Departments of the Union Government and the State Governments, particularly in the social sector will strive to make identifiable allocations in their budgets for youth development programmes;
(b) A broad based National Committee on Youth Policy and Programmes is contemplated to review and assess various programmes and schemes focusing on youth. It will also advise the Government on measures for implementation of the Plan of Action of the National Youth Policy;
(c) The Union Ministry of Youth Affairs and Sports (with the guidance of this Committee) will be the Nodal Ministry for all such programmes and schemes and will oversee the implementation of the provisions of this Policy;
(d) An effective mechanism to coordinate the activities of the Central Ministries/Departments, the State

Governments and Community and Youth Organisations, would be evolved in order to facilitate timely execution of youth development programmes; and

(e) A National Youth Development Fund will be created through contributions, including Non-Governmental Organisations, which would be utilised for youth development activities. Income Tax exemption would be sought for contribution to the Fund.

Review

The National Youth Policy, 2003 would be reviewed after 5 years from the date of commencement of implementation.

Youth* Population by Sex in India (1971, 1981 and 1991)

Year	Population (Million)			Youth Population (Million)			Proportion of Youth Population to Total Population		
	Male	Female	Person	Male	Female	Person	Male	Female	Person
1971	284.05	264.11	548.16	85.5	82.14	167.67	30.1	31.1	30.6
1981	353.37	329.95	683.32	113.43	107.24	220.67	32.1	32.5	32.2
1991	439.23	407.07	846.3	146.04	138.97	285	33.1	34	33.6

Note : * : Relates to the Population of Age-group 15-34
Source : India Yearbook 2002, Manpower Profile.

Unemployment Rates* amongst Educated Youth—1993-94

Year	Secondary Education and above			All types of Technical Education		
	Rural	Urban	Combined	Rural	Urban	Combined
1983	20.4 (2.5)	30.0 (10.7)	20.7 (4.2)	25.0	23.9	24.4
1987-88	15.9 (3.8)	16.6 (12.1)	16.2 (5.4)	24	20.7	22.1
1993-94	17.0 (2.9)	20.8 (10.8)	18.5 (4.6)	29.0	25.9	27.3
1999-2000	12.5 (3.7)	18.3 (11.2)	14.8 (5.4)	22.8	24.5	23.7

Note: * On usual Status Basis
Technical education comprises of additional diplomas or certificates in agriculture, engineering/technology, medicine, crafts and subjects.
Youth means age group 15-29
Figures in parenthesis show the unemployment rate among youth as a whole.
Source: Economic Editors Conference, October 17-19, 2001, Planning Commission, Government of India.

Coverage of Women among Trained Youth (TRYSEM) and Beneficiaries under Other Schemes in India (1992-1993 to 1999-2000)

Year	*Women*	*SCs/STs*	*Benf. In SGSY*	*Old Age Pen. Ben*	*NFBS*
1992-93	134929	116464	—	—	—
1993-94	153981	145298	—	—	—
1994-95	137822	126978	—	—	—
1995-96	124662	133930	—	—	—
1996-97	195522	173502	—	—	—
1997-98	132841	118369	—	—	—
1999-00	—	—	58019	1426122	29541

Abbr. : SGSY : Swarnjayanti Gram Swarozgar Yojana.
NFBS : National Family Benefit Scheme.
TRYSEM :Training of Rural Youth for Self-Employment
Source: Indian Cooperative Movement—A Profile 2002, National Cooperative, Union of India.

Coverage of Women under TRYSEM

(No. in Lakhs)

Period	*Women*
Sixth Plan	3.42
Seventh Plan	4.59
Annual Plan	
1990-91	1.16
1991-92	1.6
Eighth Plan	
1992-93	1.35
1993-94	1.54
1994-95	1.38
1995-96	1.24
1996-97	1.95
1997-98	1.32
1998-99 *	0.46

State-wise List of Youth Development Centres in India

States/UTs	*Number of YDC's Set up*
Andaman & Nicobar Islands	—
Andhra Pradesh	91
Arunachal Pradesh	—
Assam	205
Bihar	32
Chandigarh	—
Delhi	1
Daman and Diu	—
Dadar & Nagar Haveli	—
Goa	—
Gujarat	18
Haryana	39
Himachal Pradesh	45
Jammu & Kashmir	11
Karnataka	84
Kerala	161
Lakshadweep	—
Madhya Pradesh	79
Maharashtra	158
Manipur	76
Meghalaya	7
Mizoram	—
Nagaland	5
Orissa	91
Punjab	5
Pondicherry	11
Rajasthan	29
Sikkim	2
Tamil Nadu	118
Tripura	13
Uttar Pradesh	86
West Bengal	146
India	1513

Source: Lok Sabha Unstarred Question No. 1362, dated 26.02.2003.

Percentage Distribution of Youth* Population by Sex and Level of Education in India (1981 and 1991)

Education Level	*1981*			*1991*		
	Male	Female	Person	Male	Female	Person
Illiterate	36.11	64.7	50	30.44	56.52	43.15
Literate (without educational level)	8.51	5.43	7.01	6.71	4.84	5.8
Primary	16.78	11.54	14.24	15.15	15.86	13.55
Middle	16.16	8.36	12.36	19.49	11.84	15.76
Matriculation/ Secondary	12.57	5.88	9.33	14.56	8.04	11.38
Higher Secondary/ Intermediate/ Pre-University	5.21	2.06	3.69	7.1	3.5	5.35
Non Technical Diploma/certificate not equal to degree	0.05	0.04	0.04	0.15	0.11	0.13
Technical Diploma/ certificate not equal to Degree	0.55	0.16	0.36	0.73	0.19	0.46
Graduate and above	4.06	1.83	2.97	5.67	3.1	4.42
Total	**100**	**100**	**100**	**100**	**100**	**100**

Note : * : Relates to the Population of Age-group 15-34.
Source : India Yearbook 2002, Manpower Profile.

Workforce Participation Rates of Youth* by Sex in India (Census 1981 and 1991)

Year	*Population (Million)*			*Workers (Million)*			*Work force Participation Rates*		
	Male	*Female*	*Person*	*Male*	*Female*	*Person*	*Male*	*Female*	*Person*
Rural									
1981	97.3	77.52	156.82	63.37	19.4	82.77	79.91	25.03	52.78
1991	102.51	99.1	201.61	78.75	28.55	107.3	76.82	28.81	53.22
Urban									
1981	31.06	26.7	57.76	20.35	2.69	23.04	65.52	10.07	39.89
1991	41.7	37.84	79.54	26.69	4.09	30.78	64	10.81	38.7
Total									
1981	110.36	104.22	214.58	83.72	22.09	105.81	75.86	21.2	49.31
1991	144.21	136.94	281.15	105.44	32.64	138.08	73.12	28.84	49.11

Note : 1981 Census figures exclude Assam
1991 Census figures exclude Jammu and Kashmir.
* : Relates to the Population of Age-group 15-34
Source: India Yearbook 2002, Manpower Profile.

Budget Provisions/Net of Receipts and Recoveries and Plan Outlay for Department of Youth Affairs and Sports in India (1999-2000 and 2000-2001)

(Rs. in Crore)

Particulars	Major Head	1999-2000 Budget			1999-2000 Revised			2000-2001 Budget		
		Plan	Non-Plan	Total	Plan	Non-Plan	Total	Plan	Non-Plan	Total
Revenue		186.15	40.08	226.23	178.15	40.06	218.21	213.15	44.97	258.12
Capital		3.85	0.01	3.86	1.85	0.03	1.88	1.85	0.03	1.88
Total		190.00	40.09	230.09	180.00	40:09	220.09	215.00	45.00	260.00
A. Budget Allocations, Net of Recoveries										
Secretariat-Social Services	2251	0.30	3.56	3.86	0.30	3.56	3.86	0.30	4.00	4.30
Sports and Youth Services										
Youth Welfare Schemes										
Nehru Yuva Kendra Sangathan	2204	19.85	14.00	33.85	29.16	14.00	43.16	21.90	15.00	36.90
National Service Scheme	2204	4.18	2.40	6.58	2.50	2.40	4.90	4.05	2.79	6.84
	3601	20.29	2.54	22.83	16.10	2.54	18.64	22.07	2.65	24.72
	3602	0.03	0.06	0.09	0.03	0.06	0.09	0.03	0.06	0.09
	Total	24.50	5.00	29.50	18.63	5.00	23.63	26.15	5.50	31.65
National Discipline Scheme	3601	-	5.00	5.00	-	5.00	5.00	-	5.00	5.00
National Service Volunteers Scheme	2204	18.00	-	18.00	6.00	-	6.00	6.00	-	6.00
	3601	-	-	-	-	-	-	-	-	-
	Total	18.00	-	18.00	6.00	-	6.00	6.00	-	6.00
National Integration Programme	2204	3.00	-	3.00	4.00	-	4.00	4.00	-	4.00
	3601	-	-	-	-	-	-	-	-	-
	Total	3.00	-	3.00	4.00	-	4.00	4.00	-	4.00

Youth Hostels	2204	0.15	-	0.15	0.15	-	0.15	0.15	-	0.15
	4202	3.85	-	3.85	1.85	-	1.85	1.85	-	1.85
	Total	4.00	-	4.00	2.00	-	2.00	2.00	-	2.00
Rajiv Gandhi National Institute of Youth Development	2204	4.50	0.05	4.55	1.00	0.05	1.05	2.00	0.20	2.20
National Reconstruction Corps	2204	-	-	-	0.61	-	0.61	12.00	-	12.00
Other Schemes	2204	9.12	0.82	9.94	11.57	0.82	12.39	10.89	1.41	12.30
	3601	0.07	-	0.07	0.07	-	0.07	0.10	-	0.10
	Total	9.19	0.82	10.01	11.64	0.82	12.46	10.99	1.41	12.40
Total—Youth Welfare Schemes		83.04	24.87	107.91	73.04	24.87	97.91	85.04	27.11	112.15
Sports and Games										
Sports Authority of India	2204	54.50	6.77	61.27	61.50	6.77	68.27	70.25	7.89	78.14
Laxmi Bai National Institute of Physical Education	2204	2.18	2.25	4.43	2.18	2.25	4.43	4.00	2.75	6.75
Grants to Sports Federations	2204	13.50	1.73	15.23	15.81	1.44	17.25	15.00	2.00	17.00
Grants to Universities and Colleges	2204	5.00	-	5.00	5.00	-	5.00	5.00	-	5.00
Incentives for Promotion of Sports Activities	2204	4.00	-	4.00	4.00	-	4.00	4.00	-	4.00
Creation of Sports Infrastructure	2204	2.00	-	2.00	2.00	-	2.00	2.00	-	2.00
	3601	6.31	-	6.31	6.31	-	6.31	7.75	-	7.75
	3602	0.25	-	0.25	0.25	-	0.25	0.25	-	0.25
	Total	8.56	-	8.56	8.56	-	8.56	10.00	-	10.00
Laying of Synthetic tracks and surfaces	2204	6.00	-	6.00	4.00	-	4.00	8.50	-	8.50
Sports Talent Search Scholarship Scheme	2204	3.00	-	3.00	3.48	-	3.48	3.00	-	3.00

(contd.)

(contd.)

Particulars	Major Head	1999-2000 Budget			1999-2000 Revised			2000-2001 Budget		
		Plan	*Non-Plan*	*Total*	*Plan*	*Non-Plan*	*Total*	*Plan*	*Non-Plan*	*Total*
National Sports Development Fund	2204	5.50	-	5.50	0.50	-	0.50	5.50	-	5.50
Grants to Karnataka Government for National Games	3601	-	-	-	-	-	-	-	-	-
Other Schemes	2204	4.42	0.74	5.16	1.63	1.01	2.64	4.41	1.06	5.47
	4202	-	0.01	0.01	-	0.03	0.03	-	0.03	0.03
	Total	4.42	0.75	5.17	1.63	1.04	2.67	4.41	1.09	5.50
Total Sports and Games		106.66	11.50	118.16	106.66	11.50	118.16	129.66	13.73	143.39
Other Programmes	2204	-	0.16	0.16	-	0.16	0.16	-	0.16	0.16
Grand Total		190.00	40.09	230.09	180.00	40.09	220.09	215.00	45.00	260.00
C. Plan Outlay:-										
	Head of Development	**Budget Support**	**IEBR**	**Total**	**Budget Support**	**IEBR**	**Total**	**Budget Support**	**IEBR**	**Total**
Sports and Youth Affairs	22204	189.70	-	189.70	179.70	-	179.70	214.70	-	214.70
Secretariat-Social Services	22251	0.30	-	0.30	0.30	-	0.30	0.30	-	0.30
Total		**190.00**	**-**	**190.00**	**180.00**	**-**	**180.00**	**215.00**	**-**	**215.00**

Note : Department of Youth Affairs and Sports is under Ministry of Culture, Youth Affairs and Sports.
Source: Budget Documents, Ministry of Finance, Government of India.

State-wise Cumulative Figure of Prime Ministers Rozgar Yojana for Educated Unemployed Youth (Programme year 2000-2001)

(Rs. in Lakh)

States/ UTs	*Target*	*No. of Appli-cations Received*	*Total Loans Sanctioned*		*Total Loans Disbursed*		
			No.	*Amount*	*No.*	*Amount*	*% of Total Loans Sanc-tioned to Total Loans Disbursed*
Northern Rgion							
Haryana	8600	14370	8043	5192.16	5239	3094.15	65.1
Himachal Pradesh	2500	3479	2277	1483.93	1958	1304.02	86.0
Jammu & Kashmir	4000	2148	938	807.95	660	503.27	70.4
Punjab	9000	16613	9305	6177.62	7064	4432.58	75.9
Rajasthan	16600	30130	15606	9134.75	9578	5273.01	61.4
Chandigarh	100	166	61	48.02	44	34.96	72.1
Delhi	5000	4982	882	623.76	660	453.66	74.8
North Eastern Region							
Assam	6600	9152	3530	3179.51	1534	1135.97	43.5
Manipur	1000	741	344	257.20	336	231.00	97.7
Meghalaya	600	570	448	322.15	406	267.78	90.6
Nagaland	200	32	21	27.65	19	24.25	90.5
Tripura	1300	1440	365	295.85	26	15.57	7.1
Arunachal Pradesh	500	519	414	606.17	118	107.52	28.5
Mizoram	250	472	251	326.70	245	274.00	97.6
Sikkim	50	110	50	25.64	40	19.55	80.0
Eastern Region							
Bihar	21900	21105	10494	9550.95	7014	5773.20	66.8
Orissa	15500	16272	8116	6121.45	1503	930.33	18.5
West Bengal	22500	8971	2572	1779.31	1763	1198.00	68.5
Andaman & Nicobar Islands	150	271	132	113.86	109	88.48	82.6
Central Region							
Madhya Pradesh	32400	66573	28769	20503.35	12776	8415.58	44.4
Uttar Pradesh	52200	76370	41852	28685.08	28640	18256.10	68.4

(contd.)

States/ UTs	*Target*	*No. of Appli-cations Received*	*Total Loans Sanctioned*		*Total Loans Disbursed*		
			No.	*Amount*	*No.*	*Amount*	*% of Total Loans Sanc-tioned to Total Loans Disbursed*
Western Region							
Gujarat	14700	14849	8618	4519.99	7873	4119.27	91.4
Maharashtra	45000	61492	30896	17336.23	18610	10892.89	60.2
Daman & Diu	50	26	17	11.24	17	11.20	100.0
Goa	625	485	303	247.50	274	279.15	90.4
Dadra & Nagar Haveli	50	58	22	17.60	22	17.60	100.0
Southern Region							
Andhra Pradesh	33800	23478	13678	7991.45	8010	5082.53	58.6
Karnataka	22000	24187	12322	7474.78	7420	4777.19	60.2
Kerala	23700	23799	13707	7960.04	9845	5617.42	71.8
Tamil Nadu	18500	23190	11868	5797.39	8665	4192.01	73.0
Lakshadweep	50	60	19	13.45	14	11.10	73.7
Pondicherry	625	522	269	115.85	141	63.42	52.4
Not Specified	1327	461	127	70.68	77	40.23	60.6
India	**360050**	**447093**	**226316**	**146819.26**	**140700**	**86936.99**	**62.2**

Source: Lok Sabha Starred Question No. 64, dated 05.03.2002.

Unemployment Rate among Youth (15-29 Years) on CDS Basis in India (1999-2000)

Age Group (Year)	*Unemployment Rate (Per cent of Labour Force)*	
	Male	*Female*
Rural India		
15-19	13.1	12.8
	(9.0)	(8.3)
20-24	11.7	12.1
	(10.3)	(8.2)
25-29	9.2	7.7
	(7.7)	(6.5)
15-29	11.1	10.6
	(9.0)	(7.6)
Urban India		
15-19	19.0	18.0
	(16.2)	(18.6)
20-24	17.1	25.9
	(17.0)	(28.5)
25-29	10.3	13.1
	(9.3)	(15.5)
15-29	14.7	19.1
	(13.7)	(21.2)

Abbr.: CDS : Current Daily Status.

Note: The figures in parentheses give the corresponding rates for NSS 50th round (1993-94).

Source: Employment Generating Growth, May 2002, Planning Commission, Government of India.

Percentage Distribution of Youth Workers by Status of Employment and Broad Industry in India (1999-2000)

Status of Employment	Industry Codes	Rural			Urban			Total		
		Male	Female	Person	Male	Female	Person	Male	Female	Person
Self Employed	(0)	38.28	45.78	40.94	3.05	8.09	.4	29.32	41.05	33.08
	(1-9)	12.92	9.39	11.69	37.25	35.98	37.02	19.11	12.76	17
	(0-9)	51.2	55.17	52.63	40.3	44.07	41.01	48.43	53.82	50.16
Regular Salaried/	(0)	1.23	0.56	0.99	0.31	0.43	0.33	1	0.54	0.85
Wage Employee	(1-9)	7.04	2.67	5.48	38.24	34.06	37.45	14.97	6.59	12.28
	(0-9)	8.27	3.23	6.47	38.55	34.49	37.79	15.97	7.13	13.13
Casual Labour	(0)	29.94	38.3	32.9	2.18	7.82	3.24	22.88	34.46	26.59
	(1-9)	10.59	3.3	8	18.97	13.62	17.96	12.72	4.59	10.12
	(0-9)	40.53	41.6	40.9	21.15	21.44	21.2	35.6	39.05	36.71
Total Workers	(0)	69.45	84.64	74.84	5.54	16.34	7.57	53.19	76.06	60.53
	(1-9)	30.55	15.36	25.16	94.46	63.66	92.43	46.81	26.94	39.47
	(0-9)	100	100	100	100	100	100	100	100	100

Note: 0-Agriculture, 1-9-Non-agriculture

Source: India Yearbook 2002, Manpower Profile.

Percentage Distribution of Youth* Population by Broad Activity Status and Sex in India (1993-94 and 1999-2000)

Activity Status	Year	Rural			Urban			Total		
		Male	Female	Person	Male	Female	Person	Male	Female	Person
Employed	1993-94	81.9	47.7	64.94	69.04	19.95	46.04	78.35	40.62	59.91
	1999-2000	79.07	43.43	61.17	66.83	16.83	42.38	75.55	36.28	56.08
Unemployed	1993-94	2.37	0.7	1.54	5.63	2.72	4.27	3.27	1.22	2.27
		(2.82)	(1.45)	(2.36)	(7.54)	(11.99)	(8.48)	(4.01)	(2.91)	(3.65)
	1999-2000	2.76	0.93	1.84	6.09	2.08	4.17	3.72	1.23	2.49
		(3.37)	(2.09)	(2.92)	(8.36)	(10.98)	(8.86)	(4.67)	(3.29)	(4.25)
Student	1993-94	13.78	5.58	9.71	23.02	17.65	20.5	16.33	8.66	12.58
	1999-2000	15.22	7.66	11.42	24.09	18.73	21.52	17.77	10.64	14.23
Others	1993-94	1.95	46.02	23.81	2.31	59.68	29.19	2.05	49.51	25.24
	1999-2000	2.95	47.98	25.57	2.99	62.36	31.43	2.96	51.85	27.2
Total		**100**	**100**	**100**	**100**	**100**	**100**	**100**	**100**	**100**

Note: Figures within parentheses are the unemployment rates with respect to Labour Force; 'Others' include domestic duties, rentiers, disabled, beggars, etc.

* : Relates to the Population of Age-group 15-34

Source: India Yearbook 2002, Manpower Profile.

Coverage of Women among Trained Youth (TRYSEM) and Beneficiaries under Other Schemes in India (1992-93 to 1999-2000)

Year	*Women*	*SCs/STs*	*Benf. In SGSY*	*Old Age Pen. Benf.*	*NFBS*
1992-93	134929	116464	—	—	—
1993-94	153981	145298	—	—	—
1994-95	137822	126978	—	—	—
1995-96	124662	133930	—	—	—
1996-97	195522	173502	—	—	—
1997-98	132841	118369	—	—	—
1999-00	—	—	58019	1426122	29541

Abbr. : SGSY : Swarnjayanti Gram Swarozgar Yojana.
NFBS : National Family Benefit Scheme
TRYSEM : Training of Rural Youth for Self-Employment
Source: Indian Cooperative Movement—A Profile 2002, National Cooperative, Union of India.

Index